Digital Channels and Social Media Management in Luxury Markets

T0384278

Fabrizio Mosca - Chiara Civera

Digital Channels and Social Media Management in Luxury Markets

Routledge
Taylor & Francis Group
LONDON AND NEW YORK

G. Giappichelli Editore

First published 2017 by Routledge

2 Park Square, Milton Park, Abingdon, Oxfordshire OX14 4RN
52 Vanderbilt Avenue, New York, NY 10017

Routledge is an imprint of the Taylor & Francis Group, an informa business

First issued in paperback 2019

British Library Cataloguing-in-Publication Data
A catalogue record for this book is available from the British Library

Library of Congress Cataloging-in-Publication Data
A catalogue record for this book has been requested

ISBN: 978-1-138-57246-1 (hbk)
ISBN: 978-0-367-89066-7 (pbk)

Typeset in Simoncini Garamond
by G. Giappichelli Editore, Turin, Italy

The manuscript has been subjected to the double blind peer review process prior to publication.

CONTENTS

LIST OF ILLUSTRATIONS

Figures

Tables Appendix 1

Tables Appendix 2

PREFACE

In recent years, luxury goods markets have faced significant changes that have influenced both the dynamics of the competition as well as their strategies. The principal changes include the following:

- New geographical market developments, such as in the Far East, India, and some parts of Africa (these countries are added to a list of existing countries that are involved in luxury goods consumption, such as the Emirates, Russia, and South America).
- New consumers are streaming into these luxury markets.
- Diffusion of new media and new technologies in communication, which is characterized by a high degree of interaction.
- The evolution of distribution channels underway – these channels are moving toward new forms of integration that utilize both physical channels and digital ones.

With respect to new markets and new consumer development, we are facing a situation where an increasing numbers of consumers are interested in luxury goods consumption. These consumers are not fully educated about global brands, but they are looking for products that are able to differentiate themselves and/or guarantee unique experiences. Luxury players have to understand the factors that affect people who are making purchasing decisions, and they also have to be aware of the dynamics that characterize consumers' buying behaviors.

Concerning the diffusion of new digital technologies, in recent years, the increasing importance of the digital channels and the globalization of markets have changed both consumers' roles and the nature of the competitive landscape.

This has forced firms to revise their strategies and implement multichannel marketing strategies to continue to operate in increasingly international markets that are characterized by more demanding and informed consumers.

Recourse to a plurality of channels has proven to be a necessity for luxury goods, especially because digital platforms now constitute communication channels in their own right. From this standpoint, the digital channels serve as a meda that interacts with demand, and it further adopts a hybrid connotation: it can perform functions that are informative, transactional, and relational, and it alternately or simultaneously uses both physical and virtual contact modes. Based on this perspective, multichannel management policies can contribute significantly to establishing a brand's loyalty from existing consumers while acquiring new market segments. Although luxury firms initially had some reservations about using the Web as a distribution channel – especially given that they did not think it would be able to reproduce customers' experiences from the physical point of sale, and that it created a distance from buyers with high spending power – in recent years, the opportunities offered by digital channels have become clear. In this way, the logic underlying the development of digital channels for luxury players is one of integration with the physical channel; it is not to be viewed as a standalone distribution channel, but as one that completes the physical channel.

The book focuses on:

a) Up-to-date internet and social media strategies adopted by luxury companies with their brands.
b) How luxury companies are managing their communication and distribution channels to compete in the market and what the impact of digital marketing on their competition is.
c) What are the main models of direct and indirect distribution in digital channels.
d) Identifying the different social media strategies for luxury companies.

This digital channel has enabled firms to extend their market to new consumers who have different sociodemographic characteristics and are located in emerging countries. High-symbolic-value goods are traditionally considered incompatible with the digital channel; even today, some companies that maintain extreme brand positioning believe it inappropriate to develop distribution activities in the digital channel. Most luxury players have developed a direct presence in the digital space; this strategic distribution option has largely been successful. The digital channel is increasingly connected with the activities of physical distribution, and this integration makes it possible to enhance the consumer's shopping experience, while also maintaining long-term relationships.

The latest trend in brand development centers on the growing integration between UGC and the various distribution channels. Brand communication in luxury markets has undergone further development with social media marketing that has dovetailed into both the digital and physical distribution space. The consumer is ready, even in luxury markets, to receive information from a specific brand, to share that information, and to respond by liking the product and purchasing it in a digital or physical channel. This growing integration between distribution and effective communication (both online and offline) follows a circular approach, whereby information channels and their flows surround the consumer. This is one of the frontiers of marketing high-symbolic-value goods.

The main issue of the book is to identify: how the Internet works for luxury players, today? What are the main models developed by Luxury Players and Pure Internet Players? How luxury players manage their distribution and communication channels? How luxury players are using social media today? How they develop integrated distribution and communication strategies by integrating digital and physical channels? How consumers are reacting to the actual multichannel strategies? What are the actual trends: social commerce and corporate social responsibility and how companies are reacting?

Channel integration in markets for luxury goods lies, in practice, in the introduction of innovative technologies to points of sale, in the integration between two-way communication activities in social networks, and in the physical channels of distribution. With regard to the first path of integration, the use of technology in luxury-brand stores clearly helps intensify consumers' feelings and stimulates their senses. New technologies make it possible to entertain customers, while enhancing the communication process.

The monograph is structured into six chapters: the first is titled marketing and digital innovation, the second digital channel in luxury markets, the third digital channels: reference models for direct and indirect distribution, the fourth social media and integrated communication in luxury markets, the fifth, the frontiers of luxury goods marketing: social media systems and channels integration and the last one the frontiers of luxury goods strategies: corporate social responsibility and online communication.

Turin, April 2017

Fabrizio Mosca
fabrizio.mosca@unito.it
University of Turin, Italy
Department of Management

Chapter 1

MARKETING AND DIGITAL INNOVATIONS

1.1. Introduction

At the end of the XX century, a completely new concept was introduced, having an immediate deep effect on the economic, social and cultural macro-environment and – in line with the topic of this work – on the way we understand marketing and company management today: the advent of digital systems which, in a wider perspective, include distribution and digital communication channels and *User Generated Content*.

A revolution in marketing activities has taken place since then, starting from consumer behaviors. Marketing activities have in fact been and keep being affected and deeply modified by the advent of digital systems.

Companies started a process of strategic and operational adaptation with the aim of acquiring the necessary tools to interpret the new mentality which stands at the origin of this change and gradually assimilating all new technologies, taking advantage of their potential.

The digital innovation can rightly be defined as a revolution, which doesn't overcome traditional marketing solutions but assimilates with them providing a fresh impulse.

"*The idea that the Internet would have replaced traditional business models overturning their known advantages dominated the scenario for some time. [...] The Internet doesn't usually replace but integrates companies' traditional processes and competition strategies. Virtual actions do not provide a substitute for physical actions. On the contrary, they tend to magnify their importance. Moreover, the Internet creates new opportunities to satisfy customer needs more effectively*" (Lambin, 2012).

It is important to highlight how the digital revolution has been – and still is – a cultural event and not a mere technological phenomenon. Toward the end of the last century, people started to feel the need for different, more horizontal ways to connect and express themselves. Digital systems intercepted this need and provided the necessary technology to satisfy it. However, in doing so, digital systems didn't only affect the external form of the need they aimed to satisfy but modified its core substance in ways that are currently not predictable.

1.2. The virtual market

Within a marketing perspective, it's still difficult to identify all possible new scenarios that will present themselves in both the creation of marketing strategies and plans and the understanding of company structures. However, we can already analyze some changes, which are currently underway.

The first noticeable change has to do with what the market considered as a whole is: The worldwide market without any distinction by sector – in this market, the exchange of information is increasingly becoming more crucial than the exchange of goods. The digital innovation has brought forward an increased dependence on goods based on information, especially in more advanced societies and we can identify a convergence between the digital and the physical world. The environment in which consumers and companies act could be defined as "infosphere". (Vernuccio, 2014).

What is the current size of the infosphere and, therefore, of the digital market? According to data from January 2016[1], Internet users in the world are more than 3.4 billion, over 2.3 billion of whom are active on social networks. Both figures increased by a staggering 10% in only one year.

People can constantly be connected to the world-wide web from anywhere using integrated devices such as computers, tablets and smartphones, exchanging information, goods, services and opinions in a faster, cheaper and more aware fashion than they have ever done in the past.

The traditional market characterized by the exchange of goods has not disappeared but it is operating side by side and in integration with (for now) the electronic market (Guo and Sun, 2004).

For example, from a distribution point of view, the physical channel – characterized by many retailers all over the world – is gradually integrated with a digital channel made up of new intermediaries and old, recently evolved players. These new economic subjects are a threat to the traditional distribution players.

"GEM [Global Electronic Markets, e.d.] produce and distribute digital products and services worldwide whereas GTM [Global Traditional Markets, e.d.] work with EGM to fulfill the use phase or to implement the physical phase of production and distribution. Traditional companies direct their demand and offer to GEM while electronic market companies create new demand and offer for both GTM and GEM. "A spin off of GEM, the new market operators are become increasingly more important" (Lambin, 2012).

Besides, it is important to distinguish between the global electronic market and the e-marketplace. The former consists of a network through which all market players – consumers, providers, distributors and sellers – exchange and share information, sell and buy goods. The latter (e-marketplace) has to do with B2B transactions and can be defined as an information system for providers and buyers. Using previously provided credentials, these companies can access the system to check in real time the situation of raw material, work progress, products and prices, bypassing the typical administrative hindrances responsible for supply chain slow downs.

The integrated double arena of exchanges conceived by Lambin consists of both electronic and traditional markets. The difference between the two doesn't have to do with the participants but with their motivations and the benefits they expect to receive.

Easy, quick and cheap access to information makes the customer's role in transactions stronger. This increases awareness of the relative value of different offers. Customers expect to find a large variety of products and more personalized services to choose from, comparing prices and exchanging information with other consumers around the world. Moreover, customers get access to a higher volume of information in a quicker and cheaper manner, and transaction costs are reduced.

The traditional consumer's limited sense gives way to a higher awareness, which takes consumers themselves to a perfectly rational microeconomic model. In fact, digital systems have modified consumer behaviors making a series of more precise and up to date information on prices, product availabilities, variations, delivery methods and times available to users.

Target markets are virtually increasing without limits, reducing (due to process automation) transaction costs and overall expenses, mainly on digital products.

Manufacturers can produce an almost limitless catalogue, offering infinite versions of the same product at almost insignificant adaptation costs. That is the "long tail" conceived by Chris Anderson (2004) – decreasing significantly the distribution costs of digital products (music, movies, news, services) removes the economic and physical restrictions limiting the variety of tangible goods. Companies operating in this field can therefore still profitably afford offering products that are not in big demand. The long tail creates market fragmentation, diversifying it into countless niche products. This is particularly true for consolidated markets.

The digital channel allows manufacturers to increase their market and drop production, distribution and supply costs. Manufacturers, like other market players, benefit from the integration between traditional and digital market (Guo and Sun, 2004).

Vernuccio's virtual market analysis (2014) investigates some aspects of

B2C and their evolution during the Internet era: parties involved, relationships and subject of the exchange. The advent of the Internet has deeply affected the identity of both parties involved – companies and end customers – and has modified consumer behaviors.

"*Beside the more traditional segmentation analysis techniques, consumers/users can be clearly identified and better known using the Internet. Internet websites, in fact, are often available to identified users only. Consumers leave their status as anonymous and indistinct components of a segmented market to become individuals representing their own identity*" (Vernuccio, 2014).

In this regard, *User Generated Content* as the main social media and blogs are powerful tools available to companies to obtain real-time information about the quality of services provided, prices and customer's current and future expectations in relation to the product concept. For example, when a new smartphone by Apple or Samsung – just to mention the two main manufacturers – are placed on the market, Internet blogs are inundated with positive or negative comments generated by global users. This massive amount of information is in fact a market research assessing the gap between the expectations and the actual new product performance and it is free of charge.

This new situation is beneficial to consumers also. In fact, consumers are more easily identified by companies, which – in return – are more visible and transparent to the consumers themselves. Digital media provide customers with information on products and services as well as company's good and bad behaviors and this can be easily accessed by potential customers from anywhere and at any time.

Consumers are empowered by the opportunity of receiving more information on brands and their products in a cheaper and quicker manner. This is now a renowned fact on which academics, consumers and Internet users agree.

A number of factors have a role in balancing out the relationship between companies and final customers: they can now compare competitors' different offers, purchase from anywhere in the world after finding the best offer, give and receive information about the quality of services, using blogs and posts – in a kind of contemporary word of mouth – and create a positive or negative buzz around a product, a brand or a company. Consumers can elude marketing activities by ignoring website advertisements and classifying unwanted emails as spam. On the contrary, the same consumers can actively take part in the creation of marketing campaigns by, for example, posting product tests run by them on YouTube.

This new power is not limited to digital systems users considered as consumers but involves their personal, cultural, political and social interests also. Internet users have now all the necessary tools to express their real time opinion on any topics, taking part in the social, political and cultural life of their own country as well as the entire world's. The widespread success of Movimento Cinque Stelle in Italy, a political movement that started off from an Internet blog, as well as the diffusion of the revolution in the Arab spring with Twitter, are meaningful examples of this. For this reason in several anti-democratic countries the use of the Internet is severely restricted and websites spreading opinions not considered in line with the system are temporarily shut down. However – we should briefly mention this here – we all know digital systems have also a dark side to them. They have favored criminals too, making them even more dangerous.

The direct consequence of consumer empowerment is a change in the relationship between companies and their customers. Beside the traditional linear and one-directional top-down/one-to-many approach, where companies are active players while consumers are mainly subject to their decisions, and beside the direct marketing's one-to-one type of approach, a new dimension is starting to emerge. This new dimension – not removing but integrating the already existing dimensions – is characterized by a many-to-many type of approach, based on "non-hierarchical networks" (Vernuccio, 2014) based on dialogues and conversations that express market relations in a context of customer advocacy (Urban, 2005). Companies – now more open and transparent than ever before – have to gain their customers' trust providing them with clear and honest information on products and services (Winer *et al.*, 2013).

Winer *et al.* (2013) cite a direct and meaningful extract by John Deighton, professor at Harvard Business School:

"Marketing operators do not control the market anymore. They are invited guests. They will stay in the game only if they are stimulating, relevant and fun. If they try to dominate the market, they will be excluded".

The Internet virtual market turns both physical and digital products into bits, making them a fundamental aspect of the network. Today's marketing strategies cannot avoid considering how the consumer's user experience has now become a virtual experience too.

New digital technologies allowed the creation of a new market space and now provide consumers with a series of instruments to access it.

Internet, emails, social networks, Extranet and Intranet networks are available digital media which allow users to be constantly in touch with each other through a large variety of devices like computers, smartphones, TVs and tablets.

This system based on digital media and technical supports represents an interesting challenge for companies. In fact, companies need to change their marketing actions making them really interactive, open to sharing and exchanging and available for activities of co-creation of information and content with the market, in a process of systemic supply and demand co-evolution.

Among the Internet connecting devices, Winer *et al.* (2013) consider smartphones bear stronger marketing potential, thanks to a wide range of functions, can be considered nowadays mobile marketing platforms which enable users to receive product information, exchange opinions about brands, gather information and make purchases.

Distribution and communication both physical and digital are now integrated in order to improve efficacy and effectiveness with the aim of winning over the final user.

For example, in some cases, retail outlets are the point of contact between the physical and the digital channels. Products are available on the shelves but can be purchased and personalized online by customers while they are browsing the shop. The opposite can happen too: customers buy their products online and collect them in a retail outlet.

1.3. New application areas

One of the main issues companies face nowadays is determining to which marketing areas these new technologies can be most effectively applied.

There are essentially four areas, two of which pertain to non-digital marketing also but acquire different connotations when operating on the net: B2C (Business to Consumer) and B2B (Business to Business). The other two areas can be defined as "native digital" since they are typical of e-marketing. In fact, before the digital era, they were almost irrelevant if compared to the importance they have today: C2C (Consumer to Consumer) and C2B (Consumer to Business).

B2B, which entails the direct sale of goods and services to consumers, is still the most popular one. People buy any kind of product online no matter what price range they belong to, from commodities to luxury goods. However, as previously mentioned, digital systems allow buyers to lead the exchange process as they can compare quality, prices and similar offers in order to make their final decision based on what product feels more convenient. Moreover, buyers can share the outcomes of their online investigations contributing to the good or bad name of the different products, services and brands.

B2B is mainly an information exchange space among companies. B2B avails of the Internet to make offers, issue invoices and provide before and after sales assistance.

One of the most significant differences between B2B and B2C is the number of buyers (as highlighted by Pellicelli, 2012). If buyers are only a few, then providers tend to be known (Pellicelli, 2012).

This is very important when considering companies' actions on the web for at least three reasons. First of all, B2B providers do not need to do online advertising while B2C providers must show their presence using internet ads, search engines priority lists and banners on other websites. Secondly, given the limited number of buyers, companies tend to maximize customers' retention, acquiring (and keeping up-to-date) as much information as possible on potential customers' needs and purchase histories (first purchase, new purchase, etc.) in order to provide the best possible offer on their websites. Lastly, customers can easily find all the information they need about providers operating on the market. These providers, in turn, upload to their websites a lot of information (new products and services, closed contracts, other customers' references, etc.) with the aim of retaining the highest number of buyers. This information virtuous circle has, however, a flipside: it provides competitors with a lot of useful information.

C2C and C2B key application domains are Internet related and testify how both customers' power and awareness have grown. The former has to do with the direct exchange of information, products and services among consumers, like an online auction. Word of mouth on a brand or a character is an important marketing strategy which falls into this category and is a key factor in companies' reputation.

The latter, on the other hand, bears some similarities with the B2B model as it has to do with how easily potential buyers (final customers) can find information on sellers and, possibly, make purchase offers, ask questions, file complaints and give suggestions.

1.4. Strategic and operational changes

The widespread use of the Internet and digital technologies changes both the marketing operational tools and the strategic approach to the market (Vernuccio, 2014). This brings along several different advantages (Lambin, 2012) in relation to how physical markets used to work and the way they can be approached.

The benefits of the Internet can be explained using the four strategic elements of Ansoff's product-market growth matrix (Pellicelli 2012): Market penetration (as it provides the opportunity to sell more products and services to those market where companies already operate), market development (as it opens up new markets without the need for infra-structures and local intermediaries), product development and diver-sification (as companies can offer new products and services, also to new markets, diversifying their ranges through the long tail (Chaffey, 2000; Hughes and Sweetser, 2009).

The marketing management's approach to the market has radically changed without losing completely its traditional channels, still efficient and effective on physical markets.

The change is however happening and it seems unstoppable as the two realities are perceived as more and more integrated and similar to each other (and often even confused) to the point that, with the necessary adjustments, the advantages of virtual reality are considered fundamental for the physical reality too (especially by click and mortar companies).

The approaches to marketing are shifting from a linear, one-directional, top-down and deterministic perspective to a reticular, interactive, decen-tralized, dynamic and cooperative one, more typical of digital markets (Vernuccio, 2014).

Traditional markets are characterized by a continuous and linear company-customer relationship while virtual markets entail the use of different links mirroring the architecture of the Internet network and therefore lacking a unique center. The relationship is thus fragmented into several possible connections between the company and the individual customer and among the customers themselves.

This reticular relationship is decentralized and highly interactive. Communication becomes bidirectional and increasingly multidirectional. Companies have to interact with their customers (for example through corporate blogs or official firm generated content) and are forced to reduce their traditional position of unique source of communication. Finally, marketing management gets very dynamic and cooperative as we mentioned when talking about the new Consumer to Business application area. Customers refuse to be placed in any specific target-segment by companies. On the contrary they actively decide which segments or temporary bubble demand (Brondoni, 2002) they belong to and take initiative in asking questions about products and services.

Clients turn from passive consumers into prosumers[2] (Toffler, 1980), actively taking part in the process of finding new solutions to create a higher value proposition and the Internet is *"an important tool to deeply understand the customers' problems. [...] the role of potential customers entails the development of new products and the identification of a provider able to realize it. [...] Consumers, as members of the online community, can play an active role in the innovation process, from the generation of ideas to the conception, design and testing"* (Lambin, 2012).

Tapscott and Williams (2008) talk about *Wikinomics* highlighting how digital technologies are democratizing the creation of value through a process of mass cooperation of Internet users. Users, in fact, get together and freely work inter pares to find new solutions to their problems.

Companies, intended as economic open social systems (Ferrero, 1980), operate in the market with the aim of satisfying the market needs sooner and better than their competitors. In this scenario, the goal of marketing is to safeguard the co-creation and the exchange of value with the market and the consumers.

Nowadays we can think of a dematerialized enterprise in which a growing number of activities of the value chain could be externalized and only one activity is still directly managed and strategic: the relationship with the customer.

Customer orientation, even in a digital scenario, is still fundamental and, according to Lambin (2012): *"the emerging pattern of "prosumer's centrality" relates to a model where customers actively and constantly take part in the creation of the products. Actually, consumers co-innovate and co-produce the goods they use and they do so for themselves, their networks and their own purposes"*.

1.5. Structural changes for enterprises

Companies are changing, some more quickly than others, to partially or fully adjust to the new competitive digital arena. Moreover, new companies are emerging beside the old (and often changed) ones.

New technologies increase the technical and economic efficiency of all those activities of the value chain, which are based on the processing of information. Moreover, they lead companies towards an e-business strategy, making them rethink their value creation processes like the supply chain, the design of the offer system, the distribution and the management of the customer relationships. In other words, they are adopting a new business model (Pellicelli, 2012).

As of today, the majority of academics divide companies operating in the market in three large categories, reflecting the importance of digital marketing in their strategies: bricks and mortar, click and mortar and click only dotcom (or pure player).

Bricks and mortar companies, which are still the most common form nowadays, operate on a traditional business model generating most of their turnover – and sometimes all of it – in the physical market. However, even those companies are not completely resistant to e-marketing (no company can afford that anymore). But they use digital platforms as a tactical – more than a strategic – tool, investing little both financially and in terms of human resources on e-marketing. Their online presence is limited to a website showcasing in a static fashion (exactly like a shop's window) the essential information on the company, its products, services and contact details. It seems like these companies never made a conscious decision to open up to digital marketing but instead were forced to act as the other competitors. On the contrary, click and mortar companies have made a quite different decision, bringing forward an articulated e-marketing strategy and adopting an integrated or even new business model. In fact, differently from the typology mentioned above, these companies have not merely tried to defend their market, "planting a mole in the enemy's side". Click and mortar companies started their business in the traditional market but have since begun operating in the online market too. Websites evolve from a static window to an e-commerce digital platform, offering customers an alternative to traditional retail outlets (although still widespread) for their purchases and the possibility to interact with companies, making comments and suggestions on products and services. The integration between online and offline activities is becoming critical and some companies might be missing the organizational synergies within the company itself.

Companies allowing their customers to purchase online and collect their products in an outlet store afterwards, or surf the products, personalize them and buy them online while they are in the shop are good examples of integration between traditional market and e-commerce. This is borderline with click only dotcom companies. These companies started their activities online, making use of all the advantages of both the Internet and electronic devices. It is very difficult, almost impossible, to predict the structural evolution of companies in the near future. All companies – bricks and mortar as well as pure Internet players – will almost certainly transform in the future as a consequence of the progressive and relentless spread of digital technologies to all sectors of society.

"*Enormous changes in the way companies are managed can be predicted. Although it is still difficult to predict all changes in detail, we can already foresee the direction of the changes. In fact, we can envision a society based on information in which the acquisition, transformation and exchange of knowledge and information are the key factors. If intelligence – intended as the ability to produce and reproduce knowledge and information – represents the energy of any economic system, then marketing, dealing with the exchange of information, will go through a profound revolution*" (Guatri et al., 1999).

This recalls the idea of infosphere – a fundamental concept for companies willing to adopt a marketing strategy fitting into the economic, social and cultural context of the new millennium.

1.6. The main drivers of change

Let's now try to identify the new drivers leading the e-marketing and the new business models that companies have to assimilate to remain competitive in a market which is rapidly evolving and is today already much different from the traditional model.

Digital systems are spreading broadly and quickly mainly because, as already mentioned, they are easy to access and use. Even though the Internet doesn't cover the entirety of our planet yet, we can easily say that, in the West, everyone can connect to the net from anywhere and at any time. The web as a new technology was immediately and globally accepted – that had rarely happened in the past. The question for any company's management isn't then "why" digital technologies should be adopted but, at most, "why they have not" been adopted yet.

Digital systems are user friendly too. That makes them accessible even to people who don't usually feel comfortable using technology, like the elderly people. Low costs of Internet devices and network subscriptions make them affordable to people with lower incomes also. Sometimes, in fact, they pool together and subscribe collectively to phone companies and providers' offers to gain access to what is now considered an essential service.

More complex activities like the creation of a website or a blog are now within everyone's reach and relatively cheap. A company willing to create a basic showcase website can easily do so on a very low budget.

When a company lands on the Internet, it becomes a knot of the global network. That means that no matter how small the company is, it gains exposure to virtually all users around the world. However, even if a company doesn't have an online presence (for example a small shop), its products and services can still be known through word of mouth. The Internet has therefore now become an essential tool for business makers at any levels.

Another important factor to understand the way digital systems operate is their strong synergy with traditional media. TV channel websites are a good example of that. These websites allow viewers to re-watch old programs and watch current ones live, giving them the opportunity to send comments or cast votes online through specifically designed blogs, which have now become an active part of the show itself. Another example is the newspaper and magazine's websites, which exist alongside their relative paper editions. Those websites are not a mere copy of the paper edition but are actually a richer source of information which includes videos and ad hoc comments and sometimes, as in the case of Turin's "La Stampa", are a portal to access the newspaper's historical archive, containing all articles ever written since the foundation of the newspaper.

At this stage, the crucial question is: How can a company maintain and develop its long-term economic value using digital technologies effectively? Let's keep considering the newspapers as an example: How can they still make a profit when the same content (and sometimes an even larger one) is available to the readers online for free? In other words, which business models can a company operating on the digital market adopt to create value for both its customers and its stakeholders, generating adequate revenues? And are these business models competing methods?

The answer to the latter question is that the main types of online revenues can operate side by side within the same e-business model (Vernuccio, 2014).

The main kind of e-business, as the most common online source of revenue, is the advertising based model, particularly when managing a traditional website or when dealing with social media. Advertisers pay for a space on the website which is visible to their target customers. In this respect, it is very important for this business model to assess the volume and quality of traffic generated by the website in relation to the advertiser's targets. This can be based either on the number of visualizations of the webpage showing the advertisement, for example through a banner or a targeted link, or on the actual number of openings of the advertisement link.

Another option could be asking users to make a subscription to get access to special services and content in a formula defined premium. For example, if we consider newspapers and magazines, that would mean having access to integral articles or interviews about particularly important facts, comments or people.

Companies creating applications for smartphones and tablets generally adopt a compromise between the two solutions mentioned above. These apps can be downloaded from several digital stores and are available in free versions (containing ads) or in paid versions (free of ads).

Pay-per-view is a similar solution to subscriptions: Users pay exclusively for what they actually use, for example watch a movie or listen to a song. However, this proves to be a weak solution as users can now download for free the same content from other websites (usually hosting advertisement links). Several users, in fact, settle for lower quality content and do not hesitate to break copyright laws in order to save some money. This is a consequence of the fact that the Internet is a free space and it is perceived as such by the majority of the people.

Affiliation is yet another online business model aiming at increasing both the visibility of the brand and the customer base. The affiliating website hosts a link connected to an affiliate website. The latter, then, pays the affiliating a percentage of the profitable sales.

This is a more systematic and complex system than, for example, eBay, which provides users willing to sell their products with a digital platform and charges a commission on the revenues.

For the sake of completeness we should mention the mark-up-based model, in which the website operator increases sales prices, and the production based model, usually adopted by companies selling their products directly online.

As already mentioned, in the trade and distribution field the progressive integration between physical and digital channels is progressively becoming the successful model. Direct and indirect sales outlets exist along with the Internet and customers can buy products online and collect them in a shop or, vice versa, buy products on the net in a shop and get them delivered at home.

1.7. The integration between digital and physical channels in luxury markets

As mentioned above, until recently, companies were considered the only source of communication messages and brand related content, developed to influence consumer behaviors and create brand-equity. With the advent of social media, one-way communication has given way to a two-ways form defined as peer-to-peer-communication (Hautz and Füller, 2014); consumers can now generate and distribute their UGC – *User Generated Content* – (Ertimur and Gilly, 2010).

In the days of the web, companies are forced to develop their marketing relations in a completely new environment. Post-modern consumers are gradually changing their purchasing habits; the most significant aspect of this change is the way they relate to their purchases. Consumers are becoming more independent thanks to their ability to master the Internet, a fundamental tool that allows them to carry out this new kind of interaction and activism with the brand.

New consumers are more competent as they have acquired further information about their purchasing options and have gained an adequate level of knowledge to make the right choice. New consumers are very different from the unprepared old consumers of the past. In fact, they are demanding and expect producers to provide them with services and attention, preferring quality to quantity.

In order for a luxury good to be successful in the digital channels, two conditions need to be satisfied: A correct and personalized identification and a multisensory experience (Kapferer and Bastien, 2009).

In recent years both consumers and the competitive scenario have seen a change due to the increased importance of digital channels and the globalization of the market. This has pushed luxury companies to develop new marketing strategies to keep operating on markets that have become more and more international and are characterized by more demanding and better-informed consumers.

Luxury players are developing a presence in a plurality of channels. In this perspective, digital channels become a hybrid means of interaction with the demand: They perform informative, transactional and relational functions using physical or virtual procedures either alternatively or simultaneously.

Multichannel management policies are fundamental to retain existing customers and win over new market segments.

Luxury companies were reluctant to use the web as one of their distribution channels at first, considering it as lacking the customer experience provided inside the physical retail point of sale and far removed from wealthier buyers. Things have recently changed as the importance of digital channels has become clear to all brands operating on high symbolic value markets.

Luxury players have therefore adopted digital channels alongside the physical channels. Traditional shops still retain a significant importance when buying a luxury good but the great success of digital channels makes them an essential tool for high symbolic market players. A web strategy is nowadays necessary for luxury brands.[3]

Marketing strategies involving social media and the web place the consumer at the center of the process and communicate the brand's values through entertainment, involvement and fun. Consumers become the central characters and companies can implement engagement activities and use word of mouth in a proactive and dynamic way.

Multi-channeling is a process aiming at placing information, products and services, before and after sale, on the market using two or more channels. The management of the demand is not tied to single and independent channels but gives value to the potential of tertiarization of the economy and the diffusion of digital technologies.

This perspective overcomes the information and distribution difficulties typical of traditional sales outlets, taking full advantage of the division between physical and informational flows. Each consumer can therefore interact with the company, or any of its specific departments, at any time and in a discretionary way (Rangaswamy and Van Bruggen, 2005).

In a managerial perspective, multi-channeling becomes a process aimed at understanding, designing, coordinating and valorizing the different channels. This with the objective of increasing the value generated by the customer base (customer equity) through specific acquisition, retention and development actions.

This approach to multi-channeling allows companies to manage all different types of demand using the communication flexibility offered by digital technologies.

Multichannel management policies can have a fundamental role in winning over new market segments and therefore expand the market's dimensions. At the same time, customer relationship management can benefit from a careful use of the channels, gathering new and unusual pieces of information on consumer's habits. In this respect, the digital environment is a privileged observation laboratory for consumer behavior.

The diffusion of a multichannel behavior on the demand side opens up to an increase of competition and provides more chances for the consumer to identify the best combination good-service-price. In order to understand how consumers use the different channels available, new models of segmentation of the demand must be adopted. These models should take into account the actual reasons underlying the choice of digital or physical channels (Miceli, 2008). Luxury players need to develop a strategy integrating the digital and physical channels instead of a stand alone digital policy.

Considering that luxury market main players have developed a strategic path using the digital channels and that positive business models have been created by both luxury brands and independent subjects with a distributing role – like the Pure Internet Players –, the new frontier is the identification of integration paths between digital and physical distribution and communication channels.

In a multichannel perspective, virtual channels are often integrating and complementing traditional channels. Digital channels have significantly changed the activities of the distribution chain. In fact, products that are purchased online are often the same that are bought offline, only with a different service and set of information. Physical and digital channels must be integrated in order to have a global perspective on customer behaviors (customer journey).

The diffusion of the digital space has increased channel management opportunities whilst opening up to new forms of competition. New technologies have contributed to the definition of a hybrid space in which pre and post digital revolution pattern exist side by side.

The spreading of digital spaces in their different forms is the main reason for the growing number of consumers taking up new activities along with their traditional purchasing habits. Digital instruments allow consumers to search for information on products and brands, compare prices and choose the closest sales outlet.

We should take into consideration that consumers who usually buy products on channels at full price tend to maintain their choice to use a second channel for longer if compared to those who use less expensive channels both on a monetary and cognitive level (Venkatesan *et al.*, 2007).

The simultaneous use of different channels is a point of reassurance for the consumers and it therefore translates into higher revenues in comparison to different approaches (Berger *et al.*, 2006). In fairness, we should mention the opinions of those academics who firmly appose digital channels supporting the opinion that they reduce transactional costs making it easier for customers to leave the client base. This goes against all efforts put into customer acquisition and relationship management. Moreover, the presence of digital channels in the channel mix would discourage the use of alternative channels, reducing the opportunities for interaction (Ansari *et al.*, 2005). In actual fact, a multichannel strategic approach is beneficial to both companies and consumers. The diffusion of multichannel marketing (Ricotta, 2009) enhances customer interactions and helps companies to promptly identify market changes.

Companies have many advantages in using several platforms to reach out to customers:

- Increased chance to receive full feedback on what customers expect and how companies can improve their services. Increased customers' brand loyalty. In fact, customers are prepared to pay a higher price.
- Increase in sales. Offering a variety of points of contact with the customer, multichannel sales make the whole purchasing experience easier and more pleasant, thus increasing profits.
- Increase in productivity. Employees can use new technologies to make the customer service more efficient. The best way of managing a multichannel strategy is focusing on the customer more than on the channel itself. Customers are, in fact, nowadays considered as an integral part of the productive process.

A multichannel approach benefits consumers also:

- Easy access to information. The abundance of information enhances customer awareness and allows buyers to deeply assess all possible purchasing alternatives.
- Saving time. It is one of the most important advantages in comparison to the physical channels. The use of several channels allows consumers to compare quickly and effectively.
- Desire for interaction. Virtual spaces foster more interactions than physical spaces, assuring the involvement of the consumers, who are naturally attracted to social relationships.
- Quick delivery time. Consumers often prefer digital and virtual outlets as they guarantee the product's ready availability.

1.8. Some questions

The tendency to integrate traditional and digital channels typical of click and mortar companies (see above) is nowadays becoming widespread. Furthermore, E-marketing is proving to be more effective for some specific product categories like financial products, travels and hotels booking, books and digital music (despite the already mentioned copyright issues).

For other products, users still look for information on the web but then prefer to buy the products at a traditional sales point. It is the case, for example, for expensive goods like cars or less expensive and very common ones like clothes, even though some successful pure players profitably operate in this field too.

Another obstacle for companies operating online is the so-called "background noise" generated by the web. This is the excessive presence of online proposals and information, which can confuse consumers and hide services and products of those companies that are struggling to come up in search engines.

Users' privacy issues and the security of online transactions, then, should not be underestimated either. There is, in fact, the real risk that personal data collected for online transactions be used for different ends (like – for example – predicting customer's purchasing habits without their authorization) or for criminal purposes.

Companies are exposed to hackers and industrial or political espionage too. Although strict norms regulating both privacy and security are in place, it is often difficult to identify and prosecute the perpetrators of these crimes.

Notes

1   Data taken from *Digital in 2016*, a document published by We are social (wearesocial.net).

2   A neologism springing from the union of *producer* and *consumer*.

3   According to the third edition of the *Digital Luxury Experience (DLE)*, a survey carried out by Fondazione Altagamma in cooperation with McKinsey in 2012, revenues for luxury goods sold on line have reached 7.5 billion Euros, 4% of the total sales. Experts (BNP Paribas, 2015) predict an increase to 6% in 2017, for a total amount of 17 billion Euros. The survey highlights how multi-brand websites selling products at full price have shown the highest increase. In fact, digital channels cannot be considered simply as a virtual space where consumers look for bargains anymore. Luxury customers look for good services and complete offers, exactly as they do in the physical channels. The role of smartphones and tablets becomes then ever more central: 50% of luxury consumers search for information on a mobile device. Moreover, there is a strong correlation between sales increase and number of web pages visited: Companies showing a page per visit higher than the average of the panel, have known an increase of the 16%.

Chapter 2
DIGITAL CHANNELS IN LUXURY MARKETS

2.1. Introduction

When analyzing the digital channel and their players as possible intermediaries in the market distribution of goods with high symbolic value, we should first question its actual capacity to represent a valid option for luxury brands.

Until 2005, the opinion of managers and researchers on the subject was in the majority either skeptical or very negative. The main doubts expressed can be summarized in the following questions: is the WWW able to guarantee a shopping experience to the consumer of luxury goods? What is the actual number of consumers buying luxury goods online? Do luxury companies have the necessary know how to sell via the Internet?

From then until now the evolution of digital channels in the marketing of goods with high symbolic value has been rapid, with the judgments expressed at the time on its marginality having been surpassed by the facts.

In just a few years its role has changed due to several factors; the main one being the evolution of technologies such as the development of broadband, the widespread use of new devices such as smartphones and tablets, increased inter-connectivity, consumers' ability to 'share' and the development of social networks (Heine and Berghaus, 2014).

The disposable income of consumers from emerging markets such as China, South America and Africa, has also increased and is characterized by a higher propensity to use the Internet. Another factor to be considered is the progressively increasing use of digital channels by a broad range of customers belonging to the more mature areas of the market, who are showing increased confidence (or less distrust) regarding online purchases.

Further on in this chapter we will return specifically to the main doubts surrounding the use of digital channels in the luxury goods market and how today they have been assuaged by the evolution of the market, technology and consumer attitudes.

Today it can be said, therefore, that the digital channel has assumed strategic importance for companies operating in the market for high symbolic value goods; in fact, both use by consumers and turnover achieved by companies are constantly increasing (Okonkwo, 2010). As a result, for luxury players, creating experiences on the online becomes the imperative (Okonkwo, 2010). This need is strengthened by luxury consumers, who are more willing to take part in the process of sharing brands' values through the online platforms (Rifkin, 2000; Mosca *et al.*, 2013). Furthermore, some recent studies (Boston Consulting Group, 2015) study clearly points out that the omni-channel communication represents the challenge for luxury players, to make their online presence more effective, from institutional websites to specialized platforms.

Luxury players seem to strive more than others to modify and integrate their products offer and communication on the online, because they have to adapt to a "pop" culture without loosing their unique character and exclusivity (Aiello and Donvito, 2005; Mosca *et al.*, 2013).

In order to survive in the current competitive market, communicating through online platforms is a growing and necessary tendency. Top global luxury brands such as Vuitton, Chanel, Gucci, Burberry, Cucinelli and many others have worked together with broadcasters and app developers in order to intensify on the online their story telling over brands' heritage.

2.2. The advantages of digital channels: firms and consumers side

The Internet is a digital space for making transactions[1] (Rayport and Sviokla, 2004) in that it activates an innovative distribution channel, which offers distinguishable benefits based on the people who potentially benefit from them (Dall'Olmo Riley and Lacroix, 2003): companies and the consumers (Figures 2.1 and 2.2).

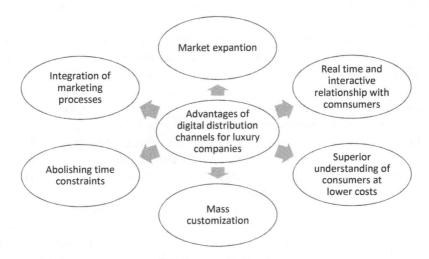

Figure 2.1 The advantages of digital distribution channels for companies

From the point of view of supply, electronic channels generate the following benefits for companies (Kalakota and Whinston, 1997):

- Expanding markets: the potential market is being expanded beyond every imaginable geographical limit with the result that, at least in theory, a small or medium size enterprise can expand its offerings without having to invest in physical distribution structures in foreign markets. Kalakota Whinston demonstrated that the costs for accessing virtual stores are exceedingly low and independent of distance.
- Development of direct two-way communication in real time: companies have the opportunity to establish a communicative relationship with the consumer (Otto and Chung, 2000). The advantage of the channels' interactivity means that access time to digital sales points is zero (Hoffman and Novak, 1996).
- Information about consumers: a corollary of this possibility to develop two-way communications is that the Internet provides superior understanding of the consumers with whom the company develops transactions, through low-cost acquisition of information. In fact, the consumers themselves provide, on request, their data and/or information on their tastes, demands and lifestyles (Daugherty, Eastin and Bright, 2008).
- Mass customization: even in the midst of numerous contacts with consumers, it is possible, at reasonable cost, to establish a per-sonalized and unique relationship with each individual. Customer loyalty therefore can thus be effectively optimized, not only with regard to communication, but also in relation to offer contents (Sciarelli and Vona, 2000).
- Abolishing time constraints: digital channels enable companies to make sales that are not bound to any point in time, thus overcoming the physical time barriers of non-digital distribution (Spar and Busgang, 1996).
- Integration of marketing processes: collecting information from the market, designing new products, the sales process, collecting orders, logistical management, accounting and finance can all be integrated with greater effectiveness and efficiency in the digital channel arena (Mandelli, 1998; Alba *et al.*, 1997; Klein and Quelch, 1997; Kalakota and Whinston, 1997).

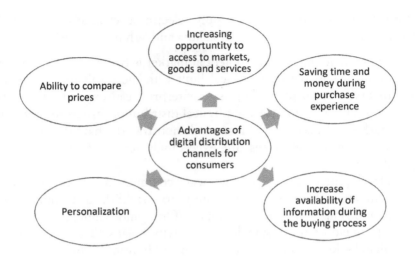

Figure 2.2 The advantages of digital distribution channels for consumers

The advantages to consumers of using digital channels can be summarized as follows:

- Increased opportunities to access markets, goods and services: the consumer can overcome physical time limits, which hinder search and selection, thus expanding access to products, services, geographic markets and an increased number of companies. The traditional limited rationality of the consumer, as understood in marketing studies, tends to decrease during the purchasing process via digital channels, in which the consumer's capacity to gather information increases exponentially.
- Reduction in the expenses incurred by the consumer during the purchase process; costs resulting from physical movement while searching for a product or service and the amount of time to be devoted to the purchase are decreased. The consumer can access the market in real time, with no limits on time or day of the week.
- Increase in basic information during the buying process: the consumer has a direct flow of information from the manufacturer, in real time, without the presence of intermediaries who may distort it (McKnight *et al.*, 2002).
- Greater personalization: the product available can be more effectively customized based on the specific demands of the consumer.
- Ability to compare prices: the customer can avail of an efficient and reduced marginal cost system to make comparisons between the

prices of products and services. This possibility makes consumers more rational and increases their power over the market.

In the face of numerous, widely shared benefits, interpretation has highlighted a number of structural weaknesses within digital channels.[2] These, however, are not the specific subject of our discussion, which is limited to goods with high symbolic value.

Here, however, we are confronting the incompatibilities between the Internet channel in general and the consumer of luxury goods, historically reported in various studies on the subject. The principal ones being:[3]

a) No emotional features to the purchase.
b) Lack of point of sale experience.
c) Inadequate relationship with the vendor.
d) Poor activation of fiduciary relationships with the vendor.
e) Inability to find the desired product.

Three more theories ingrained within the digital channel arena in all markets, which however take on special significance in the area of luxury goods, should be added to the list.

The first can be attributed to the problems related to security of transactions, which for high-end goods are more evident to consumers, since the average value of each sale is higher than sale occurred in consumer good markets. The second reason for incompatibility is linked to the counterfeiting of luxury branded products, which promotes doubt among consumers that they are making a purchase that is not guaranteed. The third is the presence of cognitive barriers in use of the medium.

The presence of these obstacles, while in the process of being overcome, still means it is very easy to make mistakes in choosing and managing digital channels within the market goods with high symbolic value, especially in a rapidly changing scenario.

Figure 2.3 shows some negative opinions held by management on the use of digital channels.

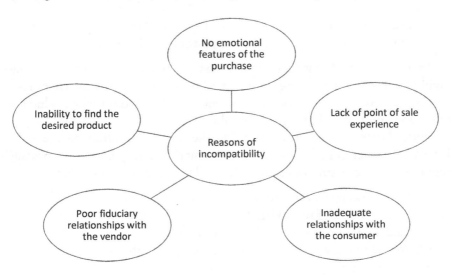

Figure 2.3 Negative opinions held by management on digital channels

The advantages attributable to company and consumer – as previously identified – were not, in the past, actually achievable in the market for goods with a high symbolic value. Taking as reference the classification of barriers to the development of digital channels according to their technological, economic, psycho-cultural, juridical-legal and socio-cultural nature,[4] (Sciarelli and Vona, 2000 and 2009) it was mainly the latter that assumed particularly relevance in the arena of the high symbolic value goods market.

The preference for face to face,[5] interpersonal contact with the seller; the importance attached by the consumer to physical, multi-sensory contact (Castaldo and Premazzi, 1999) with the product and the recreational significance connected to the purchase process made the Internet a difficult option for distribution.

In order of importance, the barriers to the development of digital channels in the market for high symbolic value goods were:

- Features of the purchase process for the consumer and the product.
- Management mistrust.[6]
- Potential conflict with physical sales outlets.
- Lack of skills and an increase in logistical costs.
- Inadequate consumer IT culture.
- Increased perception of risk.
- Lack of referent business models.

The case of Boo.com, whose intention was to become a digital intermediary in the market for high symbolic value goods, is a reminder of the potential for failure due to the incompatibility issues highlighted above.

Boo.com. The company was founded to become the first global e-tailer of fashion and prestige products, where client services were offered in the language of their respective countries. The digital sales point had been designed to offer luxury/fashion products in the US and Europe.[7]

The project involved launching a global brand label (Miller, 2000) and the corporate vision was described as "bringing beautiful clothing to the world" (Goldstein, 1999).

The features and objectives of the digital intermediary, Boo.com, were as follows:

- Premium brands: to make over twenty high-end brands available to the consumer, with a particular focus on sportswear products.
- Presence in key international markets: Boo.com would have distributed products to eighteen markets. The logistics centers were located in the United States and Germany.
- To offer a unique virtual environment, organized to provide the consumer with a shopping experience. The site was equipped with advanced features, designed to not only offer consumers the possibility to choose colors, price ranges and brands, but also various product categories according to sporting activity.
- Increased options for customization and development of personal one-to-one relationships with consumers: a distinctive element of the virtual store was the option to personalize and inspect product characteristics prior to payment.[8]

The principal strategic error that caused Boo.com to fail as a digital intermediary in the market for high symbolic value goods was a lack of consistency between marketing mix variables and a horizontal conflict between the physical sales points and the digital intermediary, which was perceived as a direct competitor.

Products sold on the digital channel were no different to those in the physical channel: the offer of Boo.com was characterized by a mix of branded products that spanned the development or maturity phases of their life cycle. Consumers therefore did not perceive any real product differentiation and their attention was thus focused on the price.

In reference to this variable, Boo.com chose to fix prices in alignment with the market conditions of the physical intermediaries, considering this to be supporting its brand image.[9] The consumer, however, looking for an emotional experience and in light of price parity, opted to buy from the physical intermediaries.

The horizontal conflict between organizations on distribution channels is intense because intermediaries are perceived by consumers as being scarcely differentiated one from another, both in terms of the price variable and range of products. In general, brand manufacturers are concerned that the excessive development of digital stores may cause disintermediation (Collesei et al.,

1999), to the detriment of traditional physical entities through which the major share of the market is created.

Boo.com's collaborative agreements with certain major brands of high-end sports clothing, such as Nike, were not implemented because the brand manufacturers did not want to create conflict with the traditional channel.

In addition to the lack of consistency, this being the principal strategic reason for Boo.com's failure, there were other aspects related more closely to operational marketing mistakes during the launch of the digital store. The main ones being: lack of prepared management; high logistical expenses and other significant costs incurred for the launch of the advertising campaign; the use of technologies that were not yet in widespread use by the target consumer and in addition, a slowdown in sales potential. [10] Also the decision to simultaneously trade in eighteen countries right from the initial development phase of the digital store – overestimating globalization factors in relation to the local peculiarities of the individual markets – contributed to the failure of the initiative. The management of Boo.com did not take into consideration certain operational factors related to digital transactions. [11] Lastly, the publicity campaign was entrusted to the traditional media. [12]

2.3. Consumer behaviour in online purchasing of high symbolic value goods

In recent years, as already pointed out, the reference scenario for the use of digital channels has totally changed. This also applies to the consumption of luxury goods. The numerous success stories of independent e-commerce sites, such as Yoox.com and Net-a-porter.com (now belonging to one single group), Victoriassecret.com, Bagborroworsteal.com, Neiman-marcus.com, Gioie.it, Bluenile.com and sales websites directly controlled by the luxury players such as LVMH, Christian Dior, Burberry, Gucci, Armani and others, have highlighted the increasing importance of digital channels within the distribution strategies for high-end goods.

Studies on the spread of digital channels, opinions of managers and experts, and empirical case studies indicate a scenario of rapid change, in which the main incompatibility issues for consumers of high symbolic value goods, while resisting certain barriers, are being surmounted. [13]

There is no doubt that consumers have progressively and quickly changed their attitude toward buying luxury goods on digital channels in recent years (Bijmolt *et al.*, 2010) and it is important to note that online shopping behavior is different from that offline in several respects. Also, new consumer profiles have recently emerged (Bowden, 2009).

The new scenario is taking shape and it is possible to identify certain needs and specific behaviors that must be kept in mind when relating to the digital consumer of goods with high symbolic value:

-   Emotional connection: the consumer's emotional connection with the brand, which is determined by its heritage and image, is highly relevant.
-   Online experience: the consumer is also consciously or even unconsciously searching for an experience within the digital channel, via experiential digital content.
-   Development of fiduciary relationships: with experience the consumer develops trusting relationships within the sphere of digital channels. The individual channel's functional features (i.e. ease of use), familiarity, habit, interaction and availability of additional content, form the basis of these relationships.
-   Alternative models: the consumer follows different buying patterns, for which interpretative models have been proposed. See, for example, Mohammed *et al.* (2002) in their book *Internet Marketing. Experience Hierarchy* (Okonkwo, 2009). This model has four phases and is constructed on the principle that the sum of the customer's online experiences contributes significantly to forming his/her opinion of a site, which in turn influences future visits. The online experience also has an effect on the general perception that the consumer has of the company and will help determine the possibility of further purchases. The model is illustrated in Figure 2.4.

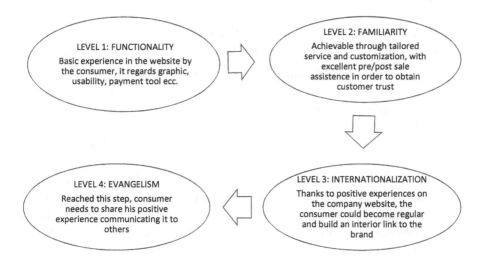

Figure 2.4 The Experience Hierarchy model

Evaluation of the consumer experience stresses the need for companies to provide consumers with a positive and pleasant sensation during the online purchase. The fundamental requirement in achieving this is the capacity of the digital channel to highlight the characteristics of the brand and to make the experience unique and special for each individual. Some important socio-cultural factors that influence the behaviour of luxury goods consumers who use digital channels should also be noted. Consumers who purchase luxury goods are more highly educated, young and are innovators. These individuals have superior knowledge of alternative offers and have a wide choice of brands available across digital channels, with lower switching costs (Van Doorn *et al.*, 2010). This means they have the option to view different products and make comparisons, selecting the most suitable product possessing the desired characteristics, without wasting time. Consumers of online luxury goods also have very high expectations. In particular it is important that, even though a site may be accessible to millions of people, the luxury companies must be able to design it so as to reflect exclusivity (Okonkwo, 2007).

Some researchers have tried to divide online consumer communities based on purchasing influences. Other studies have looked to the distinction between buying behavior in digital and traditional channels. Typical online consumer profiles can be identified by adopting, for example, the classification proposed by Jakob Nielsen in his book *Designing Web Usability* (Nielsen, 1998).

On the basis of this subdivision, the typical profiles of consumers in relation to their attitude toward using digital channels are the following:

- *Social shopper*. Individuals who associate the purchase of goods with pleasure and social gatherings. This is the least likely group to use electronic commerce (Stephen and Toubia, 2010).
- *Habitual shopper*. Individuals who always make purchases in the same shops and do not frequently change brand. This group will remain faithful to traditional trading for a long time to come.
- *Ethical shopper*. Individuals who are mostly concerned with ethical issues when they purchase, such as the origin of materials and the working conditions of employees rather than the brand. Their potential for Internet purchasing is average and sites concern themselves with meeting their ethical expectations.
- *Value shopper*. Individuals who are looking for added value in terms of product quality, price and service offered. It is therefore likely that they will look for these features in an online purchase (Huang and Benyoucef, 2014).

- *Experimental shopper.* Individuals who are open to trying new brands and purchasing channels. This group is very likely to purchase online.
- *Convenience shopper.* Individuals who prefer to purchase without wasting time. This is the largest group of target customers most suitable to digital channels (Cotte *et al.*, 2006).

Most consumers of luxury goods online fall into experimental and convenience shopper groups.

2.4. Overcoming the main constraints to adopting digital channels in markets for high symbolic value goods

Until a few years ago, as highlighted at the beginning of the chapter, many luxury brands put up strong resistance to the adoption of digital channels.

Let us examine their main restrictions in more depth.

Less brand loyalty. Despite online consumers tending to switch brands frequently, they are likely to repeat their visit and also their purchase in the event of having a positive experience on the site. At the same time, after a negative experience, a repeat visit to the online channel is less likely than to the traditional one. This is because the traditional selling point, even though it has not fully met the consumer's expectations, is often characterized by economies of proximity for the consumer. In the case of online sales the latter obviously do not apply, because everything is virtually "close" and the consumer has no difficulty in identifying alternative purchasing options.

Even on digital channels, management must know how to grant consumers a unique shopping experience, focusing on aspects that stimulate the sensory receptors. In general, the key elements or sensory stimuli for transferring emotions during the purchase process are: touch, sight, sound, accessibility, and personalization.

Figure 2.5 shows some examples drawn from analyses, referring to numerous cases in point, such as how sensory stimuli can be used in digital channels.

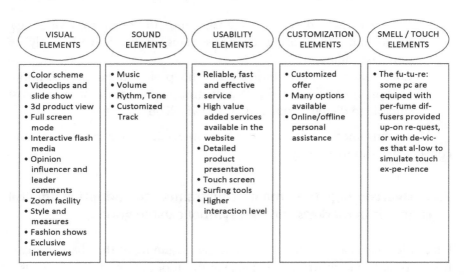

Figure 2.5 Key elements for transferring emotions to the consumer in digital channels

Lack of purchase experience at the point of sale. Many consumers, especially young people, prefer to buy high-end goods over the Internet, which guarantees unlimited options, speed of purchase, accurate information and online presentation of the product with high-quality images.

When making the purchase, the physical experience is replaced with a virtual one: more immediate, faster, more intense, less repetitive, with more detailed information available to the consumer who wants more in-depth product knowledge (Babin, Darden and Griffin, 1994).

The phenomenon of the online purchasing experience, difficult to predict even only a few years ago, is spreading in line with the evolution of digital media such as YouTube, Facebook, Instagram and Pinterest (Pöyry, Parvinen and Malmivaara, 2013).

To the above it should be added that many consumers buy luxury goods online inasmuch as they are not available in shops in their towns or countries. The phenomenon is particularly evident by observing the distribution of the turnover of certain online luxury goods sites, which shows, for example, that there are numerous Chinese consumers in smaller cities. These individuals buy online luxury goods because a physical sale point for their preferred brand is not yet available in their city.

Inadequate interaction with the vendor and poor creation of relationships of trust. Digital channels with configurations that show products from different viewing angles and dimensions, along with a wealth of information and details, including the ability to communicate online or through Skype with a seller, enable young consumers particularly to overcome the need for a direct relationship with the sales assistant.

Inability to find the desired product. The evolution of digital channels has enabled firms to provide online products and services with an increased degree of personalisation and variety (Wang and Zhang, 2012). The availability of advanced logistics platforms servicing Internet sites enables companies to manage variety at an acceptable cost.

Technological constraints. Finally, historical issues related to the inadequate technological evolution of digital channels and lack of security surrounding transactions, are gradually being overcome.

Retracing the theoretical advantages for the consumer and companies that derive from the use of digital channels, it can be said today, therefore, that digital channels have assumed a strategic and growing importance for companies operating in the market for high symbolic value goods.

This does not however permit the assertion that there is now a zero risk factor. It should be noted, in fact, that the main danger today in the inappropriate use of digital channels for goods with a high symbolic value, is still the potential damage to brand image.

In this regard, Kapferer (2000) explains that e-commerce is at the same time both an opportunity and a threat for luxury brands. The opportunity exists in being able to reach potential consumers who do not have easy access to physical sales outlets or are intimidated by them. The threat comes from the risk of cheapening the brand image, either being referenced by other websites, with the risk of product resale (Kapferer, 2000) on uncontrollable channels, or the ever present danger of being subjected to the scams resulting from the marketing of counterfeit products.

2.5. The case of Yoox Net-a-Porter

Yoox.com, born in the late nineties, is a pure, independent Internet player operating in the luxury goods market. It has a presence on the main markets – Europe, USA, Canada, Japan and China – with positive operating profits and a turnover that is growing exponentially.

Each month the Yoox.com site is visited by five million people and sells over a million products to consumers in the global markets where it operates. Just three months after the start of its activities, Yoox.com achieved one million purchase orders; revenues, cash flows and earnings also remained positive in subsequent periods.

Turnover in 2008 was 132 million, in 2009 it was up to 152 million and in 2012 they recorded 29.1% growth. The increase remained constant over the following years, until it reached an increase of 15.1% in 2014. Total investment stated by the shareholders at the end of 2014 was 127 million euro.

The company was listed on the Milan stock exchange in 2010. The merger in March 2015 between Yoox and Net-a-Porter, resulting in Yoox Net-A-Porter Group Limited, was implemented via a Yoox share-exchange. The group became an independent leader in luxury e-commerce with estimated aggregate net revenues of 1.3 billion euro and an EBITDA of about 108 million euro.

As sole shareholder Richemont maintains 50% of the shares, while the rest are owned by Yoox shareholders. To maintain the company's independence, Richemont has only 25% of the voting rights. The objective of the merger was the union of two companies characterized by highly complementary businesses, in order to reach all the luxury markets and involve different categories of consumers. The company's intention is to occupy a unique position within the luxury fashion e-commerce market, creating synergies between Yoox (which holds partnerships with leading luxury brands) and the global presence of Net-a-Porter as multi-brand online retailers.

With six proprietary online stores the fashion and luxury markets are covered throughout the entire life cycle of the product. The organisation is structured as follows: Net-a-porter.com, Mrporter.com, Thecorner.com and Shoescribe.com make up the in-season multi-brand channel, while Yoox.com and Theoutnet.com serve as off-season multi-brand channels.

They expect to cover more than one hundred and eighty countries with expected aggregated net sales of 28% from North America, 15% from the UK, 7% from Italy, 30% from the rest of Europe, 15% from Asia Pacific and 5% in the rest of the world. [14]

Origins. Since the start of operations (Lovelock *et al.*, 2007; Depperu, 1999), Yoox.com's role is that of disposing of unsold products that are heading toward the end of their life cycle and consequently it uses the price variable to attract consumers, who have the opportunity to buy at prices reduced by 40 to 70%. Products sold on the digital channel are the previous season's collections, with a variety of limited ranges and a wider assortment than any physical sales outlet. Of particular interest is the product presentation model on Yoox.com's digital sales point: after selecting the products, the company has them photographed and placed on the site with a careful description of their physical and technical characteristics, colours, sizes and personalised alternatives available.

The customer, after purchasing, receives the product to try within forty-eight hours and has the option to return it within a day if it does not conform to his/her expectations. The consumer therefore perceives only a limited risk in making a purchase.

The strengths of Yoox.com. The reasons for the success of Yoox.com can primarily be summarised by the consistency of the role played by the digital intermediary. The option to focus distribution on products that are reaching the end of their life cycle and the decision to offer a price reduction are consistent with both the nature of high symbolic value goods and the characteristics of the consumer, as represented in Figure 2.6. Without this consistency between the marketing mix variables (product, price and distribution) it would not have been possible for Yoox.com to survive as a digital intermediary. As a consequence of the above, Yoox.com is able to avoid the risk of horizontal conflict within the distribution channel, between the digital intermediary and the physical one.

The second basic reason for the success of Yoox.com lies in the fact that horizontal conflict is minimised. The intermediaries are perceived by the consumer as highly differentiated one from the other both in terms of the price variable and range of products, there being no risk of arbitrage between the digital intermediary and the physical sales points.

Finally, the third reason is linked to the network of inter-systemic cooperative relationships that have been activated with other fashion-luxury companies. The cooperative relationships develop in three directions: relationships with other pure internet players, producers of high symbolic value goods and with Internet search engines.

Yoox.com has developed relationships with a consolidated network of Internet portals dedicated to fashion and luxury, carefully selected among the most efficient on the European, American and Japanese markets, to which it provides content for their sales sections devoted to fashion-luxury products.

These affiliates give Yoox.com "virtual storefronts" with highly visibility on their portals, in exchange for the opportunity to present products for sale on the Yoox.com site and also to insert promotions in the periodic newsletters sent to its customers.

This network of relationships makes Yoox.com an accessible and visible site, which consequently favours the expansion of its potential market.

Relationships with brand manufacturers are another strong point. The digital intermediary offers its collaboration within the channel, positioning itself as an exclusive partner in relation to the brand manufacturer. Yoox.com also presents itself as a guarantor for the brand image producer in the area of transactions with consumers based mainly on price.

The quality of services and the mix of brands offered on the Yoox.com digital intermediary allow the former to establish privileged relationships with the major manufacturers in the fashion-luxury arena, who also have the opportunity to dispose of unsold products on the digital channel without the risk of losing control.

The third relationship exists with Internet search engines in the form of a communication tool, along with a solid network of affiliates, to which various programmes are made available, including a specific section on the site dedicated entirely to affiliates. Network advertising has grown on a level commensurate with the company's development.

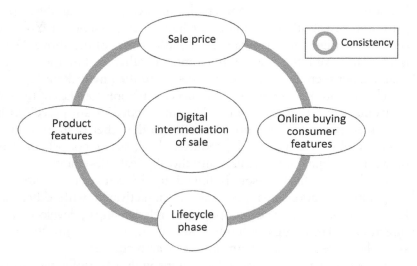

Figure 2.6 Yoox.com: consistency in managing controllable variables

The structure and style of Yoox.com. The Yoox.com sales point is light, graphically specific and understandable, containing all the information along with numerous promotions, a boutique open 24 hours a day, designed to offer added value to customers with fast deliveries, no additional charges and the option to return purchased products.

Having typed the site's browser address, a web page opens that is already adapted to the customer's home country. Even periodic communications to consumers via newsletters are often differentiated, as well as product prices, which vary depending on the market to comply with the individual retail price charged by the brands in different areas.

Customers can see all available products; software for warehouse management monitors an inventory of more than six thousand products, controlling restocking and the insertion of a hundred products per day.

The garments and accessories are sold in a digital environment characterised by a sophisticated style, where it is possible to view the products, filtering them by brand, sector category, gender, height, colour and other search variables.

The consumer can use the magnification and rotation functions to display the front and back of the product so as to evaluate it in detail. Alongside there is data sheet that provides the product description, its composition or dimensions, including colours, available sizes and price.

In the case of clothing products, consumers can personalise their products via the special "Mirror" function, which allows combinations to be created, inserting all desired items and offering a visual image of how they match.

Purchase is made using a cart, in a special area where the customer can choose the type of delivery (standard or express) and payment mode (credit card or cash). This is the first step in the completion of the order form. In the next step, the site requests personal information for delivery; payment and confirmation of data follows via e-mail, which confirms the order and its implementation. A further feedback e-mail is sent to the consumer at the time the products are shipped.

Attention is also paid to the packaging and it can be seen on the site. Delivery is guaranteed at the most in three or four working days. The agreement between Yoox.com and Banca Sella secures the transaction via the *Verified by Visa* system, which enables cardholder authentication at the precise moment the online purchase is made.

Although the physical characteristics of a virtual space may not on first analysis be considered a sustainable source of competitive advantage for a company, as they are easily imitated, the reality in certain cases is that they are the real reason that a long-standing customer relationship can be maintained. For example, the success of Amazon.com with regard to other virtual libraries such as barnesandnoble.com, is due to its superior ability to maintain long-term relationships with customers, the improved quality of their bibliographic search services and, not least, a better graphical interface.

Yoox Group lines of business. Yoox presents multi-brand and single-brand lines (see Figure 2.7). The first is divided into three e-commerce sites: Thecorner.com, the online boutique whose range is composed of the best-known brands combined with emerging designers; Shoescribe.com, dedicated to women's shoes; and Yoox.com, the flagship line handles customer assistance and management of certain fashion and luxury brand online stores.

Integration with Net-A-Porter enables further retail development with its presence on all the channels.

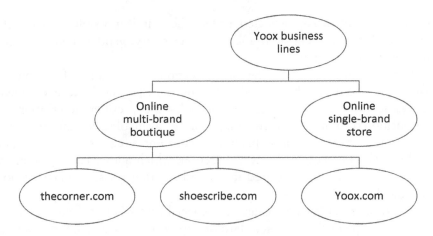

Figure 2.7 Yoox.com: business line

Logistics management. Another aspect to be highlighted is the management of logistics, often a key factor in e-commerce success. The selected products are collected in the central warehouse, where they undergo quality control, are photographed and entered on the server with careful, accurate descriptions. Subsequently the products are transferred to shipping warehouses. When the product is purchased online, the logistics flow includes a final packaging and preparation for shipment stage. Consumers can then check their order status at any stage both on the website and via call centres.

Figure 2.8 shows the logistics management flow.

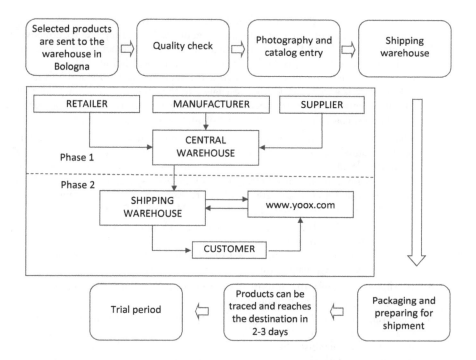

Figure 2.8 Yoox.com: logistics flow

Customer profile. The characteristics of people accessing the site are constantly changing. The latest figures reveal that access is mostly by female consumers, aged between 18 and 35 years old, with medium-high income and third level education; Asian consumers form the majority. The site does not show significant seasonal peaks in demand. Finally, consumers demonstrate an increased level of loyalty to the site by buying repeatedly.

Notes

1 In this sense it has been defined as a marketspace, to distinguish it from the marketplace, which is understood as the place where physical transactions are conducted.

2 Some weaknesses highlighted have already been overcome or are in the process. The main ones are: the Network bandwidth is not sufficient to be able to manage considerable increases in traffic and especially the transfer of multimedia content with efficient methods and timescales (Nemzow, 1997); transaction security issues are still not completely resolved; mechanisms to protect Network-connected corporate information systems from intrusion by

unauthorised individuals are still complex and costly (Nemzow, 1997); digital reality environments that enable the human-machine interface to effectively simulate the physical reality of customer-vendor interaction are still not available; there is no specific, internationally valid legislation that governs the legal and fiscal management of network transactions (Kalakota and Whinston, 1997); there is social and cultural resistance to the substitution of the traditional purchase with a digital transaction, also taking into consideration the recreational and social components of the act of shopping (Mandelli, 1998).

3 The compatibility constraints between consumers in the luxury market and digital channels were also analysed by a research carried out in France in 1997 on a sample of consumers, in which the authors came to the conclusion that there was no compatibility between goods of high symbolic value and digital channels (Dall'Olmo *et al.*, 2003). Other researchers of the phenomenon have also subsequently presented similar theories (McCusker, 2008).

4 The technological barriers can be attributed to poor operational speed and safety. Economic obstacles consist of high logistical operating costs, while the juridical-legal constraints are related to difficulties in configuring network sales in the context of typical contractual formats.

5 In digital channels the intermediary role is created through the computer (computer mediated communication).

6 Research conducted on a sample of company managers in the fashion-luxury sector in France in 1997 highlighted that a significant percentage of them proved to be against the use of digital channels as they were considered incompatible with the brand image. In particular, sales activities (e-commerce) conducted via the Internet were held responsible for deterioration in brand image (Nyelk and Roux, 1997).

7 The range of products offered included brands such as Adidas, Puma, North Face and niche brands such as Cosmic Girl and Vans.

8 There was for example, an electronic fitting room, a virtual room that allowed both male and female consumers to improve their digital experience by pairing any style or product from the various brands to create their own personalised clothing; or the creation of Miss Boo, a digital sales assistant, able to guide the buying process and provide real-time personalised answers to consumers' questions. Other features of the digital sales point included the option to accurately delineate the profile of the consumer and thus monitor his/her interests and requirements. The presence of a team of customer service staff trained in sport and fashion facilitated this customer assistance activity. Consumers were given the opportunity to make calls to customer service, send e-mails or communicate in real time with a call-centre system located in New York, London, Monaco and Stockholm. There was also an interactive international sport magazine, with high-quality photographs and images.

9 Although it should also be remembered that Boo.com, in an attempt to recover the enormous losses it had already accumulated, made the further mistake, during Christmas 1999, of launching a promotional programme with discounts of over 40%, which had a strong negative effect on its distributional branding positioning.

10 The technologies adopted were too sophisticated for an unaccustomed target

market that lacked training in their use. The photographs of the products, for example, should have been a distinctive factor in comparison with other virtual sales points. Thanks to this technology, consumers were able to zoom into images, rotate, change colours and e-mail them to friends. Access to the site was slow. Forrester Research noted that 99% of domestic users in Europe and 98% in the US did not yet have access to sufficient bandwidth to appreciate the sophisticated Boo.com animations. These technical difficulties limited access to the majority of consumers in the first phase of the project's development. To remedy this, Boo.com developed a more modest version of the site in February 2000, but in doing so the characteristics that made it a unique digital store were inhibited.

11 For example, the failure to consider the complexity of working with different currencies and tax systems. The content of a web site regarding final prices, terms of payment and the protection of privacy must, in fact, be different in each country, in relation to tax and customs legislation. Information about transaction security was not included in the first version of the site, but was added later, thus compromising the trust of potential customers.

12 Banner advertising and e-mail marketing were rarely used for online promotion.

13 In this regard, certain studies, subsequent to the initial ones conducted on the subject, confirm the trend of the 2000s. A French study conducted by Direct Panel (2008) showed strong growth in online sales for jewellery and watches with the launch of several new sites. See Direct Panel, *Barometro E-commerce & sites merchands*, press release, Gene Editing, 6 May 2008. Another study of the British Luxury Industry undertaken with Forrester Research, interviewed 178 luxury, fashion and high-end retailing sector managers in Europe, Asia and the United States. The interviews revealed a growing interest in the development of sales activities on digital channels and the majority of companies that did not yet have an e-commerce site declared their desire to create one. As for research on the question, Forrester's Consumer Technographics Research reported that: "*Eight out of ten High-net-worth Consumers make daily use of the Internet and actively research and buy luxury goods and services online on a regular basis.*" (Bracewell Lewis, 2008).

14 Other quoted and compared sources of reference relate to the sites: www.borsaitaliana.it, *Merger of Yoox Group and Net-a-Porter Group*, 31 March 2015; www.ilsole24ore.com, *Marriage of Yoox and Net-a-Porter: the online luxury front-runner has arrived. Marchetti at the wheel*, 31 March 2015.

Chapter 3

DIGITAL CHANNELS: REFERENCE MODELS FOR DIRECT AND INDIRECT DISTRIBUTION

3.1. Introduction

One of the major factors that contributed to the evolution of digital channels for luxury goods in recent years, alongside technological developments and the changing consumer culture, is the improved logistics management capabilities developed by luxury companies.

In the operative reality of these companies several main reference models can be observed, which show the various degrees to which these channels can be exploited and, consequently, the different levels of difficulty for the purpose of product sales. [1]

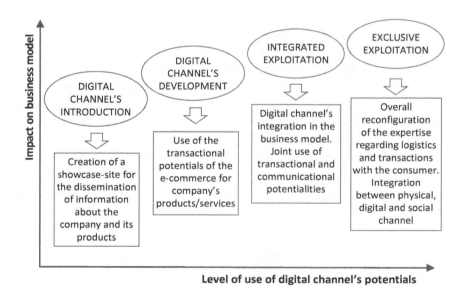

Figure 3.1 Presence levels of high symbolic value branded goods on digital channels

3.2. Distribution via direct digital channels

The company that follows this strategy monitors and manages digital distribution and/or communication channels, addressing its online products to the end consumer. Within this option different approaches are adopted and demonstrate variability in the exploitation of digital channels in relation to the objectives that the business intends to pursue.

Direct management digital channels with a communication function. The digital channel, when used to communicate with consumers, presents itself as a showcase on the virtual network where consumers can find information on the company related to its mission, activities, values, brand, history, heritage, corporate social responsibility activities, results achieved and products (Seringhaus, 2005).

The market approach at this level is not changed and transactions do not yet occur. The website assumes value as a communication medium, sometimes also interacting with the consumer, and transferring information flows (De Matos and Rossi, 2008).

For the main companies in the luxury-fashion sector during the period 2000-2005, digital channels were configured as showcase sites used for one-way communication.[2] For example, the portal conceived as a digital showcase for Louis Vuitton Moët Hennessy contained all the information on the Group and was the access point for a multitude of sites arranged by brands and products marketed. Trussadi performed along the same lines with a site full of information about the company and its products, as did Bulgari by presenting all the latest news about its collections of watches, jewellery and accessories but with no option to buy them.

Even today, companies retain the brand's showcase site, where no sales occur, but alongside there are one or more dedicated e-commerce sites.

LVMH. One example of a luxury brand with a showcase site is LVMH. The site is informational only and no option to purchase online is provided. It contains information on the Group, the various brands and product categories, investors and the latest news. It is available in three different languages. To view the products you first choose the desired category and then the brand that interests you. On the Louis Vuitton website, however, goods can be purchased.

Tiffany. Offers an international information-only website, except in certain countries where it becomes an e-commerce site, which shows all the different product categories and where the Blue Book can be consulted. It also presents the history of Tiffany, the latest news and information concerning the brand's social responsibility commitment.

Boffi. For Boffi, choosing to have a purely informative site is a consequence both of the technical characteristics of the product and the fact that its customers require personalized products that may not be included in the online sales. The site, which is in Italian and English, shows the kitchens, bathrooms, outdoor items, furnishings and the different collections. Sections are devoted to the history of Boffi and its corporate social responsibility.

Bulgari. Bulgari also presents a showcase site where you can view the various products by category – perfumes, accessories, watches – gifts for men & women section, all the news and information about the brand. It has a wishlist where you can enter the products you desire. A special window allows you to search a Bulgari boutique based on location and desired product category.

Direct management digital channels integrated with direct physical channels. This model foresees that the digital channel directly managed by the luxury brand is integrated with the direct physical channel. In some cases the directly managed digital channel could also be integrated with indirect physical channels, but this option is less frequent.

Via the digital channel consumers can choose your product and personalize it within the realm of the options offered.

The digital channel identifies and invites the customer to visit their physical sales outlets, where the personalized product can be collected. Payment is made at the directly managed physical sales point or online if the product is personalized.

The advantages of this solution are mainly due to the absence of logistical distributive operating expenses, which are generally connected to sales on digital channels and to minimizing conflict with physical inter-mediaries, who can consider the digital channel as a valuable support toward sales development and not a threat to their market share.

This option provides for a pluralistic and integrated distribution model, which means the company must exercise extreme care in the management of its direct channel, also with the goal of preventing direct digital distribution cannibalizing direct physical distribution.

Numerous companies that adopt mixed distribution systems tend to integrate the physical and the digital channels. Swarovski, for example, chose a predominantly direct distribution strategy in the physical channel and is present on the digital channel with both a website dedicated exclusively to communication and an e-commerce site.

Directly managed digital channel for a full-price luxury brand. Some luxury brands have taken advantage of the evolutionary development of digital channels to sell their full price products directly online. They have created genuine online stores that echo the brand values in a digital context with the goal of keeping the brand image intact. Cartier, on its website, does not immediately declare the price of its products, but first requires the customer to subscribe to the site or even make a phone call to the sales manager.

Bell & Ross. One of the first luxury brands to open up to online sales was Bell&Ross, who has made all their watches available, with the exception of limited series.

The bellross.com site opens with an initial video showing its latest collection and heightens brand awareness. On the homepage you can access all the collections and see the latest news on the brand's products. It is also possible to search your nearest sales outlet. A site map is also available, which directs the customer to the e-boutique, the products and a summary of the company's history.

Direct management digital channels for marketing products coming to the end of their life cycle. This option requires that the previous season's luxury item, or at least that which is no longer stocked at direct sales outlets, be marketed on the digital channel at a reduced price using a site managed directly by the luxury brand.

Direct management digital channels are often adopted for marketing products that are coming to the end of their life cycle. Management of the digital channel can be assigned to a dedicated business unit, or to third parties. The life cycle of high symbolic value products, especially in the specific area of the clothing and fashion market, is complex. The time span between the launch phase and decline is often reduced to just a few months (see Figure 3.2).

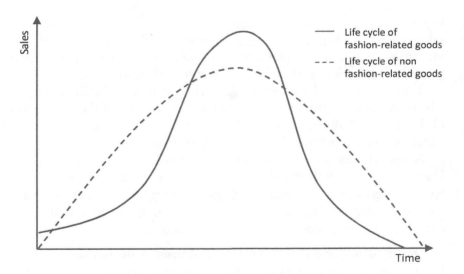

Figure 3.2 The life cycle of fashion-related goods

Digital channels enable the disposal of previous collection items in less time, mainly inducing consumers to buy with the use of price reductions.

This model[3] allows for several advantages:

- Reducing the risk of the uncontrolled spread of unsold items: the channeling of products in digital systems reduces the possibility that they are disposed of on parallel markets,[4] with serious damage to the brand image. The ever-present risk that unauthorized individuals will acquire online products for subsequent resale in the physical channel remains and cannot be eliminated.
- Different segments of the market: the consumer who buys on digital channels belongs to a different market segment than the traditional or occasional consumer who buys at physical intermediaries. For the consumer buying luxury goods on digital channels the elasticity of the demand price ratio is very high and the emotional component of the brand is perceived with less intensity.
- Price discrimination: the price differences applied to the product can be justified by keeping the channels and times when the product is sold, separated.

With this approach the consumer who purchases through the physical channel perceives the product available on the digital channel in a bidding system that is not comparable and therefore does not notice the injustice of a reduction, although significant, in the sale price.

Direct management digital channel aimed exclusively at the intermediary market (business to business). In this case the digital channel is dedicated to wholesalers and retailers, who can place online orders to establish or extend their assortment of brand products. The end-users are unable to access it. The business to business digital channel can be used by the company that controls the brand to supply both direct sales outlets (such as DOS for example) and independent outlets.

3.3. Distribution via indirect digital channels

In the years from 2010-2016 the rapid spread of the digital channel, the growth of online sales and their percentage compared to total sales in the luxury goods market, has favored, and gradually consolidated, the spread of innovative approaches to marketing luxury goods on the web.

The various indirect digital distribution models have in common the fact that the digital channel is managed by pure Internet players, i.e. companies that operate as independent intermediaries, selling various luxury brands.

Pure Internet cut-price multibrand players. This model requires the presence on the digital channels of an independent agent who sells luxury goods at a cut-price (Chevalier and Mayzlin, 2006). The products are disposed of on digital channels by using the factory outlet center logic. This is the case of Yoox.com and other independent companies, who, especially in the early stage of their development, sold cut-price, previous season, top of the range goods on the digital channel.

Currently the most successful pure Internet players, such as Yoox Net-A-Porter Group, have modified their business model, also selling special products exclusively online, sometimes at very high prices. This new trend highlights the opportunities that digital channels offer to managements to launch new collections on the market that are characterized by originality and innovation and aimed in particular at a young target audience.

As a result of the global recession in 2008-2009 some players on digital channels with luxury e-commerce sites reorganized their online activities, returning to appear as showcase sites, specialized in fashion and luxury trends, acting as access portals to sales sites, often directly controlled by a single brand.

Full-price, multibrand, Pure Internet players. This model requires the presence on the digital channel of an independent agent who sells luxury goods at full-price, positioning themselves, as intermediary, in direct competition with luxury brand e-commerce sites, as well as the physical sales outlets. This is the case of net-a-porter.com in the first phase of its development, mytheresa.com and also neimanmarcus.com, which represents a useful reference model.

Net-a-porter.com. Net-a-porter.com is a website launched in 2000 for the sale of current season clothing, footwear and fashion accessories at full price. As already discussed in the previous chapter it merged with Yoox.com in March of 2015. After only eight years in development, net-a-porter.com has become the leading e-commerce site, becoming the pure Internet player with the fastest growth rate in the UK. Natalie Massenet funded the launch of the project with 1.3 million dollars; in 2004 the site had already made a 400,000-dollar profit, with total sales of over 21 million dollars. In the same year it was voted best shop of the year by the British Fashion Council. Even more recently net-a-porter.com has continued to increase its revenue and operating profit. The site is constantly increasing its customer base, a high proportion of whom purchase on a regular basis. During its growth, net-a-porter.com acquired the site girl-shop.com and as a result had access to a database of more than ten thousand contacts. Another significant growth operation in terms of external lines was the acquisition of fashion.com. All this has enabled it to rapidly expand the number of clients in the site's database. Net-a-porter.com has in addition, opened a distribution center in New York, thus optimizing distribution costs and the market share in the US.

Analysis of the site's structure and layout. A distinctive skill of net-a-porter.com is the way it has structured its site, providing the visual impact of a traditional fashion magazine, while at the same time the ease of consulting a catalogue. The homepage is streamlined, to-the-point and allows users to reach the different sections effectively, without complicated steps; it automatically selects the country of origin and currency of the buyer, while the cart is replaced by a shopping bag. "Magazine" is the first section where the customer has the option to make purchases. Instead of finding a list of products broken down by categories, the consumer consults the index of a fashion magazine, where various trends are presented; "Specials" on certain items of clothing or designers and information related to the product's style. Across the various sections consumers can access a number of resources, mainly photographic services, which represent the central point of the new purchasing process: passing the mouse over the different garments worn by the models, the consumer can access the description page of the item of clothing, where they can decide whether to purchase the product. Areas relating to styles, brands, trends and products are developed in collaboration with journalists, stylists and forecasters from Vogue, Tatler and Elle, in order to guarantee that consumers are constantly updated on events concerning fashion, new products and new trends. Even while reading an article the customer has the option to move the mouse over a picture to obtain all the information necessary to complete a purchase. The second section of the site instead assumes the graphic design of a classic online catalogue, where customers select the product according to various categories, offering a more traditional approach to buying. The last section concerns seasonal sales, where the consumer has the opportunity to buy clothing at a discount.

Description of success factors and business model. The site displays items that have appeared in fashion shows in London, Paris, Milan, New York and Los Angeles from more than 120 high-fashion brands. The line-up includes designers such as Miu Miu, Prada, Jimmy Choo, Bottega Veneta, Fendi, Missoni, Marc Jacobs, Moschino, Dolce & Gabbana and others.

Whenever net-a-porter.com inserts a new brand, the site gains new customers, also by word of mouth. Net-a-porter.com pays particular attention to illustrating the management's privacy policy, service and efficient delivery, since the management maintains that these elements are particularly relevant for consumers of goods with a high symbolic value. Customers can order certain products online before they are officially launched on the market (it guarantees priority to deliveries of reserved products), and be updated in real time about new products on the market.

In 2015, the site had more than 30,000 customers and about 300,000 visits each month and 60% of net-a-porter.com customers reside outside the United Kingdom and the majority live in the United States. Newsletters sent to subscribers number over 250,000. The average purchase receipt per individual order is about 1,000 dollars. Net-a-porter.com is a reference model in the context of the digital channel throughout the world.

Analysis of the average profile of net-a-porter.com customers. The average customer is a woman between the age of 25 and 35; visits to the site diminish with age. Visits also increase in line with income and educational level; the peak is reached with those who have completed post-graduate courses.

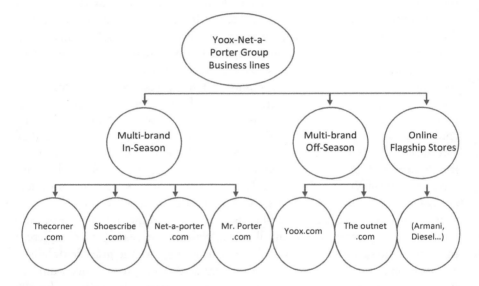

Figure 3.3 Net-a-porter.com: lines of business

Neimanmarcus.com. Neimanmarcus.com is an independent intermediary that sells numerous high-end brands on digital channels, integrating its online bidding system with physical department stores and traditional catalogue sales activities. Created in 1999 by the Neiman Marcus Group, the site positioned itself from the beginning as the main competitor (and follower) of net-a-porter.com. Annual sales on the digital channel were over 300 million dollars and have seen steady growth over the years.

The Neiman Marcus Group has a long history and in 2007 exceeded one hundred years in business. In 1907, Carrie Neiman and Herbert Marcus founded the company with the opening of a luxury goods store in Dallas. Right from the early years the commitment of the founders in identifying and developing new markets and especially new clients became clear, with advertising in local newspapers, mail drops, telephone, and subsequently fax. In 1926 Neiman Marcus offered the first Christmas catalogue: direct sales to consumers took off and grew rapidly. Since 1969 the Group has opened outlets in over thirty cities including: Chicago, Atlanta, Beverly Hills, San Francisco, Boston and Las Vegas.

In 1999 the neimanmarcus.com site was conceived under the control of the Neiman Marcus Direct Division, which had already started to sell via catalogues. Today, Neiman Marcus is one of the few Groups with over a century of history that continues to sell with its original name and maintains its headquarters in the same city where the business started. The Neiman Marcus Direct Division still prints the catalogue and manages the various Internet operations with the use of three different brands: Neiman Marcus, Horchow and Bergdorf Goodman.

Analysis of the site's structure and layout. The homepage echoes the style of net-a-porter.com in layout, clean and simple, in which there are all the elements of a virtual store: sales assistance, cart (or shopping bag), and the option for the potential customer to search for products via a search engine. There are numerous product categories: in addition to those classic ones related to clothing for men/ women and accessories, there are additional categories not available from competing sites, such as consumer electronics, household items and products for children. At the bottom of the page there are links offering access to particular sections of the site, such as that dedicated to wedding lists or the store locator. The site is the digital version of a large catalogue with no particularly innovative elements; product descriptions are simple and often there are no photos of the products from different angles.

Description of success factors and business model. The site sells a wide range of products and high-end brands, relying mainly on the price variable to attract consumers. Neimanmarcus.com initiated an upward re-positioning process with a view to marketing full-price luxury brands.

Their main strengths are:

- High level of customer service and expertise in logistics management. The consumer has always been at the center of the company's strategies. Neiman Marcus has created a customer care center with over two hundred employees in the US and another one with five hundred in Canada. Brendon Hoffman, CEO of Neiman Marcus Direct Division, noted that: *"The creation of a website is the simplest component to produce when you decide to start your own business on the web. Many have focused on creating complex sites with eye-catching designs, without placing the same importance on the necessary logistics. The true core of the business is in fact the logistics"*. Neiman Marcus delivers about thirty thousand different orders and can accept up to ten thousand product returns. The customer care center is equipped to receive voice calls, emails and establish live chat connections around the clock, seven days a week; more than 80% of online orders have some sort of interaction with the customer care center. In addition, Neiman Marcus Direct Division produces daily personalized newsletters, according to the indications provided by the customer when subscribing, so as to reach the appropriate segment of consumers in line with their communication policy. Communication activities such as newsletters are not only updates on available products, but also on discounts, best-sellers, promotions and special offers.

-   Extensive range of products and luxury brands. The availability of a wide and diverse range of products in all major categories – both related to classic luxury brands and young trendy designers – is a key success factor. Neimanmarcus.com includes over six hundred brands at full price as in the physical channel. Within the site an extensive range of top-range discounted products is available in the "Sale & Value" section.
-   Capacity to develop active relationships. The site has created a network of relationships with certain online high-end, designer and fashion brand marketing sites, placing links on its website. For example, salvatoreferragamo.com and davidyurman.com have inserted a link with neimanmarcus.com. The system of online site relationships and connections is an intangible asset, a source of sustainable competitive advantage, as it is the basis of the increase in long-term sales.
-   Synergies between the physical channel, catalogues and the digital channel: neimanmarcus.com has developed synergies between the different channels in which it operates, avoiding the risk – present in the early stages of the development of digital channels – of cannibalization between channels. The data show, for example, that digital channels are used intensively during the evenings and weekends.

Analysis of the company's average customer profile. The neimanmarcus.com site has a high incidence of monthly visits, equal to approximately one and a quarter million. The trend shows a slight decline during the summer months. It should be noted that a high percentage of people visit the site several times in the same month (about 6% are considered to be addicted); but all the more remarkable is that 60% of surfers are considered as regular. Customers are mainly women, aged between 18 and 34 (even though the 35 to 44 years age group is quite well represented). Visits to the site increase in line with increased income and education.

Mytheresa.com. An e-commerce site and world leader, it is focused on selling high fashion designer clothes, coming directly from the runway fashion shows in cities like New York, Paris and Milan. Mytheresa.com was founded in 2006 as an online boutique associated with the multi-brand store. Its collection comes from 170 of the most important global brands, such as Burberry, Gucci, Stella McCartney, Alexander McQueen and Balenciaga. Every week it presents five hundred new arrivals directly from the fashion show collections and guarantees safe shipping to one hundred and twenty countries. The success of the online boutique is also confirmed by its acquisition, in September 2014, by the Neiman Marcus Group.

Analysis of the site's structure and layout. The homepage is characterized by simplicity and a refined style, consistent with the items on display. Prime position goes to the images from the latest fashion shows and collections. The new arrivals are also updated daily.

Success factors of the business model. This site is based around giving the consumer the option to buy clothing and accessories coming directly from the runway shows of the world's main fashion cities.

Multi-brand pure Internet player focused exclusively on the intermediary market (business to business). Here we witness the presence on digital channels of an independent intermediary who sells luxury goods, directing its offer to other physical or virtual intermediaries, such as sales outlets or other sites. This intermediary, in other words, does not sell directly to the final consumer, but maintains an intermediary position in the distribution channel.

Brandsdistribution.com. Brandsdistribution.com is a recent Italian start-up that has experienced notable development in the field of B2B marketing in the high-end fashion and accessories sector. Brandsdistribution.com focuses its attention on small retail stores, helping to increase sales and profits with quantitatively small (but continuous) product orders, through continuous modernization of the collections without warehouse and operating costs thanks to drop-shipping. Recently the company has developed a website dedicated to the Chinese market – xiu.com – and has developed synergies in the e-commerce arena for the North American market.

Multibrand pure internet player integrated with the physical and digital channels. The approach entails the presence on the digital channel of an independent intermediary who sells luxury goods, integrating its sales system with the presence on the physical distribution channel as well.

The products can be searched and selected online and picked up at the physical sales point or, conversely, the purchase can take place in the store and the products can be shipped to the consumer's home. In these instances the development routes can be bidirectional: from an initial physical presence with outlets on the territory, to an online presence, or from an e-commerce site that turns into a network of physical outlets. In this context, we are witnessing the recent years' most interesting innovations in distribution strategies, with the realization in practice of integration processes between physical and digital systems.

In many cases the integration between the physical and digital channel starts from the former and extends to the latter, first consolidating the credibility and reputation of a physical sales point to then develop the digital version of the said physical store.

Luisaviaroma.com. This intermediary was originally an independent multi-brand store that, as a pioneer, had developed an online marketing site. Over the years it became one of the most important online retailers and established brands in the fashion industry, with brands such as Dior, Dsquared2, Dolce & Gabbana, Givenchy, Lanvin, Rick Owens, Roberto Cavalli, Yves Saint Laurent. Luisaviaroma.com offers the Buy it first service that allows customers to buy collections in advance. In addition to being an authorized dealer, the site has a section that serves as a magazine – LVR Diary – where items of the new collections are presented, including interviews with the most famous current personalities. Items from the collections presented can be purchased through the editorial publications.

Colette.fr. Another case of integration between the digital and physical channel is the e-commerce site, colette.fr, conceived from the need to offer web products found in Colette offline stores.

The structure of the site is original: the homepage has the form of a virtual warehouse, where the predominate color is blue. Smaller images appear in the background, each connected to a specific collection of products. The consumer can make online purchases simply and directly, read the news about the latest collections and access a blog; it is also possible to sign up for a newsletter. Checkout is effected using the classical trolley method and payments comply with the safety standards required to operate on the Internet.

The strategy of this site is based on a stockholder logic, which aims to bring the goods and services of sales outlets in the physical distribution channel online, often at lower prices.

The colette.fr customer is young, aged between 20 and 25, with a high level of both income and education.

There are also examples of the reverse integration process that, starting from the digital channel, arrives in the physical arena. This is the case with gioie.it.

Gioie.it. This e-commerce web site merged with eprice.it in 2013. The case of gioie.it demonstrates during the first period of its development, the route from the digital channel to the physical one. Part of the Italian jewelry industry, the site represented the case of a medium enterprise which was at the beginning of his history one of Europe's leading digital intermediaries in the sale of high-end gold-work and jewelry and is one of the main sites selling Italian-produced jewelry over the Internet.[5] The digital intermediary had an assortment of approximately eleven thousand models with a total of about twenty-five thousand variants. The markets served were predominantly the United States and France, followed by Germany, Britain and Scandinavia. Of lesser importance are the Spanish and Italian markets, despite the fact that gioe.it has its origins in the latter. Every day new products are launched by the network of suppliers, chosen from among the companies that produce jewelry designed by the most skilled of Italian goldsmiths, selected from the districts of Valenza, Vicenza, Arezzo, Naples and Milan. The digital intermediary completes the offer with a range of prestigious brands. Top range full price products, secondary lines and discounted collections from previous years are all available. Gioie.it also offers jewelry products to a younger target market, while maintaining certain basic requirements that are considered fundamental: excellent quality, competitive prices and innovative design.

The initial competitive strategy of this company had the sole objective of reaching the final consumer via the digital channel, applying competitive prices due to not having the intermediary margins of the physical channel. The next stage of development is, instead, characterized by intermediate forms that anticipate an intensive, physical presence on the territory. Evolving from the digital channel to the traditional forms of distribution, gioie.it therefore followed a reverse growth path compared to the traditional development model of distribution in the market of luxury goods, in which the digital option is to follow an established and significant presence on the traditional channel.

Sugar.it. Sugar is an online store founded in Italy in September 2016 by Beppe Angiolini. The founder is the actual owner of a well known boutique in Arezzo, Sugar, and is famous in the fashion global market for his long experience as a buyer and stylist. Angiolini, together with a team of digital artists has created a web site characterized by a unique design, organized in three main sections: "men", "woman" and "no sugar please". The first two include further sections, some devoted to the sale of different product categories, one dedicated to the "new season", a showcase one dedicated to vintage clothes and another section allowing user to access to thematic rooms dedicated to the famous designers involved by Sugar like Gucci, Burberry, D&G.

The "no sugar please" section depicts the innovative character of Sugar at whole; it is indeed divided into different product rooms whose name (short and preceded by a hashtag i.e. #sugarbaby), strongly evoke the social media language. Within the site products are sold mainly at full price. The website provide user with a positive experience: it is indeed user friendly, with a unique menu which allows to access to the main sections. The "no sugar please" section with its endearing design gives a touch of exclusivity to the web site. The product range is more selected compared to Yoox-Net-a-Porter, and is composed exclusively by boutiques articles. The physical store, placed in the heart of Arezzo, is integrated with the online one. The latter provide the physical store with both visibility and a remarkable channel of communication, characterized by modern language and style and intended for millennials. The key success factors of this model concern the way Sugar communicates to its customers as well as its innovative and *glocal* approach aimed to involve local art and culture in Sugar's value proposition. Both the physical and digital store aim to become unique and innovative environments through the creation of dedicated product rooms and a club space beside the inclusion of music products and books. The integration of all these elements in the store are turned to make the shopping experience unique and raise the perception of the brand by the consumer.

3.4. Emerging trends and models

The digital technologies scenario is rapidly evolving. Therefore, remaining with our theme, the digital channel is also mutating rapidly as new trends and features appear, hence new models, unimaginable until a few years ago, particularly for the high symbolic value goods market, whose full potential is still to be explored.

New digital channel functions. With the technological evolution, the digital channel is progressively developing a special ability to guarantee the consumer of luxury goods an exceptional virtual experience, updated in real time, thus positively influencing the buying process (Villanueva *et al.*, 2008). A fact confirming this trend is the increase in online transactions for, often high-priced, luxury goods and the increase in their average value (Schivinski and Dabrowski, 2014).

The digital channel, in fact, is now also being used by the players as a luxury non-residual channel to distribute innovative collections, dedicated products and ancillary services onto the market (Adjei *et al.*, 2010). The high-end goods made available for purchase on digital channels have increasingly high selling prices. The digital channel's original function of disposing of unsold products, is thus now joined by the new marketing function of supply systems characterized by uniqueness and exclusivity at high prices (Curty and Zhang, 2011).

Two reference cases are blunile.com in the jewelry market and 20ltd.com, dedicated to collectors.

Blunile.com. The bluenile.com story begins when Mark Voden, former CEO and founder of the company, searched the Internet for some information on jewelry in order to compare prices and stumbled on the internet-diamonds.com site, one of the first jewelers on the web who offered online certificates for the color, transparency and carat weight of the diamonds on offer. Voden acquired internetdiamonds.com with an offer of five million dollars and changed its name to bluenile.com. Today it is the largest online jeweler with annual retail sales in excess of 200 million dollars, in continuous growth in recent years, except during the recession. The site has more than sixty thousand gemstones and a worldwide network of diamond suppliers. Bluenile.com is quoted on the stock exchange and still represents a reference model for sales of goods with high symbolic value on the digital channel.

Analysis of the site's structure and layout. The homepage presents bluenile.com as a classic online retailer, therefore with a lot of information on the screen. The menu is at the top, where the customer has the option to login, check cart and check their web order (via the order number, which is supplied at the time of shipping). The customer can search by product category, but also in relation to the various materials available (diamonds, pearls, gemstones, platinum, gold, silver). In different parts of the homepage, visitors can access information about the return policy and the phone number to contact customer service. The bottom of the page contain links to partner sites in Canada and the United Kingdom and references to independent institutions that guarantee the security of transactions and personal information that may be entered onto the site. The most effective section of the site is the product configuration: in fact there is no ready-made jewelry (although there are many "pre-packaged" products based on typical customer choices); using a configurator, the customer can produce their own jewelry according to their requirements and financial resources. The first step is choosing the stone. The site offers a range of specific information, such as carat, cut and color. The range is extensive and there are approximately sixty-six thousand diamonds with a price range from 280 to over 900,000 dollars (the stones weigh up to 20 carats).

Description of success factors and business model. Bluenile.com has built its business model around a specific niche market: consumers, mostly males, who buy expensive jewelry, especially engagement rings. In the online jewelry sector average spending is about 300 dollars, while the average purchaser on bluenile.com invests more than 1500 dollars in each purchase; a typical order for an engagement ring is about 5,500 dollars, compared to an industry average of about 2,800 dollars. 97% of sales occur on the US market, but the segment of customers that grows most rapidly is resident outside of the United States (Canada and UK). The key factor in its success is the attention to detail that gives customers the impression they are buying from experts. Before every order is actually shipped and packaged, the jewel and its packaging undergo twenty-six different inspections (each product is inspected with a magnifying glass in order to ensure that the characteristics declared by the certificate are compliant). Respecting the stated delivery times at all times. The main competitors of bluenile.com are: bidz.com, tiffany.com and ross-simons.com.

Analysis of the company's average customer profile. The site has more than 200,000 monthly visitors, there are no seasonal variations in sales and customers who make close repeat visits over time are rare. The referent customer is a man or a woman, aged between 25 and 34; visits to the site tend to decrease with advancing age. In terms of income, customers tend to increase in line with higher income, but with a lesser tendency than other sites that offer fashion-related luxury products.

20ltd.com. It is an online boutique of designer, vintage and photographic items, created to serve and satisfy the desires of a narrow niche market seeking quality and uniqueness regardless of the price. All products offered for sale are rare, limited editions and once sold they are no longer produced.

Analysis of the site's structure and layout. The site structure is singular: it does not however possess the common features of the classic virtual intermediary. The homepage shows a screen where images of products for sale pop up: a smaller photograph illustrates the latest item in the collection, which is changed daily, and an interactive image, in relief, highlights the collection's best pieces.

Still on the homepage there are three texts that offer the user the option to search for individual products using various methods: shopping for designer items, shopping the trendiest current designers, and shopping among photographic presentations.

The customer is not faced with a list of products which are classified by product category; instead the offer follows the style model and sought-after designs criterion. Each product is accompanied by a detailed description and the name of its designer.

During the purchase phase the customer registers for login, with the guarantee of compliance to the safety standards required to operate on the Internet. To ensure the quality and safety of its products, 20ltd.com employs skilled professionals who visit manufactures' premises to get to know the history of each product and meet the designers in person. The average 20ltd.com customer is a man or woman, attracted by art and design, with a high level of education and disposable income.

The digital channel and personalization. Another recent trend is the use of digital channels to increase the degree of product or service personalization, enhancing the perceived value of the overall supply system.

Sales are often made in the physical channel, while personalization is effected directly by the customer online before delivery of the product or in the physical sales outlet during the purchase.

Digital channels and product life cycle. Digital channels, traditionally for marketing products coming to the end of their life cycle, are used by some companies to present and sell luxury goods that are being introduced onto the market. Numerous launch campaigns for new products are created using an online presale of a limited number of copies, sometimes numbered and personalized (Phau and Prendergast, 2000). Strategies to strengthen the concept of uniqueness and exclusivity of some brands marketed via Yoox Net-a-Porter include dedicated collections, exclusive areas on the site for experimental brands and innovative partnerships with certain luxury brands in the development of initiatives that integrate art, design and fashion. The use of digital channels in this approach has the function of transferring the idea of the luxury product's uniqueness and limited availability at the moment of its introduction onto the market.

Thecorner.com. Thecorner.com is a multi-brand line belonging to the Yoox Net-A-Porter Group. It presents itself as a luxury online boutique that is distinguished by retail concepts, mini-stores, corners dedicated to different designers and platforms reserved for various brands where the latest news can be found. Its distribution network covers more than fifty countries and its service is sophisticated and impeccable. Consumers accessing the thecorner.com can directly purchase items of clothing that interests them, or get an update on the latest news clearly displayed on the homepage.

Shoescribe.com. This second multi-brand line belonging to the Yoox Net-A-Porter Group is a website dedicated to women's footwear. The site presents a mix of e-commerce, exclusive services and editorial content, with a large selection ranging from top designers to major brands. Its strong point is its capacity, also via editorial content, to involve consumers by keeping them continuously up to date on the latest footwear trends. The site is composed of various areas: just in, containing the new arrivals; spotlight, for the latest trends; newsReal, the editorial area; and most wanted, dedicated to social media.

Digital channels and virtual communities. Another frontier of the digital channel is its integration with virtual communities who unite online around a brand or style (Pentina *et al.*, 2008). Virtual communities of consumers who share interests in a product, brand or style and visit dedicated blogs can be identified and made available to the site's e-commerce system, subscribe to specific lists and be regularly informed of events, latest news, products and special offers (Brodie, 2013).

The ultimate goal of marketing activities aimed at the creation and maintenance of virtual communities in the context of luxury goods' markets is to transfer the idea of exclusive access to the community and immediate offers to the potential customer (Schau *et al.*, 2009). In this sense it is required that, for example, the new community member is presented and accepted via a selection process.

Vente-privee.com. Vente-privee.com, the market leader in offering low price unsold collection items (physiologically this is around 8-10% of the total); it is organized as a circle of invitees (club) where products are made available to purchase for limited periods of time and exclusively to the parties invited. Venteprivee.com organizes forty-eight-hour online fashion shows defined as "sales events", where members receive discounts of up to 70% of the initial price. In Italy, other pure Internet players who have adopted similar business models are born4shop.com, buyvip.com, saldiprivati.it, vetrinesclusive.it and privalia.com.

Bagborroworsteal.com. bagborroworsteal.com is the first site to have created the online rental concept for luxury goods and was created in 2004 with a network of more than 250,000 customers and more than 3000 different items that can be rented and that are selected from more than 100 different designers, including Chanel, Gucci, Prada, Louis Vuitton, Stephen Dweck and Vera Wang. Consumers choose the product they would like to borrow, they can keep it as long as they want and then have the option to purchase or exchange it with a new product.

Analysis of the site's structure and layout. The homepage is clean, simple, without the classic elements of an e-commerce site (shopping cart, order tracking, return policies and so on). The product categories available to rent are organized by collections. The customer can directly access the send order function. The luxury product can be rented both by registered customers who pay a monthly subscription, or guests. The difference between these two categories of customer is that the former are granted a discount. Customers are divided into four categories based on the amount of their subscription. Other guests do not have access to the product waiting list, which grants priority in renting products that are currently unavailable.

Description of success factors and business model. Renting the product passes through four different phases: a) selection of the item b) receiving the item, c) selection of the next item d) return of the first rented or "stolen" item.

Once the product is rented, the customer can keep it for as long as they want, provided that their account remains up to date with payments. Bagborroworsteal.com also offers services affiliated to the rental option: the first is product insurance, which enables the customer to cover accidental damage risks; the second is the option to steal it. Using their account the customer has the option to purchase the product; the purchase is not guaranteed and the offer may be rejected if, for example, the product is rare and hard to find.

Analysis of the company's average customer profile. The site has over 20,000 visitors per month, of which about 38% make return visits. There are some seasonal spikes in visits. The average visitor is a woman, aged between 25 and 34, with a reduction among older age groups.

Integration between the communication function and the digital channel. Another development path in digital channels is that of informative sites and those communicating latest news and fashion, style and design trends. In their initial development stage these sites assume the form of online media for communicating information, trends, fashion phenomena, style and design; they are often linked to a founder or a group of charismatic people who proclaim the site as a reference point (Brogi *et al.*, 2013). The next step towards legitimizing the site as a provider of information (infomediary) can be starting to develop e-commerce and luxury services.

3.5. The evolution of the digital channels towards new models

The current scenario, therefore, highlights the growth of the digital channel as an important vehicle for the distribution of luxury goods, not just for the liquidation of unsold products.

The digital channel is assuming similar characteristics to the physical one with direct distribution models, achieved through active management of e-commerce sites by luxury brands, and indirectly with the presence of product-specialized or multibrand intermediaries that are often highly innovative.

Figure 3.4 shows a two-dimensional analysis of a sample of companies:

- The main function of the distribution channel, which may be disposing of lower-priced collections and disposal of unsold products (online outlet), or selling full-price brands and latest collection products (online boutique).
- The quality of interaction with the customer, understood as the user level of the sensory elements available, in order to ensure a positive customer experience.

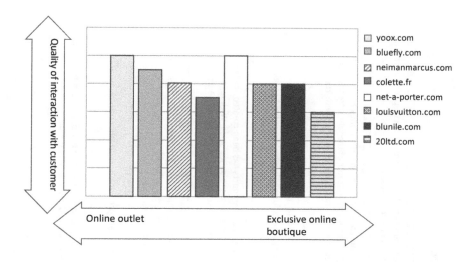

Figure 3.4 Two-dimensional analysis and classification of a sample of independent companies

FASHION BRAND WEBSITE	WEBSITE CATEGORY	COMMENT
www.chanel.com	Showcase site/ Online boutique	All information about products and brand. Now it's possible to purchase three kind of products: perfume, make up and skin care. Each of them can be bought in the related sections of the website.
www.armani.it	Online boutique	Within the site are directly sold the Armani and Emporio Armani collections, for the other ones a dedicated website has been created, incubator of new ideas by Giorgio Armani and indicator of the latest trends and fashions of young people, called Armani Exchange.com. Giorgio Armani has signed a contract with Yoox for the entire management of online sales.
www.gucci.com	Online boutique	The website is articulated in the following sections: runway (collections), women, men, children, jewelry and watches, beauty, gifts and a section dedicated to "stories", which gives further information about collections and other topics.
www.louisvuitton.com	Online boutique	Specifically for the brand Louis Vuitton, a website for the online sale of products has been created, called www.louisvuitton.com. The increase turnover percentage is growing thanks to online sales. With regard to other brands of the group's portfolio is necessary to address to individual sites, some still showcase sites, others already advanced online boutique.
www.burberry.com	Online boutique	The site devotes a special section to online shopping and allows to purchase three different collections, that are: women, men, children and beauty; it offers an innovative way to purchase within the site called "shop by look". Burberry perfumes are not sold on the web, but only in offline boutique.
www.versace.it	Online boutique	All information about products and brand. Now it's possible purchase products of different collections.
www.hermes.com	Online boutique	The website homepage asks to the user to choose the county/language and allows to buy products in the online boutique. Products sold online don't cover at whole the collections sold in physical boutique.

FASHION BRAND WEBSITE	WEBSITE CATEGORY	COMMENT
www.prada.it	Online boutique	Prada allows to purchase online from different country around the world. Within the website two collections of product are sold, that are: woman and man. Moreover is available a service called «made to measure», that allows to obtain tailor-made dresses.
www.missoni.it	Online boutique	Now is possibile to buy products directly in the website by choosing between different categories that are: #missoni, man, woman, girl, missoni home and gifts.
www.moschino.it	Online boutique	A very interactive website with advanced graphic, it now allows to buy products of the following collections: man, woman, capsule. Regarding to the last one the «shop by look» and «shop by item» options are available.
www.dior.com	Online boutique	In the website there are three online boutiques. The first allows to buy products distinguished in two categories: woman and man; in the second boutique is possible to purchase fragrance, makeup and skin care products; the third boutique is divided in three categories: jewellery, timepieces and Baby Dior collection.
www.dolcegabbana.it	Online boutique	The website could be seen as an hybrid type, it contains a section dedicated to online purchase called online store, in which is possible to buy products of the following collections: women, men, children and gifts. There are also four showcase sections, each of them dedicated to specific collections that are: beauty, watches, eyewear and jewelry.
www.ralphlauren.com	Online boutique	The company in recent years has strongly focused its activities on electronic commerce. The site allows to buy products of the following categories: men, women, boys, girls, baby, home, gifts and personalized products.
www.robertocavalli.it	Online boutique	The site divides the products sold in two categories: men and women. Within each of them, products are divided into the following categories: ready to wear, bags and accessories, shoes and fragrances.
www.jimmychoo.com	Online boutique	In the website products sold are divided into the following categories: women, man, collections, bridal boutique and gifts.
www.valentino.com	Online boutique	In the website there are three sections. One called «man» and another called «woman», in which is possible to buy four categories of products that are: apparel, shoes, bags and accessories that includes the fragrances. The third is a showcase section.

Figure 3.5 The digital channel: empirical evidence from a sample of pure Internet players

As regards the development of the digital channel by companies that retain a brand or a brand portfolio, the strategies are different and ongoing evolution is rapid. It can be stated that, at the time this volume is published, most of the leaders in the fashion and luxury markets have a presence on the Internet, some using a brand-value communication approach, others conducting sales via digital channels in specific market areas or in all major markets.

The function performed in the distribution channel is itself also interpreted in a different way. Certain companies adopt the digital channel just to dispose of unsold collections, others give the Internet a primary position in competition with other channels. The majority of companies examined use all the best techniques to ensure a positive digital experience to their referent customers. Finally, companies that retain a diversified brand portfolio only employ the digital channel for certain brands and in certain markets.

Figures 3.6 and 3.7 show a summary of the results of some research carried out by the author in the last two years on the ways the digital channel is used by a sample of global players in the market for goods with high symbolic value.

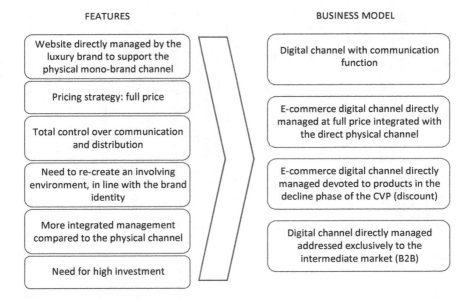

Figure 3.6 Methods of adopting the digital channel from a sample of global players in the fashion and luxury markets

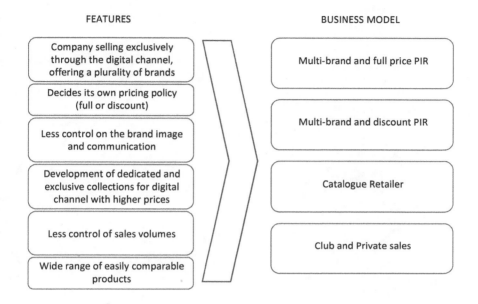

FEATURES   BUSINESS MODEL

FEATURES	BUSINESS MODEL
Company selling exclusively through the digital channel, offering a plurality of brands	Multi-brand and full price PIR
Decides its own pricing policy (full or discount)	Multi-brand and discount PIR
Less control on the brand image and communication	
Development of dedicated and exclusive collections for digital channel with higher prices	Catalogue Retailer
Less control of sales volumes	Club and Private sales
Wide range of easily comparable products	

Figure 3.7 Methods of adopting the digital channel from a sample of global players in the fashion and luxury markets

Notes

1   The observations reported are the result of analyses conducted in several case studies on pure Internet players.

2   The configuration is that of a showcase site in line with the companies' brand image: in most cases it presents an attractive graphical interface, displays collections of products (clothing, accessories, watches and so on) and interactivity with the user is limited to the option to download photos or short videos of the latest fashion shows or sponsored events, accompanied by audio tracks. All showcase sites offer consumers virtual catalogues that provide information about the company, the brand, the collection designer or designers, some bibliographic information, the list of physical outlets in the region and, at times, press reviews of events.

3   This category of virtual intermediaries, which also takes the Anglo-Saxon name e-mall, effectively performs the function of a virtual outlet.

4   Wholesalers, neighbourhood markets and unauthorised sellers in the watches and leather goods sector.

5   Gioie.it has its operational headquarters in Valencia and initiated its sales activities on the digital channel in 2000, exploiting the image and potential of the Italian territory on the world markets. The collected data show the presence of more than 15,000 individual users who visit the digital intermediary daily, with 2% of transactions being finalised (300 users).

Chapter 4

SOCIAL MEDIA AND INTEGRATED COMMUNICATION IN LUXURY MARKETS

4.1. Introduction

Communication has now become an integral part of luxury companies' brand strategies and, along with distribution, constitutes one of their two main drivers (Mosca, 2010).

Both the significant diffusion of the Internet and digital systems and a "more relaxed" relationship between customers and new technologies have deeply transformed the communication methods put in place by luxury companies over the last five years, determining a progressive integration between traditional and new digital media (Trusov, Bucklin and Pauwel, 2009).

The sales point keeps its central position as the hub of communication activities but integrates new technologies, thus allowing for pre and post sales customer service and an enhancement of the whole consumer's experience (Linda, 2010).

User Generated Content (UCG) stands out among the most significant new innovations. UCG guarantees a closer and more direct company-customer relationship and provides consumers with a completely new experience in relation to a high symbolic value brand.

4.2. Communication contents and messages in the luxury market

Products and brands defined as luxury are unambiguously identifiable for the exclusivity, quality and uniqueness they possess and broadcast. First of all, the communication message should be coherent and affirm this strategic positioning (Fionda and Moore, 2009).

The starting point for an effective marketing communication is therefore the identification of all possible interactions between potential customers and the company, its products or services. Communication should then be planned on the basis of how consumers' experiences and perceptions can be influenced and directed towards product and brand's positioning strategies, raising the brand's value and encouraging product sales (Keller, 2013).

Attributes of both product concept and brand concept should be placed at the center of the communication for a luxury good or brand: prestigious brand, high quality and preciousness of the product, heritage, history of product, producer and family, processing techniques, consumption rituals, founder's profile and celebrity status, design, style and beauty, shortage and uniqueness, high price, place of origin, packaging.

These attributes are conveyed by a message that, using both visual and descriptive images, helps consumers to identify these luxury features associated with the brand or the product.

Besides the already mentioned attributes, communication should involve the consumer experience, guaranteed by product or brand and the code of values customers must endorse if they are willing to own a specific product or use a specific service (Kapferer and Bastien, 2012).

In general, communication related to luxury goods shapes its message around some fundamental codes and elements, for example: placing the product on the foreground, highlighting its attributes of exclusivity, quality and uniqueness; using background elements to conjure up these attributes and position the product in a valued, elegant, refined and dreamlike environment; or, moreover, using accessory elements to point out non-visible features, like including specific technical data descriptions in the message.

When considering the ten possible families of advertising languages,[1] communication related to luxury goods focuses mainly on visual seduction and, less frequently, on transgression.

A message based on seductive tones can powerfully engage with consumers in terms of charm, taste and refinement, raising emotions connected to a sense of beauty and the surrounding dreamlike universe.

Fendi Painter Studio (Ironico, 2014). Fendi's communication activities aim at evoking surroundings or thematic areas connected with creativity. In a recent integrated communication activity, Fendi has showcased its products drawing inspiration from an artist studio, developing themes of collection, materials, characters and branded environments around the universe of painting. In their press communication campaign, model Anja Rubik interpreted the role of an inspiring muse for a painter who used the colors of the collection for his masterpieces. The artist was framed painting both a family portrait for the children campaign and the picture of a traditional and aristocratic woman – the model – accompanied by two purebred dogs, a status symbol and a reference to brand loyalty. This fashion tale has been introduced into Fendi flagship stores around the world, where the same settings of the campaign have been created. Mannequins, for example, faithfully reproduced Anja Rubik's features, hairstyle, make-up, poses and outfits.

Forever Now by Gucci. For its ninetieth anniversary, fall-winter season 2010-2011, Gucci started an institutional campaign as a manifesto for the fashion industry Made in Italy. Besides celebrating the brand's tradition and history, both body copy and visuals were chosen for the three subjects highlighted the values of Italian fashion. The campaign Forever Now, for example, recalled the brand's heritage in a time-referenced sequence that, conversely, showcased the brand as modern and new.

The country of origin's connotation – the Made in Italy – was evoked by placing the attention on the city where the brand originated, Florence. The city has become a model of absolute perfection through the work of generations of artisans inspired by Guccio Gucci. The Made in Italy feature was also recalled in the official website where the company emphasized the Italian origin ofthe brand and the local production.

An Italian Dream by Tod's. Tod's stages an artisanal production in its communication campaigns. The short movie An Italian Dream, produced in 2010, showed thirteen dancers from La Scala Theater in Milan interpreting the production steps to make a handmade Tod's product. According to Diego della Valle, both music and dancers' moves described incredibly well the industrious process of making a Tod's moccasin and exalted the beauty of "handcraftsmanship". This short movie was then the ideal starting point for the promotion of Made in Italy campaign both in Italian schools and universities and abroad.

Emporio Armani. In its fall-winter campaign 2013-2014 the brand involved different topics and was conceived to cover several market segments. All advertising pages were built to be read within the same narration. Frames targeting both the female population and the male population would tell the same story and would also be complementary: the meaning of the narration could be fully understood looking at the two advertising pages at the same time. The female subject depicted a woman walking in dim lighting whose attention was captured by something external to the page. The male subject, instead, showed three men in the same setting – two of the three models were looking at the woman outside of the page. A flirtatious game of glances therefore expressed the dynamics of desire among the actors.

Marketing experts, communication managers and consultants are still wondering about the best approach to communication for luxury goods, this is due to its peculiarity. In fact, communication is an essential component but these products force companies to operate in a selective manner, focusing on the reference targets, some of whom are not receptive to classical or, even less, mass approaches.

Kapferer and Bastien (2009) and others offer guidelines for correct communication in relation to high symbolic value goods. A summary is reported below.

Dreamlike and allusive communication. The communication style for consumer goods focuses on the information content directed at the transaction. Communication for luxury goods should not aim at selling a product but it should build up a dream and spread the brand values instead. It should focus on the allusive creation of a dreamlike representation of the product and the brand's universe, allowing the target audience to identify with, codify and own the brand's values. This involves a refined and artistic communication, highly codified and allusive and never referencing the direct sale.

Value communication. Companies have to communicate a product's value not linked to its price. Since luxury is often associated with money, according to Kapferer and Bastien the two terms could be confused and assimilated in a unique concept. However, doing so would deny that luxury is a "social marker". Therefore luxury and money should always be kept separate. Money, differently from luxury, does not create social stratification: a consumer could belong to an aristocratic élite no matter how substantial their financial resources are. Moreover, the two academics highlight how the assimilation of money and luxury denies the contrast between the abstract semantic void of money and the concrete semantic richness of luxury. Money does not make people dream. People dream what they can obtain through money. In fact, there is nothing luxurious to a banknote but people dream of turning it into a luxury good, giving it a real meaning.

Companies that have focused their communication on the high price of the product have got the message wrong. In fact, price is an attribute of a luxury good but it cannot alone identify it. Kapferer and Bastien highlight how a "more expensive" product can easily turn into a "too expensive" one that nobody wants to buy, instead of becoming a luxury good that everyone dreams of Thus, a direct reference to the price in communication for luxury goods diminishes and sometimes destroys the dreamlike value people place on it and the luxury positioning itself.

Communicate to support brand awareness. In luxury goods markets, each sold product takes away part of the dream and therefore weakens the perceived brand symbolic value. This is typical of high-end products, where the dream is the outcome of a consistent gap between awareness and diffusion of the brand. Communication, besides building the initial dream, should maintain the gap between dream and diffusion.

Integrated communication. Companies must develop an integrated communication approach as opposed to a simple advertisement activity in the media. Integrated communication activities are rarely found in mass media. Moreover, since a narration time is needed to represent the heritage of both product and brand following luxury codes, investments in communication should focus on tools like events, sponsorships, the tale of the product and its qualitative features and central attributes, paying attention to consumer rituals, brand ambassadors and word of mouth.

Moët & Chandon and car races. Shaking a Champagne magnum and spraying it all over the celebrating audience is all part of a ritual accompanying a car race winner. The origin of this habit is quite interesting. Back in 1950, in the event of Reims (France) Formula One stage, car races fans Paul Chandon Moët and Frédéric Chandon de Brailles presented the winner with a Jéroboam by Moët & Chandon. But the real origin of the explosion happened in 1966 when Le Mans 24 Hours' winner was given a Champagne bottle whose cork accidentally hopped discharging the wine over the exulting fans. The following year, winner Dan Gurney shook the bottle on purpose and sprayed the audience, starting a tradition which is still popular today (Kapferer and Bastien, 2009).

Structural elements for luxury goods communication. Some structural elements are strictly linked to luxury goods communication (Kapferer and Bastien, 2009): The creator of the brand; that is the person who made the brand or a specific product a work of art and not a piece of mass production. That person's face or other distinguishing features are used in sales points or in other online and offline forms of communication; Logos, usually short and visible, like Gucci's "G", Chanel's "double C", Dolce and Gabbana's "D&G" and Louis Vuitton's "LV"; The trade mark associated to the logo, for example Aston Martin's wings or Rolex's crown; A repeated visual pattern like "LV" on Louis Vuitton's bags; A brand color like Tiffany's light blue, Veuve Clicquotand and Hermès's orange, Dior's gold, Ferrari and Valentino's red; A preferred fabric like leather for Bottega Veneta or Frau, silk for Hermès; Cult of and obsession for detail, for example Louis Vuitton's close-ups on seams' thread; The celebration of craftsmanship and artisans' excellency in every product; An operational model typical of the brand like Ferrari's extreme attention to quality or Barolo Gaja's ageing process.

With regard to the communication of luxury goods, all product's attributes – ranging from the creator's signature to videos on dedicated channels – contribute to create a dreamlike universe, exclusive and elegant, which is essential for luxury itself and its consumers.

Som and Blanckaert (2015) make some interesting considerations about communication activities:

- Promotion of the brand must be obtained through rational as well as emotional messages. However, luxury good consumers do not search for a rational explanation for their purchase due to the originality and uniqueness of the goods. Goods' uniqueness can also mean unique defects, and that increases the product's desirability: for example, luxury mechanical watches are less accurate than their digital counterparts.
- Promotion's content is more important than exposition. In fact,

companies create their brand image through communication activities, which entail a high standard of quality in order to get access to selective communication channels. Brands should never imitate other brand's promotions: Hermès' strengths, for example, are different from Louis Vuitton's. Promotions should focus on points of difference in order to highlight what differentiates a brand from its competitors.

- The promotion of a luxury brand usually entails the use of evocative images and few words.
- Communication activities for a global brand should always keep in consideration the heritage, the company's culture and values, to develop a consistent image all over the world.
- It is important to value the point of view of the consumers and educate them through communication activities.
- Sales points are very important to develop the brand's image as well as events involving élite consumers and the integration of the commercial and cultural spheres.
- Digital channels cannot be ignored any longer.

According to Corbellini and Saviolo (2009), companies have three communication objectives:

- *Brand awareness*: the brand should be known and acknowledged by competitors.
- *Brand image*: consumers should associate the brand with specific values; in fact, communication activities aimed exclusively at those who share them.
- *Reputation*: is an asset whose importance is increasing and requires the alignment of shareholders, banks, local authorities and employees. Nowadays internal communication, relations with investors and social responsibility programs are as important as promotion and organization of events.

The two academics identify three levels with which different objectives can be associated and the related tools to achieve them.

- *Product*. Objectives are to support sell-in and sell-out; suggested tools are: advertisement, editorials, fashion shows and events, catalogs, websites.
- *Brand*. Objectives are to build awareness and image; suggested tools are: logo, heritage, designer or a spokesperson entrepreneur, marketing through celebrity, flagship, websites. Today's consumers are attracted to celebrities' lifestyle and seek to identify with them. This

is the reason why companies employ celebrities as testimonials and associate products and brands with VIPs or sports players who can guarantee a flow of articles, photos and PR through word of mouth.

- *Corporate*. Objectives are to improve the reputation; suggested operational techniques are: internal communication, relations with investors, foundations and sponsorship, donations, Internet website.

Some authors describe the role of communication activities implemented through new digital systems, *in primis* Internet and social networks. In relation to this, Kapferer and Bastien (2009) identify three areas in which communication integrating new digital media benefits companies:

- *Awareness*: Brand notoriety is a fundamental aspect for all luxury goods as it contributes to enhance the brand itself and feeds the dream associated to it. The development of digital systems, like websites and UGC platforms, is a crucial element that brings along an increase in brand awareness. The risk of quick and uncontrolled diffusion of bad news and gossip remains. This is why brands need to monitor the web as much as possible, trying to limit and manage all negative comments that are quickly spreading around corroding the dream created by brands themselves (Singh and Sonnenburg, 2012).
- *Communities*: They can be created on the Internet and are very important for all brands, especially luxury brands. Communities are a meeting space for a brand's fans; here they can chat, find new pieces of information and exchange opinions. Communities are a key factor for the success of a company as they reassure customers about their passion for a specific product or brand, informing them that other people share their same passion. Communities are also a powerful tool to reach out to new customers (Kaplan and Haenlein, 2010).
- *Time*: Use of digital systems facilitates communication time management. TV ads are not appropriate for luxury brands as they can't effectively reach the target audience; in fact, they are too short and focused on too large target markets and therefore don't allow for the creation of an elegant and refined dreamlike universe. The web based communication (mainly, but not exclusively, through the YouTube channel) is, on the other hand, a space where companies can create video clips long enough to build the dreamlike landscape typical of luxury brands communication or extend the communication time using several, short video clips logically connected by a common thread.

Finally, if we consider all the changes that have occurred in the communication field in the last few years, both the Internet and social media are an interesting opportunity for luxury companies to improve communication, operating in synergy with other media. Moreover, the improvements are not limited to top down communication but involve interaction among users and companies, and among users themselves.

4.3. User Generated Branding and Consumer Brand Engagement

Social web and all *User Generated Content* (UGC) platforms deriving from it are not only unique and innovative communication media attracting consumers to products and/or brands but are also multichannel instruments whose potential is currently being defined (Kim and Ko, 2012).

Before further examining some of the main tools, we should consider the User Generated Branding and the Consumer Brand Engagement as integrated communication approaches providing luxury companies management the chance to enlarge their customers base, preserving at the same time the exclusivity of the brand. Brand identity is a universe of carefully selected attributes and benefits that are communicated to customers using specific marketing activities (Keller, 2013); Firm Generated Content (FGC) identifies contents available to users and completely controlled by the marketing Function. These contents are part of company strategy and aim at creating and strengthening the relationship between brand and consumers (Singh and Sonnenburg, 2012).

Marketing reduced its central role as creator of brand stories with web 2.0 and therefore new strategies need to be put in place. New challenges involve the integration of FGC and UGC in order to communicate the desired brand identity, taking advantage of the popularity of social media among the people (Kaplan and Haenlein; Keller, 2013).

Management ability to orientate the UGC to get consumers to spread the desired message on the identity of the brand is essential (Gensler *et al.*, 2013; Schivinski and Dabrowski, 2014). This should be done through the *User Generated Branding* (UGB), that is the strategic and operational management of a specific brand in order to achieve the desired communication goals (Burmann and Arnhold, 2009).

It has been proved that UGB increases the perception of the efforts and investments made to create a consumer-brand relationship, improving the relationship itself and leading to positive word of mouth (Adjei *et al.*, 2010; Park and Kim, 2014).

Singh and Sonnenburg (2012) describe the role of storytelling in social media using the metaphor of theatrical improvisation. In fact, it is impossible to predict the outcome of the communication path, despite strategic planning.

Consumer Brand Engagement. This concept has gained popularity in marketing studies, especially in relation to new dialogue possibilities created by the development of web 2.0 and the active role of modern consumers. Different approaches have been used to examine and define CBE in literature.

According to Brodie (2013), it is a psychological state triggered by the consumer's interactive and co-creative experience towards an agent/object, for example a brand; Vivek *et al.* (2012) refer to the intensity of both participation and connection of an individual to an organization's offers, activities and initiatives, whether they are initiated by the individual or the organization itself; Hollebeek (2011) talks about a consumer's state of mind (motivational, connected to the brand and subject to the context), characterized by a certain degree of activation, identification and absorption in the relationship with the brand; according to Van Doorn *et al.* (2010), it is the customers' behavioral manifestation toward a brand or a company which goes beyond the purchasing act and is the result of motivational drivers, for example word of mouth, recommendations, cooperation with other users, blogging and reviews; Higgins and Scholer (2009) refer to a state of involvement, occupation, complete absorption in something resulting in prolonged attention.

The stronger the individuals' involvement in pursuing a target, the higher the value that is added to it. Bowden (2009) talks of a psychological process shaping mechanisms to win the loyalty of new customers and retain the existing ones; Patterson *et al.* (2006) focus their attention on the level of consumers' physical, cognitive and emotional presence in their relationship with a brand/organization.

4.4. Communication channels and new media in luxury markets

The main social web based communication tools used by companies in luxury markets to take consumers closer to their products and brand are identified as follow.

Blog. The word is a contraction of web-log, that is an "online diary". Blogging has gained significant importance in the social web environment and has proved to be one of the most interesting and innovative communication channels.

In luxury markets, blogs take on the function of web magazines, reporting comments, posts, multimedia contents and pictures aimed at informing, involving and attracting users. According to the prevalence of one format over another, a blog is called: plog (picture blog), mlog (music blog) and vlog (video blog).

Users create and directly control the contents providing their independent and influential perspective on specific topics, promoting exchange between interested parties and keeping the blog constantly updated with new and pertinent information.

Luxury market companies have traditionally influenced and oriented customers' tastes using unidirectional communication. Blog's development is changing the companies' privileged position in favor of the customers, who have more power to express their opinions and influence market trends (Okonkwo, 2010).

The bloggers' importance has now increased to the point that many companies, including luxury ones, draw inspiration from them when building their own business strategies.

Jansen *et al.* (2009) showed how users seem to trust in the disinterested opinion of strangers, in the form of online reviews (Duana *et al.*, 2008).

The Sartorialist. It is one of the world's most famous plogs. Created by American photographer Scott Schuman, The Sartorialist[2] is the website at the origin of these kinds of tools. Ranking among Time Magazine's Top 100 Design Influencers, Schuman is the world's most popular cool hunter and the first one to launch the idea of fashion blogger. Shuman's mechanism is simple and effective. He documents all new fashion trends, photographing the most original looks and mise he has found around the globe. The idea of taking pictures of completely unknown, well dressed, people (Macchi, 2011) and uploading them to the web has become a planetary success. Conversations happening on the blog obviously revolve around styles, fashion, accessories and luxury. However, the influence of these pictures goes beyond the framed styles, taking the conversation to a higher level where brands, design and models are discussed along with colors, expressions and other topics related to the images.

In an interview, Schuman explained the origin of The Sartorialist and the idea behind the fashion blog before it became a global success: "*It all started as a simple space to share pictures of fancy-looking people I had taken around New York*". Schuman had been working in the fashion industry for fifteen years and always noticed the big gap between the products sold in the showrooms and what fashionable people actually wear on the street. "*I never intended to become a fashion photographer* – he said – *but I knew that somehow my passion for both fashion and photography would come out. I never thought that could happen with a blog. The only original strategy behind my blog was taking pictures of people and styles in order to inspire designers. I am extremely happy when my pictures inspire designers. At the same time, I am still surprised when I receive email from people saying they have been inspired by the subjects of my pictures*". Finally, Schuman clarified the reasons for the creation of the blog: "*The net is making everyone equal. Differently from papers and other traditional communication media, the internet removes any filter and enables users to choose. I photograph what I see, as honestly as I can. I am not interested in spotting people who dress badly or wear expensive branded clothes. I am constantly looking out for people who are beautiful to look at*".

Scott Schuman has worked for various magazines, e.g. Vogue and Esquire, and has become the official and most sought-after photographer for important fashion brands like Donna Karan and Christopher Bailey, director of Burberry, who hired him to launch his project The Art of Trench.

Mlog and Vlog. Mlogs are interactive online magazines, which mainly use music. Several luxury brands with any kind of connection with music have their audience using a mlog.

Vlogs are set up like blogs but focus more, and sometimes exclusively, on videos and animation. Even if vlogs exclusively related to luxury brands are still not widespread, several on line communities about luxury goods and brands, fashion and lifestyle are present in YouTube and Vimeo, the most popular websites for videos.

Within these platforms, luxury brands possess and control actual web channels that are used to spread their videos, interviews and communication in general.

Hermès. Hermès' YouTube channel is used to state the brand's value and heritage in line with strong visual impact and through the creation of its dreamlike reference universe: the world of horses and riders. Hermès fosters its values on the digital channel also, making videos like Voyage d'Hermès, showing a modern interpretation of the mythological horse Pegasus, and Hobby Horses, representing models-Amazonians riding toy horses.

BMW TV. German car company BMW keeps in touch with its enthusiastic customers on BMW TV, a TV chanel where different types of videos, from innovative advertisement clips to short documentaries on historical cars, are broadcast. Their goal is a more in-depth knowledge of the brand, keeping an image of exclusivity. Virality is a key factor as videos can quickly get on blogs through links and easily spread around.

Other types of blog focusing on luxury and encompassing products or product categories, brand, services or lifestyles can be found along with the three main categories mentioned above. Blogs focusing on specific products, services or luxury goods categories (like fashion, leather goods, jewelry, watches, buildings or private jets) are extremely important for this field.

PurseBlog. It is an online community gathering more than 165 thousand luxury purses enthusiasts. When it started in 2005, PurseBlog generated more than nine million threads. In 2016 the blog showed more than 820,750 discussions and 29,576,470 posts created by its 520,425 members. Purse enthusiasts are mostly young fashionable women using PurseBlog to be constantly up to date with new tendencies and luxury leather goods. The community is where they collect information about all they need to know on purses: new models, most popular brands, shop locations, customer service experiences in different sales points, materials, prices, etc.

Blog readers value the bloggers' opinion, considering it honest and reliable and expecting some kind of loyalty and transparency from the bloggers, who should always be independent and indifferent to manipulation by the companies. This is particularly true for luxury brands and goods (Okonkwo, 2010). In conclusion, blogging is a pivotal activity for modern integrated communication of high symbolic value goods.

At this stage, two questions rise: how shall, or should, luxury companies relate to blogs? Should they start blogging?

In relation to the first question, luxury companies involve and influence bloggers through an activity of public relations, which is very similar to what they do with journalists. Chanel, for example, periodically invites the most influential bloggers to visit its ateliers, boutiques and laboratories; Louis Vuitton organizes breakfasts with bloggers to collect information on their ideas and tendencies.

With regard to the second question, then, according to some managers, luxury brands shouldn't have their own blog mainly for two reasons: firstly, blogging activities based on texts, images and some videos could disempower the dreamlike universe revolving around the brand as the subject of luxury communication; secondly, institutional blogs wouldn't be as credible as "uninterested" ones, where blogging involves only passion and not profit.

It is important to consider, however, how blogs are becoming an important communication tool for luxury companies and are generating new and unexplored opportunities.

Dom Pérignon. LVMH controlled brand Dom Pérignon is an example of how web opportunities can be used. The brand has decided to entrust the winery's chef de cave Richard Geoffroy with the task of managing a blog called Creating Dom Pérignon. On the blog, Geoffroy talks about champagne processing techniques and secrets as well as taste, bien vivre and luxury subject matters. Dom Pérignon's fans can enjoy pictures of growing vineyards and learn how to combine the right vintage with food prepared by the world's best chefs. The blog includes a newsletter and is linked to social networks like Facebook and Flickr. Readers can post comments and chat directly with Richard Geoffroy. Dom Pérignon has realized that blogs, because of institutional, need to be personalized with the introduction of the right narrating voice and need to provide users with a wider range of useful and interesting information, even if strictly connected to the brand.

Social networks. These are virtual spaces which allow users to: create and display their profiles, making them accessible, at least partially, to other users; create a shortlist of other users to communicate with; analyze their own network's characteristics, in particular, other users' connections (Boyd and Ellison, 2007). Social networks, as well as blogs, belong to the wider universe of social web and are now an important worldwide phenomenon. The most popular ones are: Facebook, MySpace, Flickr, Twitter, Instagram, LinkedIn, Qzone, VKonkacte, Cloob e Vine.

All major luxury market players in the world have an account and some of them, like Burberry, have witnessed an exponential growth in the number of users following and sharing the brand's contents (Hajli, 2014; Mosca et al, 2016).

W Hotels. It is chain of luxury hotels owned by Starwood Hotels & Resorts Worldwide targeting a young audience. The launch happened in 1998 with the restoration of the old hotel Doral Inn in Manhattan, New York. Users could upload on Instagram pictures and images of the hotels, taking part in a competition called #wdesign to win a weekend in one of the hotels of the chain in New York.

Oscar de la Renta. After selling accessories and perfumes exclusively on Facebook, the fashion designer has created a niche social network called The Fancy to sell high-end clothing. The Fancy counts about 750 thousand subscribers. It has proved a winning strategy. In fact, a relatively small social network can select its users, offering an exclusive, not for all, collection. One of his top-of-the-line products, a sweater with sequins sold for almost two thousand euros, is a good example of this.

The continuous increase of social networks is due to these platforms' characteristics, like the easy accessibility and management of one's own social networks and their ability to attract millions of users (Gensler ri al., 2013).

In general terms, these features identify social networks as mass tools and – as such – the exact opposite of anything that has to do with luxury and its offer (exclusivity, uniqueness etc.).

There are several prejudices on the use of social networks (Okonkwo, 2010). Two among them can be particularly dangerous for luxury brands:

- Social networks are mass tools. Almost all social networks are open to everyone. However, some online networks base their higher status on some sort of exclusivity. (Tuten and Solomon, 2014). Some social networks like Facebook (Dhaoui, 2014) are defined by their huge number of users, whereas other ones, like A Small World, stand out for the quality of their community members. 90% of A Small World users have an average income of 330 thousand dollars (the remaining 10% is made of millionaire philanthropists and aristocratic heirs). A Small World is therefore one of the online communities gathering the highest number of rich people on one platform in the world.
- Higher-income people do not use social networks. This statement is

far from reality as shown by several studies.[3] Rich people are very active on LinkedIn, A Small World, Twitter or MySpace (for example pop stars and their followers) and they love blogs where they can chat with their virtual friends about sailing, flying, photography and fashion (Toubia and Stephen, 2013). Social networks based on community and trust provide people with a sense of belonging and affiliation.

Cartier. Even though as early as 2016 companies were persuaded to use both online marketing and social media for their communication activities, Cartier was the first luxury brand to include a social network in its marketing strategy. In fact, in 2008, the brand created its first official page on MySpace to advertise one of its brands (Love) and a charity campaign (Luan, 2008).

Zegna. Wool mill Zegna is a Google+ pioneer with its page Zegna: the Modern Man's Manual. It is a shopping guide focusing on styles and new trends, aiming at involving all users by fostering their sense of belonging to the brand.

Michael Kors. The brand's web site is linked to Kors' Instagram profile where some pictures are marked as #IstaKors. Users can receive personalized emails reporting all features of the products shown in the images by clicking the like button.

Christian Louboutin. Chistian Louboutin is one of the most social shoe brands, coming second on Instagram, before strong and well-known luxury brands like Chanel and Burberry. Its strength being the collection of pictures narrating the history of the brand.

Burberry. Among luxury brands, Burberry has best used digital channels, providing consumers with a unique experience. The old style image of this brand has changed for the better through live-streaming fashion events, viral social media campaigns and an extremely active online community. The change has rendered the brand appealing to a young audience, aware of the brand's values.

This active social presence has made Burberry visible to web consumers, gaining it a leading position in the market. Followers can access videos, images and backstage fashion events on Facebook, Twitter and YouTube. Burberry was the first brand to broadcast a live 3D fashion event from London, while at the same time hosting other events in New York, Paris and Tokyo.

Tiffany & Co. Tiffany uses Facebook to communicate the brand's values to its audience. Tiffany & Co's profile shows celebrities wearing the company's products along with videos and pictures of dinner parties to showcase the brand's importance for the American élite.

Blog users can decide to remain anonymous or use aliases while social networks require users to display their own identity. Social network users are active, smart, curious, reactive, brave and opinionated but flexible enough to get influenced by members of the community they trust (Smith, Fischer and Yongjian, 2012).

Social networks are mainly used to gather information, entertain, exchange opinions about different topics (luxury among them), share news, contacts and experiences. Like bloggers and their users, social network members are passionate people who, however, do not necessarily get together around a specific topic or area of interest. Social networks are, in fact, independent platforms connecting individuals with different backgrounds and experiences.

Social platform users tend to create subgroups, micro communities, online clubs and other forms of community gathering people who share the same interests and passions. Social networks create a sort of online users segmentation that is almost automatic and affordable (Nambisan and Baron, 2007).

Finally, social networks have modified the way customers assess services and products (Huang and Benyoucef, 2013). In fact, customers tend to consult the community (Shin, 2013) before buying luxury goods like purses, watches, luggage, writing tools online (Jin, 2012).

Consumers are not interested in the information provided by a brand on its official website but want to know the brand's credibility and the value perceived by other customers. Companies' information is not enough to bond customers with products and services. Companies need to be in tune with consumers using online communities and social networks in order to influence and attract their customers (Jahn, Kunz and Meyer, 2013).

In this new scenario, how to approach consumers to make them spread the company's message has become the new biggest challenge. This is especially true for luxury brands which have always been detached from consumers.

The Internet must be used by companies producing high symbolic value goods as a multichannel system to reach out to new customers, strengthen the relationship with existing ones, improve brand's image, make online sales and improve the overall customer experience (Park and Kim, 2014).

Moreover, luxury companies should get access to all communities (Loureiro and Lopes, 2014) where traditional consumers of high symbolic value goods operate. They should then identify relevant micro-communities and understand their working mechanisms in order to design an adequate marketing approach.

Social networks are an important opportunity for luxury brands as they allow companies to monitor consumers' evolution (qualitative analysis) and marketing actions' return (quantitative analysis). Most of all, however, social networks are effective platforms for advertising targeting a specific audience (Park, Song and Ko, 2011). A Small World and Pinterest, for example, provide luxury brands with access to a consumers' élite segment (Yoon, 2013). They make an ideal space where brands can advertise their luxury products without sharing their communication space with mass-produced goods.

Kate Spade New York. Also known as Kate Spade Handbags, it is a design company founded in 1993 by Kate Spade. The company started off by selling purses and carried out a process of brand extension including beauty products, shoes, perfumes and raincoats. The first shop opened in SoHo, New York. The campaign Ride Colorfully for the new Vespa by Kate Spade was advertised on Pinterest. Users were asked to create a section reporting the name of the campaign with the addition of a hashtag: #ridecolorfully. The first four winning people would get a Vespa personalized by Kate Spade.

Online Brand Community. Companies can make their actions of corporate social responsibility known through online communities. For example a company's transparency, sustainable development practices, negative effects of counterfeiting, environmental accountability, respect for human rights, gender and working conditions equality (Liang *et al.*, 2012).

Finally, luxury brands can involve customers in the creation and development process of their products using social networks to launch online competitions and co-creation activities (in a controlled environment to guarantee the exclusivity of the brand). This makes customers feel appreciated and valued (Wang, Yu and Wei, 2012).

Brogi *et al.* (2013) show how Online Brand Community dynamics are positively correlated to brand equity. In particular, participation of the community and shared content production have a direct influence on brand loyalty. Marketing managers can get useful information by keeping community dynamics monitored, paying attention to its members' ideas as they represent the most important stakeholders for the brand's image and value.

Louis Vuitton. LVMH group has heavily invested in the web over the last years, creating actual live events to involve its community. An example of Louis Vuitton's web strategy to involve customers and communicate with them is the opening on the 25th May 2010 of the new brand's boutique in Bond Street, London. TV stars, journalists and popular bloggers were invited to the opening while customers around the world could follow the event online. A special live show allowed the company's fans to follow the celebrities' arrival, discover the boutique and take part in the interviews of the happy selected guests. The French maison's Facebook application allowed users to update their status with news concerning the event and post comments about the opening. Through the Facebook application Mon Monogram, users could then create a virtual bag bearing their initials, choosing both colors and monograms, and email it to their friends or buy it directly from the brand's website.

Louis Vuitton's digital strategy involves other social media like Flickr, YouTube and Twitter. Twitter is mainly used for news and events as push communication while fashion shows and presentations' pictures are collected on Flickr. Louis Vuitton YouTube channel hosts several travel videos made by emerging directors from all over the world. Louis Vuitton's example shows how social media shouldn't only be part of any luxury brand's universe but they should definitely also be a valuable platform to improve results in both customer relations and brand awareness.

We are going to explore peculiarities and possible future developments of social media dynamics in relation to high symbolic value goods in the next chapter.

Applications. Cell phones are nowadays the most personal communication tools on the market. Smartphones, in particular, have changed our way of communicating, thinking, living and interacting. The mobile revolution affects all generations, geographical areas and cultures, regardless of their economical situation. The global development of mobile technology has created several market opportunities in different fields for companies willing to take advantage of them.

Luxury players were among the first companies to use this technology employing mobile devices in cooperation with cell phone producers and through mobile marketing campaigns related to promotions, events and information on new products.

Mobile technology creates good opportunities for marketing strategies, for example: a connection between brand and customers before, during and after the purchasing experience; the chance of increasing and efficiently channeling its brand awareness; the possibility to influence the purchasing decision; the advantage of increasing the customer's experience; the opportunity to improve both service and brand loyalty.

Storytelling. This narration model, appropriate in particular for luxury brands and goods, has been created with consumers in mind and developed a relationship as deep and genuine as possible. The model not only tells the story of the brand but it highlights the passion behind the creation of a product or the life story of its designer. For example, communication in the filed of perfumery and cosmetics has always included storytelling as an essential part to sell a luxury brand's heritage. Through social media and the new available tools, brands can offer a multidimensional and multimedia narration (Lesage, 2011).

Burberry and digital development. Thomas Burberry opened his first shop in 1856 in Winchester Street, Basingstoke (UK). Burberry is now one of the main global luxury players, its revenues in constant growth: from 2 billion euros in 2012 to over 3 billion in 2015 and 2016. In recent times revenues have doubled year on year.

The Burberry Group is organized in strategic business units for distribution channels, regional macro-areas, regions and product divisions. The group is then supported by corporate functions. The main merchandise categories refer to personal luxury goods segments: men, women and kids' wear and accessories.

Burberry's products are sold through the retail channel (generating about 71% of revenues) and the wholesale channel (generating 26% of revenues). During the years, the company has made a series of global license agreements using partners' local competences. Burberry acts in three main markets: Asia-Pacific (38% of the revenues), EMEA (35%) and the Americas (27%).[4] For several years now, the brand has been considered a pioneer of digital luxury and fashion. In fact, it has allocated about 60% of all available resources to communication activities. As a consequence of that, Burberry's presence on digital channels is widespread and it has become a reference point for several players.

The official website, available in six languages, can be found in more than forty-five countries and is organized into several sections. Among them, the shopping section was created to offer a personalized service. Moreover, the service Burberry Bespoke opens up to personalization, allowing customers to design and order their own personalized trench coat.

Burberry's approach to digital channels for both communication and e-commerce highlights the strategic competence of the brand in relation to social networks management and consumers' engagement activities. Burberry was the first company to put fashion shows on live streaming and launch interesting campaigns to involve consumers using web and social networks. The success of this digital strategy is evident in the growing number of consumers following the company on social networks: YouTube, Pinterest, Instagram, Twitter, Facebook. This approach allowed Burberry to establish millions of connections, thus reaching out to an international target demographic.

Christopher Bailey and, later, Angela Ahrendts were the minds behind the company's digital channels development strategy involving the integrated management of several social media and e-commerce websites.

Burberry took advantage of its "Britishness" sponsoring celebrities like musicians, models and actors, i.e. movie star Emma Watson. The company then launched Burberry Acoustic, a TV program to spot English talent and promote their songs.

Every day Burberry shares updates, images and designers' contents with its large Facebook community of 12 million followers.

With Tweet walk, a live fashion event on Twitter, Burberry severed its ties with physical distribution, allowing customers to buy online the outfits shown on the catwalk within 72 hours. In September 2014 the button buy-now was introduced. Users can now buy a product that has just been tweeted simply by clicking on the button. Burberry was again the first company to implement this option for its nail polish collection.

Moreover, the brand launched on Twitter a campaign called Burberry

Lipsticks, focusing on engagement to promote its collection. The campaign allowed customers to send out free samples by just naming their friends on the social network. Burberry has a YouTube channel and users can download all Burberry fashion shows' background music from iTunes.

The company is present in the Chinese market through local social networking platforms like Kaixin001, Douban and Youku (the Chinese version of YouTube) and Sina Weibo, Twitter Chinese equivalent.

4.5. Sales outlet: from logistical hub to integrated communication channel

Latest marketing studies have seen the definition of sales outlet shift from a simple distribution logistical hub to an important part of the integrated communication process. This happened keeping in mind how both tangible and intangible elements of the product and brand concept can have an influence on the consumers' buying behavior and provide consumers with a unique, involving, sensorial and emotionally stimulating shopping experience.

Traditionally, studies on consumers' purchasing behavior highlighted how physical distribution and logistics have gained importance over the role of sales points in relation to influencing consumers' choices. In this perspective, sales points covered the functional role of making products available to consumers. The debate here revolves around the intensity of distribution, e.g. the number of sales points available in a specific area and their exhibition space.

Traditional consumers and, even more, occasional ones value the opportunity of buying a high symbolic value good at a sales point. Here is where the company makes an effort not only to make a range of products available to consumers but to transfer the system of values identifying the lifestyle the brand intends to affirm and communicate (Codeluppi, 2000; Mosca, 2000).

In other words, sales points are the final hub of the whole marketing strategy, conveying the image of the brand to consumers.[5] Therefore, direct control of the distribution channel is very important to maintain the set of the values communicated to the end user.

Nowadays a sales point for high symbolic value goods is an exhibition space where consumers look for products as well as the identity and the lifestyle associated with the brand, in an emotionally-charged purchasing experience.

If logistics is still an important function for luxury companies, the communication function of the point of sales becomes even more important and it should employ all available tools to involve consumers' senses, giving them the chance to experience a unique purchasing experience.[6]

Luxury goods' buyers do not make their purchasing decisions based on a rational process but are influenced by both environmental and internal factors like irrational, instinctive and unconscious drives. Therefore, experiential shopping approaches are particularly adequate to provide operational indications for sales points management (Hirschman and Holbrook, 1982; Branca, 1992; Sansone and Scafarto, 2003).

For all these reasons, both design and management of luxury goods sales points are crucial. A spectacular exhibition space definitely represents competitive advantage (Pellegrini, 2001), which improves the purchasing experience, giving a sense of uniqueness when compared to the main global luxury players' uniform offer.

Communication factors in the sales point. Atmosphere,[7] location and consistency are the three communication elements that can activate a multisensory experience for the consumer, stimulating the purchasing process and reinforcing or confirming brand identity.

Communication activities happening in retail shops may have to do with different events and situations: the shop's renovation; an opening anniversary; a special event, possibly connected to a festivity; the presence of a famous designer in the shop; a range of new products; live streaming of a fashion show; a special brand anniversary; the opportunity to show online or on TV a special event involving the brand; the beginning of the sales season or its early beginning for habitual clients, the launch of a new product. It is important for these events, even at a local level, to be tickling consumers' interest and curiosity (Chevalier and Mazzalovo, 2012).

We should highlight how a relational and sensory approach to retail shop management is usually not aimed at increasing sales in the short period but looks at strengthening the brand's image in the long term and communicating the brand style to the customers.

Therefore, the effect of a shop's atmosphere should be assessed not only on the basis of sales increase but, in a wider perspective, keeping in mind its contribution to the brand's value increase perceived by the customers.

Ralph Lauren. The brand was the first to conceive a system of sales points in tune with its own identity.[8] Values and lifestyle the way customers perceive them as their own when buying a product were transferred into the atmosphere's dimensions (Hetzel, 2002). Ralph Lauren has recently opened in Milan, based on the model of other world cities, an exclusive club. The club, like some English venues, is a place where its members can relax in a comfortable and informal environment, buying products if they decide to do so. This kind of new frontier integrates two components: service and purchase.

The image of Ralph Lauren.[9] The brand's key elements have to do with its neo-British style with reference to a romantic view of the old good times in America. The brand represents values[10] and cultural traits typical of the East Coast of the United States and, more precisely, New England and Massachusetts. Both the modern values of fashionable and wealthy American society and the traditional values of British aristocracy ("Polo" actually refers to the British elitist sport) coexist in the brand.

The connection with WASP's[11] local traditions allowed for strong identification among proposed brand, values and lifestyle. Values, which were originally established at a local level, dispersed and were taken up by a large group of consumers in the main international markets.

The brand's image reinforced through the sales point. The brand' image is reinforced by the creation and development of a network of sales points aimed at moving and thrilling the consumers before persuading them to a rational purchasing decision. Environmental factors become very relevant in this context: a Ralph Lauren shop is planned and furnished like a house; more precisely like an upper class countryside residence[12] where products are laid out without a specific order in the different rooms. The boutique is full of objects. This prevents customers from having a global perspective, keeping them engaged with each single detail instead. The physical environment is designed to convey the feeling of harmony and warmth typical of a distant past. The objects on display in the boutique are not for sale but are there to communicate the brand's lifestyle and values. The external facade is the reconstruction of a house and it gathers a series of objects, some of which are for sale. Inside, consumers are driven by a growing curiosity. The design aims at making people feel at home. The physical environment promotes the identification of the customers with the space around them, as if they were in their own house. The good and pleasant feeling experienced by customers in the boutique makes them eager to possess the objects surrounding them, in order to reproduce in their own house this feeling of an ideal home. This is Ralph Lauren's creation of value and one of the reasons for its products' high prices. Public and private dimensions combine in the boutique. As mentioned, that is a sales point as well as, apparently, a residence.[13] Visiting it, consumers can either get acquainted to the brand's values or confirm their importance if they knew them already. The objects on display are not mere merchandise but useful symbols to make the brand's cultural categories visible and stable. They deliver emotions and communicate Ralph Lauren's values: all elements converge and refer to the same code. This use of the story contributes to make the brand more credible as the creator of a system of forms and values that can transcend the brand itself.

Shop assistants. They do not wear uniforms but can choose what to wear among the shop's collections. Their outfits create a homey feeling and allow their personality to come out through the brand. Moreover, shop assistant outfits' variety illustrates Ralph Lauren's large range of lines. The variety of products, in fact, grants consumers the opportunity to express their personal style in connection to the brand's style itself.

Customers' profile. The sales point addresses cross-age groups including both sexes: collections are quite diverse and the brand features a unique, interesting mix between casual and formal clothing. Ralph Lauren's store environment strategy aims at a sort of brand's involvement. [14] Ralph Lauren intends to improve the whole purchasing experience, increasing its value for the customer and does so through specific marketing activities and services. Customers are charmed by the brand and pay little attention to prices; moreover, Ralph Lauren's highly experienced sales assistants guarantee a personalized service like the so called Made to Measure. In addition to that, the company offers a big range of products and a competent staff. Ralph Lauren's lifestyle as represented in its outlet network is well built and identified in the consumer's mind. This allows the company to overcome one of the biggest challenges, typical of the fashion industry: the coexistence of the brand and the innovation and change of its intrinsically transient products.

Communicating the sales point's atmosphere. As mentioned, atmosphere is one of the most relevant aspects when assessing the image of a sales point (Baker, Grewal and Parasuraman, 1994). Image has a big influence on the sales points' decision process, especially for high symbolic value goods (Dickson and MacLachlan, 1991), on customer satisfaction level (Cristini, 1995) and on customer retention (Donovan and Rossister, 1982; Bloemer and De Ruyter, 1997). Whatever the distribution channel chosen for luxury products, emphasis should be put on the atmosphere and the related sensory aspects of the sales point. In fact, those aspects should evoke the brand's reference values and communicate its lifestyle to the consumer. (See Figure 4.1).

Kotler (1973)'s definition of sales point as *"the creation of a shopping environment able to generate specific emotional effects – like pleasure or excitement – in people, increasing their inclination to make a purchase"*. Sometimes the atmosphere is more important than the product itself for purchasing decisions (Kotler, 2015).

Considering the matter from the same perspective, Derbaix (1987) defined the atmosphere as:

"A way of effectively organizing the space with the aim of creating impressions of well-being, welcome and joy".

The sales point's atmosphere is a multidimensional experience which influences both the decision of what sales point to go to (Stanley and Sewall, 1976; Nevin and Houston, 1980); Malhotra, 1983) and future customer's loyalty (Baker, Levy and Grewal, 1992; Swinyard,1993; Golden and Zimmer, 1986).

The prevalent dimensions of the atmosphere affecting the consumers' cognitive system and, therefore, their purchasing processes are (Vianelli, 2001): Visual (color, light, darkness, dimensions, shape, display, layout and crowding); Auditory (music, volume and loudness); Olfactory (smell and freshness); Tactile (temperature, texture); Social (interaction with sales staff and other customers) (Eroglu and Machleit, 1989; Mehrabian and Russell, 1974).

Moreover, atmosphere is not a univocal concept. The distinction between real and perceived atmosphere proves to be an important factor (Kotler, 1973). The former has to do with sales points' elements aimed at influencing consumer's behavio r and brand perception. The latter refers to the consumer's perception of the atmosphere when visiting the sales point.

Every single element of the atmosphere is important and affects consumers' choices. Customers' perceptions and, therefore, purchasing habits can be influenced by managing the different physical and social factors (Yadav *et al.*, 2013) that characterize the sales point and affect customers' sensory dimensions.

In the past few years, more and more studies have started taking into consideration the sales point's atmosphere (De Luca, 2000). The majority of these studies focus on the relationship between atmosphere and sales point, considering the former as one of several components (Lindquist, 1974; Zimmer and Golden, 1988; Lee and Geistfeld, 1995) or the main component (Baker, Grewal and Parasuraman, 1994) that can influence consumers' ideas about the quality of the product or service.

Depending on the method which is used, surveys can be divided into two groups: those considering the influence of the atmosphere's single elements on purchasing habits and those considering it as a holistic concept (Tai and Fung, 1997).

Many studies based on the first method have investigated both physical and psychological effects of individual environmental elements on consumers, like, for example, music (Areni, 1993; Herrington and Capella, 1994) or smells (Sprangenberg, Crowley and Henderson, 1996).

Studies based on the second method have considered the atmosphere globally instead, combining its multiple variables (music, light, color, design, furniture, staff) in order to understand how they affect consumers' choices as a whole.

A global approach that considers all elements together proves to be more useful to our analysis. In fact, a sales point for high value goods, due to the image it should cast, needs to pay attention to every single detail, engaging consumers' all five senses.

Lemoine (2003) carried out a study to analyze the sales point's atmosphere in a global perspective, considering the simultaneous influence of physical, architectural and human environment on consumers. He proved how the perception of the atmosphere positively influences both the amount of time consumers spend in the sales point and their willingness to purchase. The author based his study on the following model: Stimulus → Organism → Response (SOR) (See Figure 4.1).

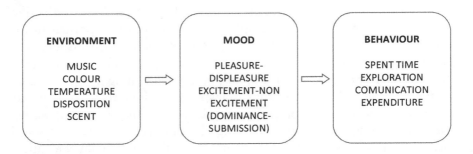

Figure 4.1 Stimulus → Organism → Response Model

Source: East R., *Comportamento del consumatore*, Apogeo Education, Milano, 2003, p. 295.

With regard to sales points' atmosphere, Mehrabian and Russell (1974) created a model (employed, with the necessary changes and integrations, from other studies about the role of emotions on consumers' behavior in a sales point) to analyze the emotional impact of environmental stimuli and its effects on a variety of behaviors.

The authors identify four different variable groups:

- *Environmental stimuli*: considering the complexity of most environments, as a multitude of several stimuli affecting all possible sensory perceptions (smell, hearing, touch, sight, taste), the authors have introduced the idea of information rate, expressed by a series of adjectives. [15]
- *Personality variables*: people are different in their inclination to hedonism and therefore differently receptive to environmental stimuli. The authors divided people into two categories: screeners and not-screeners, highlighting how the latter tend to feel, see, smell, etc. more than the formers.
- *Emotional states*: emotional states springing from environmental stimuli are: pleasure (P), arousal (A) and dominance (D). The first one refers to pleasure, happiness and satisfaction; the second has to do with excitement, stimulation and activity; the third one stems

from the degree of domination, intended as the individual's ability to control the environment.

- *Reaction variables*: individuals' reaction behaviors to the environment can be positive (approach) or negative (avoidance). [16] The evaluation of these behaviors is based on the individual's desire to be in a certain environment or to avoid it, explore it and interact with it or passively stay out of it, deal with other people dwelling in it or ignore them altogether. Moreover, it is based on results achievement, or lack of it, in relation to the expectations.

Donovan and Rossiter (1982) have applied this theory to retailing. Their model connects sales point characteristics (environmental stimuli) with individual emotions and behavioral reactions at the moment of purchase. According to the authors, the individual's emotional states in a retail shop arguably influences patronage behavior. Moreover they showed a positive connection between the degree of pleasure and the level of expenditure.

In general, then, literature supports the idea of a positive correlation between emotional experiences and resources (both financial and not) invested in shopping (Boedeker, 1996). The environment should be created to satisfy both the functional needs driving potential consumers to visit the sales point (to buy goods or gather information) and their emotional needs, connected with sensory aspects.

More recent studies have shown how the atmosphere influences purchasing behavior in three ways: as a means to create a message; as a means to create attention and as a means of perceptions (Zaghi, 2008). In the first two ways, the atmosphere directly affects the consumer's decision to prefer a specific sales point over others and become a customer; while it influencing the selection of the product and promoting a sudden purchasing decision in the third way.

Several studies identified the environment's effects on purchasing:

- Positive moods inviting individuals to treat themselves more generously and freely (Rook and Gardner, 1993).
- The whole shopping experience becomes fun and rewarding (Beatty and Ferrel, 1998).
- It makes customers spend more time in the retail shop, taking more time to assess what is on offer (Piron, 1989).
- It increases the interaction between customers and the staff.

There is no such thing as an ideal atmosphere. Each market is different and needs to be carefully studied separately. When making a purchasing decision, the situation – i.e. environmental factors defining the purchasing context – is a key element (Zaghi, 2008).

The key factors are:

- Physical environment, i.e. dimension of the surrounding space.
- Social environment, i.e. people the customers interact with.
- Time perspective; i.e. customers' time availability.
- Task's definition, i.e. the reasons for the purchase.
- Previous conditions, i.e. customer's moods and physiological states.

As mentioned, the development and management of the sales point has three main strategic goals:

- Reinforce and confirm the brand's image.
- Communicate values and the lifestyle associated to the brand. [17]
- Stimulate purchasing through a sensory connection with the consumer.

Direct management of the distribution channels and sales points by companies, for example Ralph Lauren, springs from the need to fulfill the strategic functions listed above. The affirmation of stable and well identifiable values deeply connected to the brand's image happens through direct management of all international sales points by Ralph Lauren. Luxury companies' competitiveness in the long term depends on the degree of consistency between proposed lifestyle, brand's identity as envisioned by consumers and individual collections representing goods and product lines.

4.6. Integrated communication through new technology applications in sales points

Channels integration in luxury markets concretely happens by introducing innovative technology in sales points and by integrating the physical distribution channel with bi-directional communication on social networks.

With regard to the first integration path, use of technology in luxury brand's stores positively influences consumers' sensations and stimulates their senses as described above. New technologies entertain customers and intensify the integrated communication process.

Companies use the variety of communication options available online to send out tailored messages that capture consumers' attention as they reflect their particular interests and deeply rooted habits. The Internet is a reliable tool and the effects of a campaign can be easily tracked down (Kotler *et al.*, 2014).

Companies need to define an offer and spread it in an integrated perspective. They do so using multichannel strategies aimed at developing an articulated and coordinated series of means and channels of contact between offer and demand.

It is an approach to customer that goes beyond the traditional single, usually physical, channel. This is due to the tertiarization of the economy and the diffusion of electronics and digital networks that overcome the logistics difficulties typical of traditional sales points (Ricotta, 2009).

Rohm and Swaminathan (2004) highlighted existing motivational differences between online and traditional shopping, using several motivational categories: Convenience and saving, need to gather information about products and brands, eagerness to immediately own a product, desire for social interaction, need to find a larger variety of products.

Direct sales points are the terminal of customer's relationships; companies using direct distribution have introduced progressive innovations aimed at improving customer relationship and developing a rewarding purchasing experience.

Offline and online communications in directly managed sales points are integrated. Innovation in distribution channels happens in the form of new technology used to entertain customers in the exhibition spaces, intensify upward and downward information streams between luxury brand and consumers, ensure complex purchasing experiences.

A survey of the newest technological innovations available at the moment at luxury brands' exhibition spaces allows the drafting of a short inventory.

Smart Labels. Smart labels use radio frequency signals to communicate with writing/reading fixed or mobile devices as far as one meter away. It is a system made of three components: an antenna, a reader and a transponder (tag). A smart label can contain information useful to customers like date of production or bar code. Tags are an evolution of the bar codes. In fact, tags can be read even when conditions are not ideal, for example when dust or other materials are between the tag and its reader. These labels allows multiple readings in real time.

Luxury brands like Prada, Gucci and Burberry tend to employ this technology in their sales points. That makes final products' logistics easier, guaranteeing their complete traceability.

Interactive dressing rooms. They are the evolution of traditional dressing rooms. Equipped with a touch screen that can show all different product types, in the interactive dressing room customers can go through all products they have previously tried on. This innovation aims at speeding up the purchase decision making process and decrease the number or returned items.

Several personal luxury goods distribution chains have recently introduced an evolution of the interactive dressing room in their shops: Dressing room 2.0, which is equipped with a webcam to send pictures to the main social networks, downloading an app that connects to the shop's mirror. Customers can thus get real time opinions from their friends. Boucheron's customers, for example, can try jewels on the company's website using a webcam and a face-recognition software.

Prada's Epicenter in New York is equipped with an interactive dressing room where customers can change color, luminosity and selected items.

Body Scanning. Body scanners were first introduced in Selfridges and Harrods department stores. These tools provide customers with the possibility to virtually see clothes as if they were worn, without actually trying them on. Customers' bodies are 3D-scanned and reproduced as a digital avatar on a screen. Several pieces of clothing in different sizes and colors can then be virtually tried on the 3D avatar. The screen comes in different sizes and allows customers to have an interactive experience, configuring all the collection's products and accessories.

Moreover, customers can create a personal avatar using a program installed in the room's display and use it again in any shop of the chain around the world.

This technology makes customers' experience unique, increasing their loyalty and saving their time.

A similar service is also available on the web. This technology is called My Virtual Model and is based on body scanning principles. In fact, it collects customers' body measures to create their digital avatars.

Luxottica, for example, has recently developed software associating several Ray-Ban models to customers' virtual face reproduction and has done so integrating a webcam with face-reproduction software.

Interactive window shopping. The shop window is the first element consumers encounter in their purchasing process and therefore becomes an ideal instrument for brand identity. Up to some years ago, messages were unidirectionally spread: from brand to consumer. Nowadays companies can directly interact with customers using different functions to entice them into the store. Window shopping, for example, enables customers to buy products during closing hours, becoming a huge touch screen for the customer to purchase goods and navigate around the whole commercial offer. Products available at the sales point can be reached at any time. Moreover, through window shopping, contents can be personalized on monitors visible from the outside.

Ralph Lauren was the first luxury brand to implement this technology in its stores in New York and Milan.

Chanel has set up window shopping dedicated to their trademark lipstick Rouge Allure in fifteen perfume shops. Consumer can gather useful make-up suggestions on the interactive window shopping.

Therefore, physical sales points can now provide information on the brand and its history, upcoming events, downloadable multimedia contents, news about fashion events, magazines to buy items during closing hours. All this information that was once available to digital channel users only can now be easily found in physical sales points.

QR Code. Quick Response is a matrix bi-dimensional bar code. A QR code is made of black modules laid out inside a square. It is used to collect information fast, usually through a mobile phone or a smartphone equipped with a special reading software. Luxury brands can include logos or other images in QR codes. This system allows users to read links to websites, see pictures, video, promotions and events.

NFC. Near Field Communication's technology provides short-distance (10 cm), bidirectional, wireless connectivity. NFC enables people to make wireless payments in stores using their smartphones and tablets. Moreover, information can be exchanged between devices through a peer-to-peer network. Stores can set up tablets to allow customers to make their payments more quickly than traditional cashiers.

RFID. Radio-frequency identification applies to the so-called "smart shelves". When a customer picks up or moves an item on display, the shelf gets activated and shows real-time information on prices, colors, models, etc. on a screen. This technology has been successfully spread around over the past years as it improves the shopping experience and customer's satisfaction, increasing both their involvement and loyalty.

These technologies, when integrated with advanced software, enhance purchasing awareness and represent new in-shop communication paths.

All technologies mentioned above are integrated with social media fulfilling that marketing integrated communication we discussed in the first chapter.

VIRTUAL REALITY. This technology allows the immersion of consumers in a virtual environment and could grants a global experience around the product of the brand.

Notes

1 These are: irony, intelligence, smile, fun, spectacularity, visual seduction, transgression, "classical" realism, demonstration and testimonial.

2 The reference website is: www.thesartorialist.blogspot.com.

3 A recent study carried out by the Luxury Institute shows that 72% of wealthy Americans belong to at least one social network. Luxury Institute WealthSurvey, *Social Networking Habits and Practices of the Wealthy*, 2009, in www.luxuryboard.com.

4 Data taken from Annual Report 2014/2015.

5 In relation to this, Pellegrini (2001) says: "*The sales point, where goods and information are exchanged, becomes important again. It becomes (...) a platform on which relationships are built and fed*".

6 Companies have started to explore new experiential marketing techniques aimed at maximizing customers' involvement in the sales point. In some sectors, the sales point becomes a "*permanent, constantly renewed, exhibition where products are displayed*". (Fabris, 2003; Schmitt, 1999; Carù and Cova, 2001).

7 The first studies exploring the relationship between physical environment and consumers' purchasing habits date back to the seventies and focused on sales points. In particular Kotler's (1973) proved that physical environment was among the nine main factors affecting the image perceived by potential customers. Successive literature on this topic has looked at the relationship between emotions on the one hand and customer's preferences and decisions taken on the other. In this regard, Westbrook (1981 and 1985) defined the satisfying repeated experience of buying goods in a sales point as "*the individual's emotional reaction to the whole range of repeated experiences made at a specific sales point*". Donovan and Rossiter's (1982) was the most popular model in the eighties and later. The academics proved how perceptions and behaviors of an individual-consumer in a sales point are the outcome of environmental stimuli. Environmental stimuli are at the origin of emotional states of pleasure and arousal.

8 The atmosphere's dimensions are: visual, auditory, olfactory, tactile, social.

9 Ralph Lauren was created by Ralph Lipschitz in 1968, when he decided to explore the prêt à porter market for men. The first Ralph Lauren boutique opened in 1971 in Beverly Hills.

10 In a brand management perspective, the brand acquires a specific personality and gets associated to tangible and intangible elements, creating an added value for both the company and the consumers.

11 The acronym WASP means White Anglo Saxon Protestant and connotes protestant white people of Anglo-Saxon origin.

12 Physical evidence's elements are dimmed lights, fall's classical and intense colors and antiques and modern art. Jazz and classical music are specifically thought to create a friendly environment.

13 The American company hired professional architects working in the film industry and museums to design their sales points. Giving a public place (a

shop) the identity of a private residence (the fashion designer's house) attracting customers to the brand.

14 Ralph Lauren stated: "*With our proven expertise in creating unique shopping environments, specialty retail is quickly becoming the fastest growing area of our business*".

15 In particular, Mehrabian and Russell (1974) used the following adjectives: redundant-varied, simple-complex, familiar-novel, small scale-large scale, similar-contrasting, sparse-dense, continuous-intermittent, usual-surprising, homogeneous-heterogeneous, uncrowded-crowded, symmetrical-asymmetrical, distant-immediate, common-rare, patterned-random.

16 Environmental psychology investigates what the authors have researched using the experimental method. That is how sales point's environmental variables like crowding, colors, music, noise, temperature, signs, olfactory and tactile sensations affect purchasing behaviors.

17 In relation to this, Pellegrini (2001) notes how sales points "*have become necessary meeting places with the customer: Stages where customers are invited to interpret the brand and its values, gathering the essential information to keep up the offer*".

Chapter 5

THE FRONTIERS OF LUXURY GOODS MARKETING: SOCIAL MEDIA SYSTEMS AND CHANNELS INTEGRATION

5.1. Introduction

In an era of web 2.0, companies are being asked to develop their marketing relationships in a completely new context. New consumers are progressively changing their purchasing habits; more importantly, they are changing how they relate to their purchases.

Today's consumers are more independent and know how to master the digital environment, in a context of new form of interaction with the brand in the global market.

These are competent consumers who gather sufficient information before buying products, have developed an adequate skills set and can assess different options. They are demanding and constantly expecting higher quality and performances from producers.

Therefore, two basic requirements should be satisfied for a luxury product to be successful in digital channels: a correct and personalized identification of consumers (and their needs), and a multisensory experience (Kapferer and Bastien, 2009) naturally integrated in the physical and virtual environment.

5.2. The development of special media system for luxury goods

One of the challenges, as well as one of the frontiers, of luxury goods marketing (but not limited to it) is the integration of FGC (*Firm Generated Content*) and UGC (*User Generated Content*) to communicate the brand identity using social media. The integration generates a UGB (*User Generated Brand*), i.e. UGC strategic and operational management related to a brand, aimed at achieving communication and marketing goals.

Social media's dynamics in relation to luxury brand marketing – as discussed in the previous chapter – are a relatively new and unexplored topic. In fact, even if more generic studies on general products or different fields are available, the peculiarities of luxury goods require specific considerations pertaining exclusively to the luxury market.

Jin (2012) has investigated the potential of active social media management for the marketing of luxury goods. He highlighted how consumers' satisfaction about content shared by companies generates brand affection and motivates consumers to use social media for their online shopping or to gather information before shopping offline.

With regard to social media strategies, Kim and Ko (2012) identified five essential features of social media marketing for luxury brands: entertainment (create interest and make the offered content pleasant), interaction (exchange opinions and suggestions between users and users and brand), trend (feed up-to-date content and information), customization (provide customers with effective services and information) and word of mouth (provide opinions and recommendations about products and services).

The authors have showed how the above mentioned activities, entertainment in particular, influence luxury customer relationships (made up of familiarity and trust) whereas purchasing intentions depend more on word of mouth and interaction, besides trust.

Kim and Ko (2012) have also researched the effect of these five social media marketing activities on luxury customer equity (composed by value equity, relationship equity and brand equity) and purchasing intention. They have highlighted how these activities positively influence consumers-brand long-term relationship, customer equity and purchasing intentions.

Park et al.'s survey (2011) on activities that most influence brand loyalty has shown the key role of interaction, followed by word of mouth and customization. The authors have then identified interdependence between the influence of social media marketing activities and the users' lifestyle (considering four groups: leisure oriented, ego-expression, fashion leader and early adopter), noting how social media users are less prone to be influenced and are more independent, self-referential and self-expressing.

Brogi et al. (2013) conducted another study to prove the positive effect of social activities. This study showed how user-created dynamics[1] in eight online luxury brand communities had a positive influence on brand equity and brand loyalty.

Jahn et al. (2013) emphasize how brand pages on social media prove an effective marketing tool to improve consumer relationships if two things happen: the attention is placed more on the level of user-user and user-brand interaction than on the number of fans; and offered content is assiduously created. In order to improve the relationship between users and brand, contents should include hedonistic, functional, entertaining and commercial aspects.

Dhaoui (2014) observed how the best content features for customers' appreciation have to do with the brand's heritage, its exclusivity and ability to include emotional elements in communication activities.

According to Loureiro and Lopes (2014), brand's reputation and transmission of functional values are not the main drives to online communities' involvement. Instead, an auto-generated online "tribe" able to communicate an intense emotional connection through social and individual values is the engine for a thriving community.

5.3. Integrated communication between old and new media: a reference model for luxury markets

The most innovative companies operating in luxury markets have evolved their communication plans and activities keeping in mind the progressive need to integrate traditional and emerging media. This operation led to the integration of new media generated by consumers (Bruhn and Schoenmueller, 2012) – i.e. all *User Generated Content* – which is used to directly get in touch with users and, more broadly, with the stakeholders (Schultz, Tannenbaum, Lauterborn, 1993; Krugman *et al.*, 1994; Collesei, 2002; Duncan, Mulhern, 2004; Aiello, Donvito, 2005; Collesei, Ravà, 2008; Belch, 2009; Mosca, Casalegno, Feffin, 2013).

The concept of integrated communication is strictly connected with the idea of sharing a series of common values between company, consumer and stakeholder. Among these values, company social responsibility stands out.

Porter and Kramer (2011) introduce the concept of social innovation, which considers the idea of shared values between company and community as a competitive key factor.

Communication in luxury markets is evolving according to three main trends, which are responsible for a change in consumer behavior:

- Search for personal experience and gratification;
- Technology pervasiveness and digital channels development;
- Corporate social responsibility (this will be discussed in the next chapter).

Search for personal experience and gratification. Several studies highlight how experience is nowadays a key element for consumers who look for it even before owning the purchased good. This is due to a change in consumers' purchasing patterns. Consumers are now shrewd, well informed, experience-hungry and in search of a connection with the brand, powerful and influential, individualistic but, at the same time, eager to be part of a community they can identify with.

Therefore communication activities become strategic and integrate with distribution activities in the competitive market of luxury goods. Distribution gives value to product and brand's heritage and guarantees a remarkable purchasing experience.

Technology pervasiveness and digital channels development. Innovation progressions have caused a change in consumers' purchasing behavior and role, from passive customers to active users. Customers are now willing to create content and be part of good production processes. They are involved in consumption (See-To and Ho, 2014), in a process of value co-creation.

Development of new technologies and compression of product lifecycles are at the center of new consumption mechanisms which involve sharing goods and experiences more than buying products in order to possess them (Rifkin, 2000).

Digital channel communications help luxury companies understand the role of the Internet. In fact, the Internet is not only a communication medium among others but is a multichannel platform, which should to be used along with other tools in specific integrated marketing strategies.

Communication activities through digital media aim at building consumers' trust, fostering information, sharing and exchanging opinions and content in a circular process integrating traditional unidirectional communication typical of press, radio and TV (Henning-Thurau *et al.*, 2004).

Corporate social responsibility. In luxury markets, consumers are interested in companies' code of ethics and conduct as well as implementation of sustainable practices throughout the integrated value chain. Consumers expect the highest quality standards as well as ethical decisions in relation to raw materials, labor conditions, relationships with staff (Hajli, 2014) and selection of suppliers. Companies' strategic management should therefore pay attention to all these elements, both in their implementation and coherent and integrated communication (Mosca, Casalegno and Civera, 2016).

We will discuss corporate social responsibility further in the next chapter.

A reference model. Can we identify a communication model for companies operating in luxury markets, which incorporates the above mentioned trends?

The concise model introduced here refers to seven expressions summarizing the suggested company's approach to integrated communication in luxury markets.

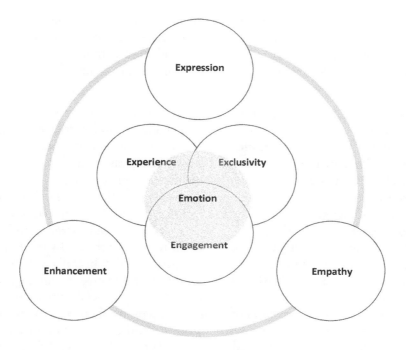

Figure 5.1 7 "Es" model

The first four expressions, already partly highlighted by some academics investigating communication in luxury markets, are:

- *Experience* (Okonkwo, 2009);
- *Exclusivity* (Chevalier and Mazzalovo, 2012);
- *Engagement* (Chevalier and Mazzalovo, 2012);
- *Emotion* (Atwal and Williams, 2009).

The interpretation of the above mentioned trends allows us to add three more expressions that are strictly connected with the opportunities generated by new technologies available to companies operating in luxury markets:

- *Expression*;
- *Enhancement*;
- *Empathy*.

Experience. Communication should aim at involving consumers, surrounding them with a universe that is consistent with the value of the brand, the heritage and the product and service concept. This will provide customers with a rewarding experience. The above-mentioned communication activities can be successfully implemented at the physical sales points. They have become the focus of integrated communication as they can broadcast the image of the brand and create a unique purchasing experience.

Burberry. London flagship store was designed to increase customers involvement and in store sales through a digital and tactile experience referring to the brand's historical and artistic heritage. The single-branded, 44 thousand square meters shop in Regent Street was created following the logical and physical design of its correspondent virtual sales point – burberry.com. The setting of the rooms retraces the website's sections, creating a digital-physical combined experience. One hundred screens, among which the world's largest indoor advertisement screen, and five hundred speakers giving voice to the exclusive videos shown by the English fashion house, guarantee a total immersion in the brand's values and products. Burberry's flagship store employs innovative technologies in relation to merchandising and inventory activities. Special mirrors turning into screens for the projection of exclusive videos are showcased along with RDIF chips. These tools are sewn to outfits and accessories and contain multimedia information on products. Moreover, iPad-equipped shop's staff has access to customers purchasing history and preferences through a specific software application. This allows for a personalized and tailored shopping experience.

Angela Ahrendts took part in the design of the flagship store when she was in charge of the distribution development (before moving to the same position in Apple). She said: "*Burberry Regent Street brings our digital world to life in a physical space for the first time, where customers can experience every facet of the brand through immersive multimedia content exactly as they do online. Walking through the doors is just like walking into our website. It is Burberry World Live*".

The store in Regent Street features specialized areas recalling the brand's values and products of the collection, a concierge, a maître and the Wi-Fi. The store often hosts events like music, cinema, theater and art's new and old talents. The physical space is not only a selling point but also a gathering place where Burberry entertains customers, organizes events that are live-streamed on burberry.com to be accessed by a global audience. Burberry's strategy in the store enhances the perceived brand's value using new technologies and creating interactive experiences, which improve the whole shopping experience. Moreover, it invites customers to dwell in the shop longer and creates in them the desire to return soon enough to repeat the rewarding experience.

Exclusivity. Exclusivity is a key factor in marketing strategies for high symbolic value goods and all elements fostering it have always been protected. Integrated communication for luxury goods should thus focus on this feature.

Digital marketing activities have generated new opportunities to communicate exclusivity (Hennings, Wiedmann and Klarmann, 2012). This has happened in spite of the initial, and still perceived, fear of a loss of brand exclusivity when using digital marketing and the Internet. The creation and development of communication platforms where community members can discuss brand or products is a reference model for the development of exclusivity on digital channels (Kim and Park, 2013). Contrary to the initial negative belief, these days, communicating luxury brands and goods using digital channels gives brands a touch of modernity and fosters exclusivity, prestige and emotions connected to their use.

Burberry. The Art of the Trench. Burberry created an exclusive platform gathering all trench-coat owners in a community called The Art of Trench. The community collects pictures taken by both famous and ordinary people. The company has therefore developed a fashion social network which combines the brand's high level contents with the users'. This platform has generated thousands of contacts and sharing in a virtuous communication process between passionate users and the brand. People can comment on pictures and share on Facebook, Twitter and Delicious. This initiative wasn't aimed at increasing sales in the short term but looked at spreading the brand's culture and values relying on its flagship product.

Engagement. Integrated communication activities for high symbolic value goods shouldn't just inform customers but also involve and touch them emotionally (Patterson, Yu and De Ruyter, 2006). Companies can achieve this outcome focusing their communication on their brand's heritage and bringing customers into the brand's universe (Hollebeek, 2011). They can do so by integrating traditional communication activities (traditional media and sales points) with digital marketing (Hollebeek, Glynn amd Brodie, 2014).

The development of new digital technologies has increased companies' abilities to involve consumers, guaranteeing a prolonged and coordinated experience based on different media (Vivek, Beatty and Morgan, 2012). Videos and online experiences, when based on touching stories and captivating content, can engage viewers, creating a unique experience.

Communication in luxury markets should not inform but create an experience fostering the future development of the brand. The main goal should be involving customers in an exclusive journey through the brand's values and products, focusing on long-term success (Higgins and Scholer, 2009).

Consumers are constantly exposed to a large amount of information, often not reliable and true. In this scenario, selected and reliable communication released by the brand becomes valuable and creates a unique and precious experience.

Louis Vuitton and web applications for visiting the world's capital cities. On the occasion of Beijing Olympic games in 2008, the French brand launched Soundwalk, a digital app providing an MP3 audio guide of Beijing, Shanghai and Hong Kong, which could be downloaded on smartphones and MP3 players. The app guided users through a one-hour walking tour of a city. The journey, as an intimate and personal experience, has always been the background theme of the French maison, which has always known how to use digital contents, turning them into a real and online art de vivre. As if in a movie, users would be surrounded by music and sounds during their city exploration. A narrating voice would lead them to the most popular city landmarks telling a love story and trying to reproduce the pace of everyday life. The guide was available in six languages: English, French, Cantonese, Japanese, Korean and Mandarin.

The natural evolution of the journey – as the natural background for Louis Vuitton's values and products – was fulfilled using a digital application providing virtual guides to visit the world's major cities. The app could be downloaded to smartphones. The tour is created by Louis Vuitton and takes the visitor to neighborhoods, shops, restaurants, interesting situations and engaging events. All of the above was created in accordance with the French brand's perspective.

Emotion. The process of creating fulfilling experiences and communicating exclusivity factors through both physical and digital channels is at the source of the emotion perceived by high symbolic value goods' consumers. The integration of different communication channels in a unique story about product attributes and service concept, enriched by local values of origin and productions, creates the emotion. For example, consumers are loyal to Burberry because they look for a *"timeless authenticity"*, stay at Ritz-Carlton hotels to feel *"away from the world"*, go to Tiffany to find *"true love"*.

Luxury brands employing the best communication strategies have since long realized how products and service concept values are not to be found in tangible attributes but in first and second level intangible elements. These are the core of the communication and can create elusive and ephemeral feelings and emotions. Physical content represents the means available to consumers to reach those emotions. This is the reason why luxury brands determine the emotional value related to the brand itself first and, only afterward, develop physical and digital expressions to communicate and make that specific emotion tangible.

The development of communication technologies has allowed the creation of a system integrating traditional tools and new digital media. This has brought forward three more advantages connected to: expression, enhancement and empathy.

Expression. Digital systems can expand communication time, which is now managed by some direct and indirect sources. Communication content is immediately available to users. An event can be known in real time or users can decide to learn about it at a different time. This is at the source of an integrated story that starts with the event happening and goes on forever, indefinitely. Companies can therefore create more suggestive, elegant and dreamlike communication strategies, reaching out to a specific target market, which is constantly in the search of content to enjoy and share. This kind of expressive results is hard to reach using traditional media only.

Enhancement. It is enhancement of product and service concept through online communications, which refer to exclusivity but in a circular sharing context involving consumers, fans and companies. In other words, company, brand and product become the center of an integrated, circular system of multi-directional communication which is more democratic but also guided and controlled.

Empathy. Companies can generate direct, personalized and sympathetic content making appropriate use of new digital media. They are at the center of a circular communication process where experiential content is constantly fed and personalized. That is how companies can give customers the sensation of having established a direct and personalized relationship with them.

Tiffany and the seven "Es". This luxury brand has set up a website called What Makes Love True and a mobile app, Engagement Ring Finder, to involve customers even more, providing them with a circular communication based on experience with the brand. Customers can tell their love story on the website and actually see the engagement ring on their hand through the app. Both these communication activities have been extremely successful. Scott Schuman, creator of The Sartorialist, and Garance Dore took pictures of couples in New York and Paris that embodied their idea of true love. These pictures were then published on the web. At a later stage, users and fans were allowed to upload their own pictures too, using mobile apps and specific filters, like Tiffany Blue on Instagram or using photo boots located in the brand's jewelry stores. What Makes Love True is divided in four sections: Love is Everywhere, The Art of Romance, Tiffany's New York and Love Stories. Pictures representing the community's idea of true love can be found in the section Love is Everywhere. These pictures show couples cycling and walking around as well as letters, personal notes and articles implicitly connecting with the emotions and to the romantic nooks of New York and Paris. The implementation of this immersive activity has allowed Tiffany to place the brand within a shared context and offer a lifestyle model based on love and revolving around the product. In fact, the brand has invested significantly in its communication campaign on the website. What Makes Love True allows customers and fans to share their own love stories using videos or songs and provides them with a map, for example a map of New York, they can use to share the location of their most important love-life events. Tiffany's communication activity has created a virtual environment integrating the stores' physical space, where the brand's lifestyle is narrated in a cooperation with customers.

5.4. The development of multi-channel systems for luxury players

Luxury companies need to use several channels, especially since digital channels have now gained official status. Digital channels are a means of interaction with the demand and have informative, transactional and relational functions which use physical and virtual contact methods, alternatively or in parallel.

In this perspective, multi-channel management policies are a very important tool in gaining customers' loyalty and conquering new market segments.

As previously mentioned, companies operating in luxury markets were initially skeptical about using the web as a distribution channel. In fact, they considered it to be both lacking the customer experience offered by sales points and too far from customers with purchasing power. This perspective has changed lately and digital channels have showed their high potential, guaranteeing their growth in popularity over the next years.

Digital channels' development logic for luxury players therefore envisages integration with the physical channel. Traditional shops still cover a central role in the purchasing experience of luxury goods.

However, digital channels are now an essential tool for high symbolic value goods market players.[2]

The interactive nature of social media marketing makes them a useful tool to gather further information about consumers and establish a better relationship with them.

Some brands are pioneers of this approach.

David Yurman. It is an American jewelry company founded in 1980 by David Yurman. The company sells its products through 28 boutiques in the United States and 4 abroad, Hong Kong among other places, and uses the social media channels solely as social commerce. The brand's widespread presence on the main platforms makes up a real, complete offer system on digital channels. Back in 2012, the company had already shown a strong attitude to social commerce building Shop behind the scenes, a Facebook application which allowed customers to get access to a FB exclusive collection.

Tiffany&Co. Tiffany's website has more than 3.500 products for sale online. Each of them comes with a detailed report on price, features and history of the collection it belongs to. The company clearly considers social media channels and new technologies as an opportunity to grow the brand's image and identity. For this reason, Tiffany&Co can be found on the main platforms like Facebook, Twitter, Google+ and YouTube. For 2015 Saint Valentine's Day, the company launched an innovative digital campaign. For a whole month, the Concierge of Love, recalling all services available in shops, supported men in finding the right Valentine's present.

The Multichannel process allows placing information, products and services, before and after sale, on the market using two or more channels. This way of handling demand goes beyond single, independent channels, promoting the potentiality of economic tertiarization and diffusion of digital technologies (Okonkwo, 2012).

This approach overcomes the informational and distributional constraints typical of traditional sales points, taking full advantage of the separation between physical and informational streams. Each consumer can, therefore, interact with the company – or its specific components – at any time and in a discretionary manner (Rangaswamy and Van Bruggen, 2005).

Under a managerial perspective, multichannel processes lead to digital channels' understanding, designing, coordination and valorization. These processes aim at increasing the customer base generated value (customer equity) through targeted actions of acquisition, retention and development. This approach to multichannel systems enables companies to manage demand growth, using the communicative flexibility typical of digital technologies.

In this perspective, multichannel management policies can be very useful in conquering new market segments, thus expanding their boundaries. At the same time, customer relationship management can benefit from wise management of the channels. In fact, new and useful information on purchasing habits can be collected and digital environments can be used to observe customers behaviors from a privileged point of observation.

Lastly, the customer base will be motivated to continue the relationship on the basis of the value generated by the offer in terms of increased availability and the systematic adjustment of contact channels with the company regarding purchasing opportunities and relationship's lifecycle evolution (Ricotta, 2009).

The diffusion of a multichannel behavior on the demand side generates increased competition and better possibilities for consumers to identify the best good-service-price combination.

After all, understanding how consumers use different channels involves taking up innovative models of segmentation of demands. These models, in fact, should bear in mind the reasons for choosing both digital and physical channels (Miceli, 2008).

As mentioned in Chapter 2, Luxury brands require a strategy integrating digital and physical channels instead of a stand alone digital policy. The main players have already strategically implemented the development of digital channels in high symbolic value markets. Moreover, positive business models have been established by both luxury brands and independent distributors (pure internet players). The ultimate goal of a multichannel approach is the integration of physical and digital channels in both the distribution and communication fields. Most of the time, this means that virtual and traditional channels are integrated and complementary.

Virtual channels definitely alter the distribution chain's processes. In fact, online and offline purchasing often involve the same products but with different service and information content attached to them.

Different sales channels – physical and digital – should be integrated in order to have a full picture of customer's behaviors (customer journey).

The popularity of digital environments has contributed to the extension of channel management opportunities, opening up new competition playing fields.

As mentioned, consumers can nowadays buy online at physical sales points or, vice versa, buy offline in shops after visiting the website. Furthermore at physical sales points, customers can access multimedia content, which add special value to the purchase.

The ubiquity of digital environments, in all their forms, is among the reasons for the increased number of consumers associating new activities with traditional purchasing rituals. Digital tools allows consumers to gather information on products and brands, compare prices in different sales points and find the closest one to them.

We should, then, bear in mind how consumers buying at full price on a specific channel tend to use a second channel for longer than consumers buying on channels considered less costly both financially and cognitively (Venkatesan, Kumar and Ravishanker, 2007).

Greater channel integration, in fact, translates into greater customer reassurance and this leads to higher profits than those made by companies adopting different solutions (Berger, Lee and Weinberg, 2006).

Let us investigate, now, multichannel development lines for luxury brands.

Using new technologies, brand's websites become a real digital hub that includes micro-pages for specific products, markets and campaigns; blogs; brand communities and e-commerce.

The main operational tools are listed below.

Search Engine Optimization. It aims at increasing traffic to a website, giving it more visibility in the most popular search engines. This is an important aspect, especially when operating in markets using a different alphabet.

Direct Mailing. E-mails are a traditional digital marketing tool. Although not particularly innovative, e-mails can be used to build relationships with luxury market customers, sending messages, information and targeted offers.

Online Advertising. Online advertising is more than a traditional tool readjusted to suit the web's needs. In order to be successful and reproduce the brands' concept, online advertising should incorporate a creative and interesting idea able to make it "viral" and motivate customers to spread around the "*dream*".

Luxury Brand Community. The goal of a community is gathering consumers interested in sharing content related to the brand. A community can be started by creating an account on social media or a blog with the intention of making consumers interact with the brand (an example of this is Burberry's The Art of the Trench).

Social Campaign. In order to involve community consumers, both content and brand story created should stand out of the social media crowd. Web storytelling and online and offline media consistency prove to be key factors.

Applications for smartphones and tablets. Apps can be used to entertain customers and channel them toward e-commerce (tablets, in particular, are sometimes used in shops). What was said about websites applies to apps also; in fact, luxury brand's customer expectations are generally very high.

E-commerce. Despite a strong debate about e-commerce, it is now an important channel for luxury brands whether it happens directly on the brand's website or through intermediaries like Net-A-Porter and Yoox. Apart from looks and functionality, other key factors are completeness of information, assistance, personalization opportunities, security of transactions and insurance, return and refund policies.

Some brands have recently shown a strong ability to integrate several channels.

Fendi: from selective e-tailer to a complete digital approach. 2015 is a turning year for Fendi's online policies. The company launched its first digital boutique on fendi.com on March 26th. Customers all over Europe can now find purses, small leather accessories, shoes, jewels, glasses, products from the last fashion show, previews and exclusive capsule-collections on e-commerce platform. *"Knowing our customers and integrating their experience through the medium of this channel is a fundamental approach to answering an increasingly sophisticated demand. Launching e-commerce is a very important step for Fendi as we are always at the forefront and attentive to market's evolutions"* said Pietro Beccari, president and CEO. Fendi's digital boutique was launched implementing a video campaign on YouTube and other social media. Fendi, however, is not completely new to e-commerce: in 2012, the brand launched a pop-up store on line to celebrate the fifteenth anniversary of one of its key products – the purse Baguette. Apart from being a strategy targeting the attention on an icon-product, this activity was a first test for the launch of the real boutique online. In the summer 2014, Fendi launched the app My Baguette for iPad and Android through which customers could create their own personalized purse and share it on social media. Each month, Fendi would select one of the shared purses and publish it on the company's profile.

5.5. The frontier of social commerce for luxury brands

E-commerce activities using social media are still quite uncommon features in social media marketing for luxury brands. However, they will grow in popularity over the next few years.

According to recent studies (Mosca *et al.*, 2015), few luxury brands have started an integration process between their social and e-commerce channels to promote products and increase sales.

Moreover, the importance of social commerce in luxury markets depends on both which social media are being used and which product sectors are considered, taking into account the big differences between available platforms and products.

This is the outcome of a survey investigating a sample of over one hundred luxury brands belonging to five different sectors: Fashion & Accessories, Automotive, Perfumes & Cosmetics, Jewelry & Watches and Wine & Spirits and analyzing the content published by brands on their official social channels – Facebook, Twitter, YouTube, Instagram and Pinterest – over a period of time spanning from 2014 to 2015.[3]

A first phase focused on assessing the brand's position in the general context of social media analyzing adoption, type and popularity of the published content. Popularity was measured considering both the brand's fan base in examined social media and the engagement rate, an index comparing different brands and platforms used to determine the best indicators to gauge brands' popularity in social media.

A synthesis indicator, the social commerce rate, was later calculated to measure the examined brands' level of social commerce policies. This indicator evaluates the posts published by brands over the established period of time, according to their higher or lower inclination to social commerce dynamics.

With regard to popularity and engagement, two main results have been achieved. The first result shows how the fan base doesn't prove a relevant indicator if we intend to measure the users' level of interaction and involvement by the brand. As per correlation matrixes, in fact, the engagement rate is the real indicator and shows little or inverse correlation with the number of fans. This means that brands should not aim at increasing their fan base in absolute terms but should focus on improving their relationships and publish engaging and interesting content.

The second result shows that brand's popularity differs on the basis of considered social media and reference sector. Among social media, Instagram shows the highest engagement rates. Based on a strong visual component that associates it to high-end products, Instagram is favored by fans in spite of its main limit: the lack of a real sharing function like Facebook or Twitter's.

On the basis of the two identified dimensions, we can define a framework highlighting four possible strategies luxury brands can implement to approach social media.

The two-dimensional matrix illustrated in Figure 5.2, which features *"Percentage of promotional content"* and *"Social commerce score"* as variables, helps to classify four strategies related to social media adoption by luxury brands, as follows.

The Social brand ambassador's strategy class (low promotional content percentage and low social commerce score) includes those brands that use social media for entertainment and user engagement; therefore, are mainly oriented toward brand identity communication rather than commerce. At the bottom of the cell, the sub-class haters category refers to those brands that are mainly inactive or that make only minor use of their social media accounts. The Social showcases strategy (high promotional content percentage and low social commerce score) includes those brands that use their social accounts as online catalogues – i.e., they provide product-related images and detailed information, but without e-commerce links or referrals. The Social infotainers strategy (low promotional content percentage and high social commerce score) includes those brands that scored high in social commerce, mainly because of the provision of informative content and brand-consumer interactions, but they were linked to more entertainment-oriented actions rather than product-related ones. Finally, the Social sellers strategy (high promotional content percentage and high social commerce score) includes those brands that have integrated social commerce into their online strategies and have subsequently exploited the potential of social media to drive online and offline sales.

		SOCIAL COMMERCE SCORE	
		LOW	HIGH
% PROMOTIONAL CONTENT	HIGH	Social showcases	Social sellers
	LOW	Social brand ambassadors Haters	Social Infotainers

Figure 5.2: Luxury brand social strategic approaches

The Automotive sector, among other sectors, has achieved high involvement values, even four times higher than the other sectors'. This ability to create an emotional relationship with customers is due to its products' high quality and technology as well as the component of admiration, dream and status symbol generated in the audience. Jewelry &

Watches and Wine & Spirits have also achieved high involvement values because of the strong symbolic component related to some of their products. Among brands showing the highest engagement rates are, in fact, Rolex, Harley Davidson, Porsche, Maserati, Möet & Chandon and Tiffany & Co but also, in the footwear market, Christian Louboutin and Jimmy Choo.

Social activities result in different levels of social commerce depending on which social media and business sector are considered. Pinterest was rated best among social media for both social commerce rate and the percentage of promotional content published by brands. The reasons being an interface reminding users of a real website, including thematic sections like departments of an online boutique. Pinterest's limited diffusion, if compared to Instagram or Facebook, is however a drawback. Facebook's multifunctional features, in particular, lend themselves to connecting with the online boutique through links, connections and social commerce targeted applications.

Interesting instances are: Tory Burch's Facebook store, Fendi's My Baguette application, Oscar de la Renta's Facebook exclusives or thematic albums sharing through e-commerce links (like Stella McCartney's album The Art of Giving, suggesting gift ideas through its purchasing link).

Twitter is also an interesting tool in relation to social commerce, as it allows the linking of images directly to the purchasing channel. Furthermore, customers can buy through their own profile (an option tested by Burberry) using the buy now button, a tool showing interesting potential.

On the contrary, Instagram's social commerce introduction is limited by its own functionality. The only interesting instance is Michael Kors', hastag #instaKors.

Luxury brands have also introduced competitions to draw fans to e-commerce. Users can win products or discount vouchers for online shopping sharing brand-related images, or using their own Instagram account to showcase products.

As mentioned, there are significant differences in the approach to social commerce according to the different product categories.

Fashion & Accessories's level of social commerce increases proportionally with the quantity of promotional content published. This, obviously, depends on social media marketing strategic choices made by different brands.

In general, however, social commerce is still not widespread. If we think of how new collections are presented on social media during fashion week, we can see how luxury fashion brands focus more on sharing show images, backstage, events and important guests rather than promoting new product ranges and providing information on them.

The Automotive sector has more objective difficulties introducing social commerce as selling cars or motorbikes online proves more difficult. Nonetheless, several brands have adopted strategies to attract customers before the actual purchasing transaction phase, taking advantage of the growing phenomenon of ROPO (*Research Online Purchase Offline*). Most Automotive brands use social channels to introduce new models and provide detailed information and technical specifications. They also often use car configuration/customization apps and a website/section selling merchandising, accessories or clothing articles. Porche, for example, has a car configuration app on Facebook, Ferrari has a unique Pinterest account as Ferrari Store, RollsRoyce shares on Facebook its models' reviews from users or specialized websites, Infiniti recently launched the contest #infinitilovesme where users could win a gift card sharing an episode about the brand's customer care.

Perfume & Cosmetics products and brands show a fragmented attitude to social commerce. Some brands have totally integrated social commerce in their social media marketing policies whereas others use social channels like online windows. A third category of players, then, moderately uses digital channels and social media.

Clinique, Shiseido and Estée Lauder belong to the first group and constantly offer new information about new products, advice on use, beauty e-consultancy applications, contests and possibilities to get discounts. Some other brands like Jean Patou, Amouage and Caron Paris don't have a social media presence and keep far away from social commerce.

Jewelry & Watches brands show divergent approaches also. Some brands have integrated social commerce in their social media marketing activities whilst others use their accounts as windows where consumers can personalize their items and find extra information before buying in boutiques or from offline distributors. Tiffany & Co is a case in point for its effort to develop several activities to draw users to products, always keeping in mind the entertainment factor. Another case in point for social commerce policies is David Yurman. The company uses its social media as real sales channels where it publishes pictures of new collections along with the links where they can be bought. Other brands using social commerce are Van Cleef & Arpels (using social media for advertising), Cartier (for example the app Mon Diamant to find personalized diamonds) and Chopard (for example, the links to buying jewels worn by the stars at the Oscars).

The Wine& Spirits sector has shown a weak interest in social commerce so far and most of the brands do not avail of an official e-commerce channel at the moment. The only reference instance is Krug. The company's app Krug ID allows consumers to read about the history and origin of each bottle, scanning the barcode on the label: Place and date of production, grapes used, processing times and techniques, combinations and tasting methods (food and wine combinations are common practice for most of the surveyed brands). Krug has then opened a section on its website called Wall of Love where users can exchange opinions and advice on the products.

In conclusion, social commerce is still seen as a new kind of approach; however, it shows interesting perspectives for the future and several companies have drawn inspiration from it to improve their online marketing strategies. Once again luxury brands fall behind other market players, being afraid of engaging with new communication and promotion strategies for fear that they could reduce the exclusivity of their products.

Notes

1 Those dynamics are: participation, generated content, interaction and brand quality's perception.

2 According to the third edition of Digital Luxury Experience, a survey carried out by Altagamma and McKinsey in 2012, luxury products' online sales reached 7.5 billion euros, equal to 4% of total sales and 6% for 2017, with sales growing up to 17 billion euros. Multi-brand sites selling products at full price show the highest growth, according to the same survey. Data show how nowadays digital channels are not a virtual space where consumers can look for bargains. Luxury customers search for good services and professional offers, as they would do in any physical shop. This goes hand in hand with the ever-growing role of smartphones and tablets in our society; 50% of luxury consumers do online investigations on a mobile device. Furthermore, there is a clear connection between sales increase and number of web pages visited: companies reporting a page per visit above panel average show increases up to 16%.

3 A proper static evaluation could be performed on Pinterest only. It was impossible to work out the relevant synthesis indicators on YouTube for the period of time considered.

Chapter 6

THE FRONTIERS OF LUXURY GOODS STRA-TEGIES: *CORPORATE SOCIAL RESPONSIBILITY* AND ONLINE COMMUNICATION

6.1. Introduction

In a context characterized by growing expectations and more complex needs expressed by all groups of stakeholders within all business sectors (Freeman and Velamuri, 2006), entrepreneurs and managers of companies – no matter the size and the industry – cannot avoid implementing strategies of Corporate Social Responsibility (CSR) and shape their business models according to sustainable practices. One of the ways to think about business ethics, beyond the logic of mere response to what society requires, is to legitimate, through corporate social responsibility implementation, managers' self-interest and profit-seeking (Freeman *et al.*, 2010). Such statement might explain why, especially in the last twenty decades, corporate social responsibility has started acquiring a core strategic importance (Sen and Bhattacharya, 2001) for the main global companies and small and medium competitive enterprises. The reason is that they aim at imposing new business models based on innovation on their markets and make it clear that the value creation they seek to achieve is economic, social and environmental at the same time.

The competitive advantages of implementing corporate social responsibility practices are clear to all and travel on a spectrum of economic benefits for the company and the society (reduction of waste, reuse of materials, decrease in social costs, etc.), differentiation in products and services design, positive impacts on customers' perception and loyalty (Pomering and Dolnicar, 2009; Xie and Peng, 2009), as well as higher chances to market products and services (Castaldo *et al.*, 2009) when the company is the first mover (McWilliams *et al.*, 2006), increase in companies' competitiveness (Hur *et al.*, 2014) and in social and environmental performances of the reference society. Some of those impacts – once CSR strategies are implemented, of course – are obtained by thorough communication strategies (Jahdi and Acikdilli, 2009; Pomering and Dolnicar, 2009; Nasruddin and Bustami, 2007) that, especially within a 2.0 era, need to be set up according to transparent rules tailored on industries and markets' specificities as well as on stakeholders' preferences, in order to work towards the expected results and perceptions in the audience's minds.

Why is the CSR implementation and its online communication so peculiar and worth of careful consideration for luxury players?

As explicit when reading the studies of classical authors of luxury markets and examining some of the latest strategies of the most well-known luxury groups, the notion of responsible or sustainable luxury has started gaining considerable attention over the past years (Vigneron and Johnson 1999; Bendell and Kleanthous, 2007; Kapferer, 2010; Janssen *et al.*, 2014). At the same time, along with the escalation and intensification of the online activities of luxury brands (Kim and Ko, 2010; 2012; Okonkwo, 2005; 2009; 2010; Mosca *et al.*, 2013; 2014; 2015), imposed by an extensive digital development and the need for more democratization, luxury players have started adopting the online channels for communicating their strategies and projects of CSR and increasing the awareness around some of their intrinsic sustainable values, beliefs and ethical concerns (Lodhia, 2006; Insch, 2008; Kaplan and Haenlein, 2010; Eberle *et al.*, 2013; Lee *et al.*, 2013; Mosca *et al.*, 2016).

The implementation of CSR and the need of communicating it online is, therefore, becoming one of the strategic imperatives for luxury players. Many reasons justify these tendencies, which will be described in the next paragraphs by underlining first the strong links between corporate social responsibility and luxury concepts and, afterwards, the need for and the configuration of online communication of CSR by luxury players that are undergoing the so-called process of luxury democratization. As a matter of facts, nowadays customers wish to take part in the creation of online content, share companies' values and recognize themselves in sustainable and responsible conducts (Rifkin, 2000; Mosca *et al.*, 2013; Okonkwo, 2005; Lundquist, 2014; Boston Consulting Group, 2015). Finding a balance between the elusive intrinsic features of luxury goods/services and the need for a larger online consumer base is a complex, strategic challenge for luxury players, that can be partially solved by the implementation and communication of CSR.

6.2. Towards a more formalized implementation of CSR by luxury brands

From the classical literature, many definitions of the luxury universe are clearly and undisputedly associated with key features and values of corporate social responsibility. If we think about the concept of raw materials high quality for instance, at a first glance, this has to deal with greater attention to the sourcing or extraction of such materials and implies guaranteeing a certain degree of respect in all processes related to that. The aim of this paragraph is, on one hand, to clarify specific characteristics of luxury products and services that evocate sustainable and ethical concerns and that can, therefore, be used as key drivers for a coherent and transparent communication on the online channels. On the other hand, some difficulties and paradoxes in the CSR implementation by luxury players will be underlined, which make the implementation and communication of CSR for luxury players challenging and interesting to investigate at the same time.

Before underlining the linkages and the barriers between luxury and corporate social responsibility, a little digression on our understanding of CSR and the theoretical backgrounds of CSR and sustainability that we acknowledge as valid to conduct theoretical and empirical investigations on luxury players is required.

Despite a common and globally accepted definition of CSR has not been provided yet (Vallaster *et al.*, 2012) because of the multi-faceted nature of corporate social responsibility and the inclusion of various practices and strategies within its conceptualization, the definition that we base the present chapter on is the result of various studies and well-recognized authors that have contributed to clarify the features of CSR. The meanings and implications of corporate social responsibility have strongly changed and evolved in the last decade, due to ongoing economic and social challenges that societies and companies need to face in their everyday business. Latest definitions of CSR aim at integrating and establishing a stronger link between social and economic logics and, therefore, overcoming the traditional and old-fashioned ways to interpret social results separated from economic achievements and performances. Under different labels such Integrated Corporate Social Responsibility (Freeman *et al.*, 2010), Company Stakeholder Responsibility (Freeman and Velamuri, 2006) or Corporate Sustainability and Responsibility (Visser, 2013), similar activities and practices can be grouped together in the form of long-term strategies of CSR and sustainability. Companies (depending on their size and industrial sector) implement and communicate those strategies to different extent in order to engage multiple stakeholders in the economic, social and environmental value creation (Freeman and Phillips, 2002), with no separation between social and economic goals (Crane *et al.*, 2013; Vallaster *et al.*, 2012; Visser, 2012; Freeman *et al.*, 2010). Accordingly and to sum up the different approaches undertaken by the above mentioned authors, we can define corporate social responsibility as the set of values, practices, norms, codes, projects, strategic and operative actions in the field of social, environmental and ethical sphere that a CSR business function within a company implements in order to establish an innovative business model based on sustainability. Under this logic, CSR is a strategy seeking for the creation of a two-way dialogue with all stakeholders for engaging them and maximizing their multiple interests and therefore increasing the value created within the economic, social and environmental dimensions. [1] In other words, nowadays CSR strategies for luxury players should be developed around business repositioning, creation of new business models, products and services – sustainable also in their supply chain – processes, components and, materials that are sustainable themselves and base their long-term objectives on social, environmental as well as economic sustainability.

According to such definition and based on several empirical and theoretical works, a description of the typical activities of CSR that luxury players have started implementing in a more formalized and standardized way will be hereby provided. Such description will serve as framework to understand on which activities and strategies the online communication of CSR by luxury players is mostly based.

The main dimensions that a CSR strategy can be built on are the following: [2]

- *Standards*;
- *Strategic philanthropy,* and;
- *Integrated outputs* (Casalegno and Civera, 2016; Mosca *et al.*, 2016).

The three dimensions refer to all the strategies and activities that a company can implement to adhere to an international standard, for instance, or to partner with a not for profit organization for a cause-related marketing campaign or, also, to employ a waste management policy in order to reduce the economic and environmental impact of their waste pre, during or post production.

In particular, the first dimension (standards) includes all the codes, norms and standards (both national and international) that a company can implement in order to show that their products, services and processes and the way they conduct, in general, their activities meet certain performances of quality, environment, ethics and human resources. Clearly, the adherence to such national or international standards imposes the respect of strict rules for the management, entrepreneurs, suppliers and employees of the company. Among the most well-known standards is worth to mention the ISO9001 for quality; ISO14001 for the environment; the OHSAS 18001: occupational health and safety assessment, the SA8000 on international work-place quality and sustainability; the Code of Ethics or other codes of conduct are used as communication of standards of professional ethical conduct. This is the most formal and standardized CSR strategy that companies use to show their alignment to business minimum requirements (they can be mandatory or voluntary laws) that are adopted by the majority of players. Therefore, this is less and less a distinctive CSR strategy utilized as competitive advantage or differentiation factor.

LVMH Group. The commitment of the Group to people and individuality is clearly expressed in the Code of Conduct that regulates all the aspects concerning human capital and aims at enabling employees to find personal fulfillment through their job. The Code of Conduct reports all the values that guide LVMH policy for recruitment, respect for gender equality, for employees with disability and older workers. Since 2011 the adoption of such Code has been compulsory for all the brands included in the LVMH portfolio, in order to establish a standard and homogeneous corporate culture around the respect for human resources. To strengthen such commitment, since 2013 the Group has been a member of AFMD (Association Française des Managers de la Diversité, a French organization promoting diversity in managerial practices) and fully adheres to its principles.

Kering Group SA. Since 2005 the Group and all brands in its portfolio have implemented the Code of Ethics and created a Group Ethics Committee with the duty of monitoring the implementation of the Code, responding to various enquires from all employees and developing the policies and actions of the Group in the area of sustainable development. The Group also commits to the International Labour Organization (ILO) standards and to the conventions to abolish child and forced labour as well as slavery. Moreover, they adhere to the United Nations Global Compact in defense of the ten principles of the Global Compact since 2008.

Bulgari. As part of LVMH Group, Bulgari confirms its commitment to the environment by adopting the best ecological practices within production and management activities. To this regard the company implements an environmental policy based on the ISO14001 standard, which aims at promoting environmental awareness among employees, suppliers and business partners as well as meeting concrete goals and performances in the waste reduction and the efficient use of materials, resources and raw materials. Energy consumption is also taken into account for improving environmental performances as well as the promotion of sustainable forms of mobility.

The second dimension of CSR activities and strategies draws attention to the company's efforts to support social causes and/or events promoted by the third sector or any artistic, cultural or sports activities which might be connected with its core business. Philanthropy, in this sense, is defined strategic the more all the actions to support social causes are related to the core business activities of the company. In this way, by activating partnerships coherent with the company's DNA, mission and main business activities, players can become competitive factors in a long-term perspective (Porter and Kramer, 2002) and, also avoid misperceptions in the audience's mind when communicating over actions of strategic philanthropy (La Cour and Kromann, 2011).

In particular, for luxury players the role played by foundations is essential within this dimension of CSR. Typically, luxury groups possess their own foundation that strategically carries out and reports the outcomes achieved through their sponsorships, cause-related *marketing activities*, donations, partnerships, community projects and employees' voluntary work.

Ermenegildo Zegna. In line with a vision that characterizes Zegna Group and Zegna family, which is based on quality, genuineness, believing in the future, responsibility, passionate participation and spirit of belonging with a great focus on their communities, since 2000 Zegna Foundation has been established in order to co-ordinate international humanitarian activities in the field of environment and cultural resources, local communities development, medical and scientific research and education and training. The commitment to the community and the involvement in the protection of cultural heritage, which is strategically linked to Zegna's core business, is expressed by Casa Zegna, an historical cultural center that aims at linking mountain culture and nature and focusing on the relationships among people, which hosts also an archive museum synthetizing history and experiences into a multi-purpose space for enhancing creativity. The foundation funds projects in co-operation with third sector organizations and a Scientific Committee has the task to select strategic projects to invest on. Moreover, since 2008 Zegna Foundation supports the realization of a series of site-specific permanent artworks, created in the Trivero area, where the Group belongs, with the aim of favouring access to contemporary art and its values by local communities.

Fendi. One of the most impacting examples of a philanthropic initiative carried out in a way that is coherent with the core business of the company and, therefore, strategic is the financial support that Fendi provided for the restoration of the Trevi Fountain in Rome in 2015. The site is one of the most well-recognized symbols and icons of the city of Rome, for Italians and foreigners. Fendi's involvement in this project confirms the Roman roots of the Maison and the caring for the city development and improvement of its aesthetic character. Moreover, the restored site is a place for Fendi to be potentially used for their fashion shows, in a unique and traditional environment. Aside from this one of a kind project, Carla Fendi Foundation is the institutional foundation of the Maison that mainly aims at carrying out projects of restorations addressed to the "Teatro Caio Melisso Spazio Carla Fendi", in order to achieve the mission of protecting cultural heritage and values from the past.

Eventually, the third dimension of CSR, named integrated outputs, can be considered the most evolved and coherent with the new meanings and implications of CSR, which see its strategies and actions integrated with the core business of the company, in a logic of new business models development and innovation. That is the design and creation of new products, services, processes and policies that are intrinsically sustainable and take into account the improved sustainability of the whole supply chain, from raw materials to distribution of sustainable goods. This is the dimension where CSR sits at the heart of the organization and where communication of tangible and achieved performances is more effective and, yet, easier to demonstrate, as the integrated output is the performance itself. Indeed, the actual integrated outputs are concrete proofs of responsibility and sustainability and extend to the supply chain for making the final good less impacting in terms of environment, for instance, or more socially responsible in terms of human resources.

Gucci. In 2011 Gucci launched on the market their first sustainable output, result of an increased commitment to the environment and their attention and concerns over material reuse and recycle to avoid waste and, therefore, improve environmental, social and economic impacts. The output is a line of sunglasses made from liquid wood–a biodegradable material that Gucci employed for the first time in the production of such goods–and an eco-friendly packaging, with the aim of increasing social, environmental and economic value creation throughout their supply chain.

Giorgio Armani. Ever since the brand have started acknowledging the negative impact that certain chemical substances employed in the manufacturing of textile and clothing products have on the environment, they have decided to implement a long-term sustainability policy that applies to all stages of the supply chain where manufacturing plants are located, in order to monitor and reduce the use of such chemical components. The overall purpose of such policy (started in 2013) is to achieve the zero discharge goal by 2020, meaning that the use of such chemicals should be eliminated by then. The action plan for this policy started with an analysis of compliance addressed to all suppliers and manufacturers in order for them to meet certain criteria of use of chemicals reduction. An audit programme is constantly conducted to test the progress of the policy and the state of the art as for environmental impacts.

The above described CSR dimensions and the evidences provided on luxury players support the idea that sustainability (or CSR in general) and luxury markets can be understood as having intrinsic similar features.

What we have pointed out so far is that despite the fact that luxury brands operate in various industrial sectors and luxury market is considered multi-faceted and transversal, general rules for CSR (especially concerning values, beliefs and social and environmental concerns) apply to the luxury universe as such. Some authors attribute distinctive features to luxury brands: the importance of building and maintaining a brand heritage that is based on the history, the myth and legend of the origins (Kapferer *et al.*, 2014), the high quality craftsmanship, the respect for materials, timelessness, a recognizable design, an emotional and symbolic appeal, the exclusivity, rarity and scarcity (Catry, 2003; Phau and Prendergast, 2000) and a unique reputation (De Barnier *et al.*, 2012; Choo *et al.*, 2012; Nueno and Quelch, 1998; Laurent and Dubois, 1994). In each of these features, as mentioned above, it is possible to find linkages and associations with CSR and sustainability matters (Vigneron and Johnson 1999; Bendell and Kleanthous, 2007; Janssen *et al.*, 2014), especially because each of them is addressed to create an image of high quality, protection of scarcity and uniqueness and respect for materials as symbol of caring, awareness and attention to the environment and social issues.

Prada. The series of portraits named "A City of Women" is one of the latest examples of the role that luxury brands play in the social sphere by implementing specific CSR projects carried out in various ways to spread their voice around certain ongoing social matters. Such artistic project is advertised on the Prada Group website and entirely funded by the group itself. The images portray women to celebrate femininity and empowerment as catalysts for social changes. Through this activity Prada aims at integrating the seductive character of women and fashion with an ongoing social debate whose purpose is to sensitize the community over diversity and power to women.

Moreover, some other characteristics contribute to make sustainability and luxury closer as concepts. When associating the features of luxury products and services concept with openness and conservation values, which are highly compatible with CSR-associated self-transcendence values (Schwartz, 1992), the assumption that luxury and CSR present some similar principles (Janssen *et al.*, 2012) becomes less unpleasant. Also, the idea that, by definition, luxury goods and services are commonly acknowledged as rare and scarce imposes a coherence of responsible consumption as well as protection of resources that luxury bases its character upon; the high dependence on resources brings with it a sort of obsession for their sustainability (Kapferer, 2010).

On the other hand, luxury goods are often perceived as wasteful and latest corporate scandals by top brands are pushing luxury companies to intensifying the implementation of sustainable and responsible practices in their manufacturing more intensively and concretely and, to communicating to their stakeholders that greater attention is put on CSR and avoid the bad repercussions of the past. Moreover, the need for protecting luxury products from counterfeiting is increasing the focus and the attention towards quality of production, selection of materials, attention to sustainable processes as differentiation factor and the communication of all these efforts to both consumers and stakeholders (Donvito *et al.*, 2016). Also, if considering that luxury consumption responds to self-actualization needs, the concept of sustainability and responsibility is highly related and coherent to the same needs and expectations that drive luxury consumers. Eventually, given that luxury brands' exclusivity is undergoing a democratization process also due to the increasing need of online presence manifested by customers for purchasing luxury goods and having evidence of their actions, events and brand values, sustainability can offer a further differentiation factor, especially on the online.

Prada. In march 2017 Prada Group promotes the event "Shaping a Creative Future" in partnership with Yale School of Management and Politecnico of Milano School of Management hosted at Prada Headquarter and Prada Foundation in Milan. The purpose of this conference is to reinforce the reflection on the impact of sustainability and innovation on luxury players' strategies. This is to prove the strong link between luxury and CSR (or sustainability) in a context in which topics such as craftsmanship, unique skills, authenticity, history, provenance, heritage and arts are discussed and connected to sustainability for improving brand and market value and, therefore, creating a sustainable value for the brand. Moreover, issues connected to the design for sustainability between innovation and tradition and value creation are considered, in the context of the event, key success factors for luxury players.

Brunello Cucinelli. Driven by the vision of its founder, Brunello Cucinelli, who states that "The great dream of my life has always been to work for the moral and economic dignity of mankind" (www.brunellocucinelli.com), the company provides a good example and live evidence of a business founded on the concept of sustainability and responsibility as core values driving operations and ways of conducting all activities. Brunello Cucinelli is defined a humanistic enterprise, which pays attention to the quality of material, particularly cashmere, as symbol of cultural tradition that lasts and does it by empowering and engaging people working on this. Employing Italian manual skills and craftsmanship shows an identity based on local context, valorization of lands and respect for traditional resources. What the company calls "The Project for Beauty", for instance, is a 360° revitalization process of the industrial area in which Brunello Cucinelli manufactures, where next to the industrial park sits an agricultural park with trees, vineyards and recreational areas for younger people. The remarkable commitment to tradition, local development and nature is well-expressed by several other projects such as "The Forum of Art" designed in 2001, which includes a theater and an Amphitheatre to host music shows and expressions of all forms of art.

6.3. The online communication of CSR by luxury brands: more efforts to increase customers' perception

Luxury brands management is often counterintuitive and requires ad hoc studies, especially after the digital revolution and concerning the implementation of online communication of corporate social responsibility. Moreover, as explained before, due to the transversal and multi-faceted character of luxury groups and their brands operating in various industrial sectors, CSR implementation and online communication need to be understood by putting an extra effort in the context of luxury markets.

As well as the implementation of CSR by luxury brands, also the online communication of sustainable and ethical practices and strategies is drawing interest and attention among both academics and practitioners. The diffuse and increasing online presence by luxury brands (Okonkwo, 2005; 2009; 2010; Mosca *et al.*, 2013; 2014; Boston Consulting Group, 2015) suggests a future development of communication messages around sustainability, connected to brand heritage, protection of lands and respect for communities, resources and human capital. Theories and concepts of online communication are strictly connected with the idea of sharing a series of common values with a plurality of stakeholders that manifest various interests and needs at the same time (Freeman *et al.*, 2010) and that can be satisfied by a common factor: corporate social responsibility.

CSR communication represents more and more a strategic decision within the company (Sen and Bhattacharya, 2001), especially with the advent of social media and the internet becoming the strongest echo consumers and all stakeholders can give to their opinions and, at the same time, that companies can give to their actions. The main issues connected to the communication of CSR stay in the content, the placement and the purposes of the messages that can influence consumers and all stakeholder in a positive or negative way (Du *et al.*, 2010; Jahdi and Acikdilli, 2009). To this regard, it is not surprising that some of the messages spread in the context of CSR might turn the audience's perception negatively, lower trust, increase skepticism among stakeholders and hit brands' reputation and image (Jahdi and Acikdilli, 2009).

How and what to communicate about CSR to all stakeholders raises uncertainty as for trust and judgment (Jahdi & Acikdilli, 2009; Pomering & Dolnicar, 2009; Nasruddin & Bustami, 2007), especially in industries like the luxury one, where the monetary component of each unique good has always been mostly associated with wasteful logics and, in some cases, also exploitation (diamonds extraction, for instance, constitutes a clear example of this).

The challenge for CSR online communication applied to luxury players is to balance out marketing and social intentions (de Ven, 2008; Hur *et al.*, 2014; Nasruddin and Bustami, 2007; Pomering and Donilcar, 2009) and appear more and more as a strategy that expresses the true DNA of luxury brands and avoid being misperceived and intended as greenwashing practice (Delmas and Cuerel Burbano, 2011).

Therefore, one of the biggest strategic efforts that luxury brands are required to make is about setting up an online communication of CSR in way that can positively affect consumers through a transparent and coherent flow of information and that does not show dystonia between promises of CSR and actual actions and achieved performances. In doing so, CSR online communication needs transparence and pragmatism performed through the paradigm *"performances vs. promises"* (de Ven, 2008; Hur *et al.*, 2014). Communicating CSR performances, for example, is more useful to increase the truthfulness of the message than a series of general statements of values, intentions, ethics and sustainability not followed by any results (generally defined as "promise"). The communication of integrated outputs in the form of sustainable products, for instance, such as the Gucci sunglasses described in the previous paragraph, which enrich the consumer with a sustainable real experience, provides the company the legitimacy to be believed as for sustainability implementation and communication. All the online messages suggesting a lack of alignment between promises and related outcomes, or focusing too much on promises and values as such, create negative perceptions and a poorer brand's image, affecting consumers' trust ultimately (Pomering and Dolnicar, 2009). Moreover, given that the luxury consumer has become more active in the online activity, companies' declarations and the alignment between their actions and communications can be easily verified online by them (Christodoulides *et al.*, 2011; Fieseler *et al.*, 2010; Kaplan and Haenlein, 2010; Du *et al.*, 2010).

Clearly, the widespread popularity of the Internet makes CSR online communication even more challenging than before (Pollach, 2003; Welcomer *et al.*, 2003; Christodoulides *et al.*, 2011; Fieseler, 2010; Kaplan and Haenlein, 2010; Du *et al.*, 2010). Consumers can now find online information on the company's behavior and verify transparency and consistency of the messages somewhere else rather than on the company's website or from any press release. In other words, they can verify the gap between promises and performances. It is the behavior of luxury consumers one of the elements that makes the investigation of online communication of CSR by luxury players more interesting. Consumers' experiences define companies' reputation and attitudes (Uwins, 2014); CRS influences consumers' purchasing decisions and opinions over companies conduct. If consumers are aware of CSR actions (Pomering and Dolnicar, 2009), both the economic impact and the business image will benefit (Demetriou *et al.*, 2009). Consistent CSR communication is key to spread awareness, foster commitment and inform customers on results.

As the Figure 6.1 shows,[3] when luxury players are communicating alignment between promises and performances of CSR they are most likely to improve economic and social benefit at the same time.

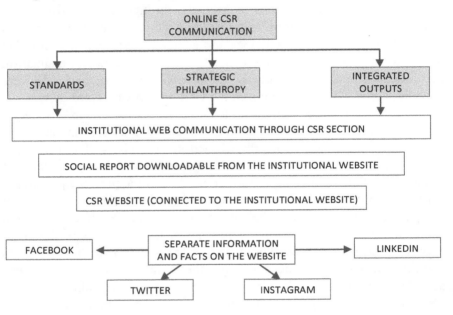

Figure 6.1 Promises and performances of CSR by luxury players

Some authors have presented luxury consumers as less affected by ethical issues in relation to products and brands. According to them, luxury consumers are aware of social and environmental problems but show little awareness when it comes to specific brands and CSR issues (Davies *et al.*, 2012). On the contrary, recent studies have highlighted consumers' growing interest in luxury brands CSR. A survey carried out by Boston Consulting Group for the Italian institute "Altagamma Foundation" in 2015, for instance, involves ten thousand global luxury consumers and shows that 73% of them considers ethics and sustainable processes a guaranty of exclusivity. Moreover, they declare they would not buy products from brands that are not compliant with those characteristics. Furthermore, as clarified by other authors (Corbellini and Saviolo, 2007;

Okonkwo, 2010; Truong and McColl, 2011), luxury consumers–properly portrayed by the effect of exaggerate consumption (ostentation), snobbish attitude (differentiation), Veblen's (1899) bandwagon (conformism)–are more informed and are becoming aware customers, who are looking at sharing experiences with high symbolic value brands in order to keep the connection with the whole community and their favorite brands.

One of the most remarkable empirical researches on luxury consumers poses a need of investigating them further as it shows a growing interest in the communication of sustainability on the online since, as Janssen (2014) states: "… perhaps more communication about luxury brands' CSR efforts would increase consumers' awareness of the social and environmental impact …" and would, therefore, increase their interest and brand perception. There are no evidences that CSR communications have a direct impact on luxury goods purchases; however, certain strategies and communications of CSR have the power to increase consumers' positive perception towards both brands and products and contribute, in this way, to increase differentiation and exclusivity of luxury brands.

That is why, in order to overcome the traditional intrinsic barriers that prevent luxury players to be well perceived when communicating about CSR, web and social media are a great opportunity for CSR communication (Pollack, 2003; Welcomer et al., 2003; Wanderley et al., 2008; Jahidi and Acikdilli, 2009) with the aim of: spreading the message more quickly, in a cheaper and deeper manner; presenting more creative and consistent content; reaching out to more stakeholders at the same time; interacting more effectively with customers (de Bakker and Hellsten, 2013; Lee et al., 2013; Eberle et al., 2013; Fieseler et al., 2010); feeding positive word of mouth; building an identity; strengthening the uniqueness of luxury goods; influencing consumers' perceptions, opinions and loyalty; building up image and reputation – when companies' messages are accepted and validated (Insch, 2008; Du et al., 2010; Kim et al., 2010; Eberle et al., 2013) – and enhancing non-voluntary communication.

Prada. The website csr.pradagroup.com can be discussed as symbol and evidence of a strategic online communication of CSR, where all the contents of CSR converge into an easy-access "place" for communications to be spread. Such strategy favors luxury customers' understanding of all the implemented CSR strategies, as the website is directly accessible from the institutional website pradagroup.com. The CSR website welcomes customers and all stakeholders with a video explaining the new perspectives of Prada Group about CSR, which unfolds three mainstreams: the know-how; the places (intended as territories and communities) and; the culture. By following a story telling approach, the online communication of CSR is centered on the activities that Prada conducts in respect of the three mainstreams. As for the know-how, a focus is put on the quality of craftsmanship characterizing all Prada brands from the attention to the raw materials to the production of goods as we know it. The work ethics is stated to guide all activities of the production process and extends throughout the whole supply chain.

6.4. The framework of online CSR communication for luxury players

The creation of online experiences has become a necessity for luxury players (Okonkwo, 2010) and this necessity is made stronger by consumers willing to take part in the process of sharing the brand's values, using online platforms. The effectiveness of luxury brands online presence can increase by using all channels, from institutional websites to specialized platforms (BCG, 2015) and fostering interactions and participation to their values by the audience (Lundquist, 2014; Eberle *et al.*, 2013; Fiesler *et al.*, 2010; de Bakker and Hellsten, 2013).

The aim of the present paragraph is to report some of the findings of previous studies conducted by the authors on the configuration of online communication of CSR by luxury players.

The first exploratory study commenced in 2013 has underlined a greater and growing use of the online platforms by luxury players when communicating in general, showing a larger use of websites and social platforms to communicate brand heritage, products features and brand events. Further studies (2015; 2016) underlines that online CSR communication is a strategy that, as a matter of facts, still belongs mostly to the corporate brands rather than all brands included in their portfolio. When investigating the way luxury players communicate online over their sustainability efforts, the communication is wide-spread and implemented formally on the websites of the main groups such as Kering SA and LVMH for instance. At a brand level, the website looks more like a shop window, with just few references to the ethical and sustainable values guiding the group owning that particular brand. The second remarkable characteristic of luxury brands' online communication of CSR is that websites are still the most utilized means for spreading information and facts about sustainability. Whilst, in an opposite trend as for communication of new products line or events widely-spread on social media, those are less likely to be used for communicating CSR and the few communications on Facebook, Twitter, Instagram or Linkedin appear just as a reflection of what formally stated by the Groups on their institutional websites (Mosca *et al.*, 2015; 2016).

Exploratory findings (Mosca *et al.*, 2015; 2016) conducted on a sample of luxury fashion brands on the use of social and web platforms provide preliminary evidences on the placement, content and purposes of CSR messages and are summarized in Figure 6.2 below. According to these findings the majority of the players at a corporate level are intensifying CSR communication on their website, presenting a CSR section where, in fewer cases, social reports are available for download. A smaller percentage of such corporate luxury brands have a dedicated CSR website (one worth of mention is Prada), which is always accessible from the institutional website. Just few of the investigated luxury brands focus their communication on sustainable goods as separated facts and information within the website. It is very rare to find an attractive communication about a sustainable policy or process implementation or sustainable products development *"advertised"* as all the core product lines within the collections. The only information and facts which consumers and all stakeholder can make experience of when navigating on the institutional website are the ones connected to strategic philanthropy, according to which luxury players confirm their engagement with communities and environment for more effectively justify the unique quality of materials and products. In addition to that, the same studies have connoted websites as *"spaces"* from where messages are simply transferred, contaminating social media content. Messages of CSR that are spread on social media like Facebook, Linkedin, Twitter, YouTube and Instagram are, at least at this stage, a mere repetition of their websites content to which they constantly refer in their posts. These results open up interesting avenues for further researches on the merge between "online luxury" and "responsible luxury" in a more strategic way, so that products can become integrated outputs of communication about sustainability on integrated channels (social media, websites and points of sale for instance) so that CSR can become more than just a policy; instead a confirmation and evidence of appealing unique goods and transparent luxury management strategies.

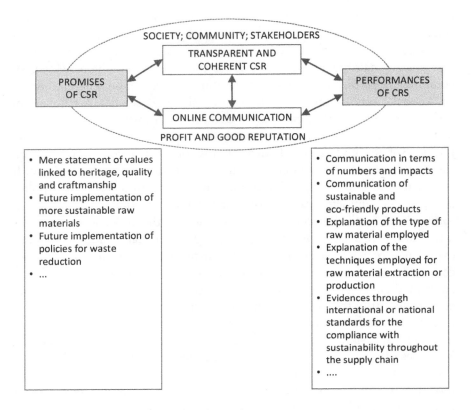

Figure 6.2 Framework of online CSR communication

Notes

1 The definition of corporate social responsibility has been adapted from Casalegno and Civera (2016) and based on the innovative characterizations of CSR, which intend it as strategy to re-shape business models through products, services and processes sustainability.

2 The dimensions of CSR group together all the main strategies and activities that a company can implement in the field of ethics, sustainability, environment and society. Such framework has been first proposed by Casalegno and Civera (2016) based on various academics and empirical researches and it is applied to the luxury players in the context of the present book in order to qualitatively investigate the spread of formalized implementation of CSR practices within luxury market.

3 Figure 6.1 is adapted from Casalegno and Civera (2016) and considers the communication of CSR spread by luxury brands at a corporate level.

REFERENCES

Aaker D.A., *Managing Brand equity capitalizing on the value of a Brand Name*, Free Press, NY, 1991.

Adjei M.T., Noble S.M., Noble C.H., *The influence of C2C communications in online brand communities on customer purchase behavior*, Journal of the Academy of Marketing Science, vol. issue, 2010.

Aiello G., Donvito R., *Comunicazione integrata nell'abbigliamento: strategie di marca e ruolo del punto vendita nella distribuzione specializzata statunitense*, Firenze University Press, 2005.

Alba J., Lynch J.,Weitz B., Janiszewski C. *et al.*, *Interactive home shopping: Consumer, Retailer and Manufacturer*, Journal of Marketing, 61 (3), July 1997.

Allsop D.T., Bassett B.R., Hoskins J.A., *Word-of-mouth research: principles and applications*, Journal of Advertising Research, 47 (4), 2007.

Anderson C., *The long tail*, Wired, 2004.

Ansari A., Mela C., Neslin S.A., *Customer Channel Migration*, Working Paper, Tuck School of Business, Dartmouth College, 2005.

Areni K., *The influence of background music on shopping behavior: Classical versus Top-Forty Music in a Wine Store*, Advances in Consumer Research, 20, 1993.

Atwal G., Williams A., *Luxury brand marketing – The experience is everything*, Journal of Brand Management, 16, 5-6, 2009.

Babin B.J., Darden W.R., Griffin M., *Work and/or Fun: Measuring Hedonic and Utilitarian Shopping Value*, Journal of Consume Research, 20 (4), 1994.

Baker J., Grewal D., Parasuraman A., *The Influence of Store Environment on Quality Inferences and Store Image*, Journal of the Academy of Marketing Science, vol. 22, 1994.

Baker J., Levy M., Grewal D., *An Experimental Approach to Making Retail Store Environmental Decisions*, Journal of Retailing, vol. 68, 1992.

Beatty S.E, Ferrel M.E., *Impulse Buying: modelling its precursors*, Journal of Retailing, vol. 74, n. 2, 1998.

Belch G.E., Belch M.A., *Advertising and Promotion: an integrated marketing communication perspective*, 4, Irwin/McGraw-Hill, New York, 1998 and 8th ed., Boston-London, 2009.

Bendell J., Kleanthous A., *Deeper Luxury Report*, 2007, in wwf.org.uk.

Berger P.D., Lee J., Weinberg B.D., *Optimal Cooperative Advertising Integration Strategy for Organizations Adding a Direct Online Channel*, Journal of Operational Research Society, 2006.

Bijmolt T.H.A., Leeflang P.S.H., Block F., Eisenbeiss, M., Hardie B.G.S., Lemmens A., Saffert P., *Analytics for customer engagement*, Journal of Service Research, 13 (3), 2010.

Bloemer J., De Ruyter K., *On the relationship between store image, store satisfaction and store loyalty*, European Journal of Marketing, vol. 32, 1997.

Boedeker M., *Recreational Shopping. The Role of Basic Emotional Dimensions of Personality*, European Marketing Academy, Marketing for an Expanding Europe – Proceedings, 1996.

Boston Consulting Group, *True-Luxury Global Consumer Insight*, 2015, in www.altagamma.it.

Bowden J.L., *The Process of Customer Engagement: A Conceptual Framework*, Journal of Marketing Theory and Practice, 17 (1), 2009.

Boyd D.M., Ellison N.B., *Social network sites: Definition, history, and scholarship*, Journal of Computer-Mediated Communication, 13 (1), 2007.

Bracewell Lewis V., *Benchmark: Luxury Sector – Business Adoption*, Forrester, 27 May, 2008.

Brammer S., Millington A., *Corporate reputation and philanthropy: an empirical analysis*, 61 (1), 2005.

Branca B., *Complessità e comportamenti d'acquisto: un approccio semiotico*, Micro & Macro Marketing, n. 2, 1992.

Brodie R.J., Ilic A., Juric B., Hollebeek L., *Consumer engagement in a virtual brand community: An exploratory analysis*, Journal of Business Research, 66 (1), 2013.

Brodie S.M., *Global Markets and Market Space Competition*, Symphonya, Emerging Issues in Management, 1, 2012.

Brogi S., Calabrese A., Campisi D., Capece G., Costa R., Di Pillio F., *The Effects of Online Brand Communities on Brand Equity in the Luxury Fashion Industry*, International Journal of Engineering Business Management, 5, 2013.

Brondoni, S.M., *Global Capitalism and Sustainable Growth. From Global Products to Network Globalisation*, Symphonya. Emerging Issues in Management (symphonya.unimib.it), 1, 10-31, 2014.

Bruhn M., Schoenmueller V., Scafer D., *Are social media replacing traditional media in terms of brand equity creation?*, Management Research Review, 35 (9), 2012.

Burmann C., Arnhold U., *User Generated Branding: State of the Art Research*, Germany: Lit, Münster, 2009.

Carroll A.B., *A history of corporate social responsibility: concepts and practices*, in Crane A., McWilliams A., Matten D., Moon J., Siegel D., *The Oxford Handbook of Corporate Social Responsibility*, Oxford University Press, 2008.

Carù A., Cova B., *Esperienze di consumo e marketing esperienziale: radici diverse e convergenze*, Micro & Macro Marketing, n. 3, 2001.

Carù A., Cova B., *Small versus big stories in framing consumption experiences*, Qualitative Market Research: An International Journal, 11 (2), 2008.

Castaldo S. *et al.*, *The missing link between corporate social responsibility and consumer trust: The case of fair trade products*, Journal of business ethics, 84 (1), 1-15, 2009.

Castaldo S., Premazzi K., *I virtual stores italiani: risultati di un'indagine empirica*, Micro & Macro Marketing, n. 2, 1999.

Catry B., *The great pretenders: the magic of luxury goods*, Business Strategy Review, 14 (3), 10-17, 2003.

Chaffey D., *Internet Marketing*, Prentice Hall, New Jersey, 2000.

Chevalier J., Mayzlin D., *The Effect of Word of Mouth on Sales: Online Book Reviews*, Journal of Marketing Research, 43, 2006.

Chevalier M., Mazzalovo G., *Luxury brand management*, Wiley, Chichester, 2012.

Christodoulides G., Jevons C., Blackshaw P., *The voice of the consumer speaks forcefully in brand identity: user-generated content forces smart marketers to listen*, Journal of Advertising Research, 51 (1), 2011.

Christodoulides G., Jevons C., Bonhomme J., *Memo to marketers: quantitative evidence for change, how user-generated content really affects brands*, Journal of Advertising Research, 52 (1), 2012.

Clark N., *Effectiveness of online advertising on luxury brands*, Marketing, 2010.

Codeluppi V., *Lo spettacolo della merce*, Bompiani, Milano, 2000.

Collesei U., *Brand Tracking*, Micro & Macro Marketing, n. 12, 2002.

Collesei U., Casarin F., Vescovi T., *Disintermediazione e reintermediazione nel commercio elettronico*, relazione al XXII Convegno AIDEA, Parma, ottobre, 1999.

Collesei U., Ravà V., *La comunicazione d'azienda*, Isedi, Torino, 2008.

Cooper C., *Hooked on Ethics*, People Management, 2003.

Corbellini E., Saviolo S., *L'esperienza del lusso: mondi, mercati, marchi*, Etas, 2007.

Corbellini E., Saviolo S., *Managing Fashion and Luxury Companies*, Etas, Milano, 2009.

Cotte J., Chowdhury T.G., Ratneshwar S., Ricci L.M., *Pleasure or utility? Time planning style and Web usage behaviors*, Journal of Interactive Marketing, 20 (1), 2006.

Crane A., Matten D., Spence L.J., *Corporate social responsibility in a global context*, Chapter in Corporate Social Responsibility: Readings and Cases in a Global Context, 2/e. Abingdon, Routledge, 3-26, 2013.

Crane A., McWilliams A., Matten D., Moon J., Siegel D., *The Oxford Handbook of Corporate Social Responsibility*, Oxford University Press, 2008.

Cristini G., *Le strategie customer-based nella grande distribuzione*, Micro & Macro Marketing, dic. 1995.

Curty R.G., Zhang P., *Social Commerce: Looking Back and Forward*, Proceedings ASIST, New Orleans, October 9-13, 2011.

Dall'Olmo Riley F., Lacroix C., *Luxury branding on the Internet: lost opportunity or impossibility?*, Marketing Intelligence & Planning, 21 (2), 96-104, 2003.

Daugherty T., Eastin M.S., Bright L., *Exploring Consumer Motivations for Creating User-Generated-Content*, Journal of Interactive Advertising, 8 (2), 2008.

De Bakker F.G.A., Hellsten I., *Capturing online presence: Hyperlinks and semantic networks in activist group websites on corporate social responsibility*. Journal of Business Ethics, 118 (4), 2013.

De Barnier V., Falcy S., Valette-Florence P., *Do consumers perceive three levels of luxury? A comparison of accessible, intermediate and inaccessible luxury brands*, Journal of Brand Management, 19 (7), 623-636, 2012.

De Luca P., *Gli effetti dell'atmosfera del punto vendita sul comportamento del consumatore: verifica empirica di un modello di psicologia ambientale*, Industria & Distribuzione, n. 2, 2000.

De Matos C.A., Rossi C.A.V., *Word-of-Mouth Communications in Marketing: a Meta-Analytic Review of the Antecedents and Moderators*, Journal of the Academy of Marketing Science, 36 (Winter), 2008.

De Valk K., Van Bruggen G., Wierenga B., *Virtual communities: as marketing perspective*, Decision Support Systems, 47, 2009.

Delmas M.A., Cuerel Burbano V., *The drivers of greenwashing*, California Management Review, 54 (1), 64-87, 2011.

Demetriou M., Papasolomou I., Vontris D., *Cause-related marketing: Building the corporate image while supporting worthwhile causes.* Journal of Brand Management, vol. 17 (4), 2009.

Derbaix C., *Le comportement de l'acheteur: voies d'études pour les années à venir*, Recherche et Applications en Marketing, vol. 2, n. 2, 1987.

Dhaoui C., *An empirical study of luxury brand marketing effectiveness and its impact on consumer engagement on Facebook*, Journal of Global Fashion Marketing: Bridging Fashion and Marketing, 5 (3), 2014.

Dickson J.P., MacLachlan D.L., *Social Distance and Shopping Behavior*, Journal of the Academy of Marketing Science, vol. 18, 1990.

Donovan R.J., Rossister J.R., *Store Atmosphere: An Environmental Psychology Approach*, Journal of Retailing, 58 (1), 1982.

Doohwang L., Hyuk Soo K., Jung Kyu K., *The impact of online brand community on consumer's community engagement behaviors: consumer-created vs. marketer-created online brand community in social-networking websites*, CyberPsychology, Behavior and Social Networking, 14 (1), 2011.

Du S., Bhattacharya C.B., Sen S., *Maximizing business returns to corporate social responsibility (CSR): The role of CSR communication.* International Journal of Management Reviews, 12 (1), 2010.

Duana W., Gub B., Whinston A.B., *Do online reviews matter? An empirical investigation of panel data*, Decision Support Systems, 45 (3), 2008.

Dubois B., Laurent. G., *Attitudes towards the concept of luxury: An exploratory analysis*, AP-Asia Pacific Advances in Consumer Research, vol. 1, (1994).

Duncan T.R., Mulhern F., *A white paper on the status, scope and future of IMC*, IMC symposium sponsored by the IMC programs at Northwestern University and University of Denver, McGraw-Hill USA, 2004.

Eberle D., Berens G., Li T., *The Impact of Interactive Corporate Social Responsibility Communication on Corporate Reputation*, Journal of Business Ethics, 118 (4), 2013.

Edelman D.C., *Branding in the digital age*, Harvard Business Review, 88 (12), 2010.

Eroglu S.A., Machleit K.A., *Atmospheric factors in the retail environment: sight, sounds and smells*, Advances in Consumer Research, 20, 1993.

Ertimur B., Gilly M., *The Impact of Consumer-Generated Advertising on Brand Associations*, NA-Advances, Consumers Research Association for Consumer Research, 37, 2010.

Esrock S.L., Leichty G.B., *Social Responsibility and Corporate Web Pages: self-presentation or agenda-setting?*, Public Relations Review, 24 (3), 1998.

Fabris G., *Il nuovo consumatore verso il postmoderno*, Franco Angeli, Milano, 2003.

Ferrero G., *Imprese e management*, Giuffrè, Milano, 1980.

Fieseler C., Fleck M., Meckel M., *Corporate Social Responsibility in the Blogosphere*, Journal of Business Ethics, 91 (4), 2010.

Fionda A.M., Moore C.M., *The anatomy of the luxury fashion brand*, Journal of Brand Management, 16 (5-6), 2009.

Fondazione Altagamma e McKinsey, *Digital Luxury Experience*, 2012.

Fournier S., *Consumers and their Brands: Developing Relationship Theory in Consumer Research*, Journal of Consumer Research, 24 (2), 1998.

Foux G., *Consumer-generated media: Get your customers involved*, Brand Strategy, 2006.

Freeman R.E., Phillips. R.A., *Stakeholder theory: A libertarian defense*, Business ethics quarterly, 12 (03), 331-349, 2002.

Freeman R.E., Harrison J.S., Wicks A.C., Parmar B.L., De Colle S., *Stakeholder Theory. The State of the Art*, Cambridge University Press, 2010.

Freeman R.E., Velamuri S.R., Moriarty B., *Company Stakholder Responsibility: a new approach to CSR*, Business Roundtable Institute for Corporate Ethics, 2006.

Gambetti R.C., Graffigna G., Biraghi S., *The Grounded Theory approach to consumer-brand engagement: The practitioner's standpoint*, International Journal of Marketing Research, 54 (5), 2012.

Gensler S., Völckner F., Liu-Thompkins Y., Wiertz C., *Managing Brands in the Social Media Environment*, Journal of Interactive Marketing, 27, 2013.

Golden L.L., Zimmer M., *Relationship between affect, patronage and amount of money spent on affect scaling and measurement*, Advances in Consumer Research, 13, 53, 1985.

Goldstein L., boo.com, Fortune Magazine, 5 July 1999.

Granitz N.A., Ward J.C., *Virtual community: a sociological analysis*, Advances in consumer research, 23, 1996.

Grose V., *Basics Fashion Management: Fashion Merchandising*, Bloomsbury Academic, 2011.

Guatri L., Vicari S., Fiocca R., *Marketing*, McGraw-Hill Italia, Milano, 1999.

Guo J., Sun C., *Global Electronic Markets and Global Traditional markets*, Electronic Markets, 14 (1), 2004.

Gwen M., *Hot Stuff: make these top trends part of your marketing mix*, 2006.

Hajli N., *A study of the impact of social media on consumers*, International Journal of Market Research, 56 (3), 2014.

Hajli N., *The role of social support on relationship quality and social commerce*, Technological Forecasting & Social Change, 87, 2014.

Hautz J., Füller J., *The Impact of Video Source and Quality on Consumers' Perceptions and Intended Behaviors*, Journal of Interactive Marketing, 28 (1), 2014.

Heine K., Berghaus B., *Luxury goes digital: how to tackle the digital luxury brand–consumer touchpoints*, Journal of Global Fashion Marketing: Bridging Fashion and Marketing, 5 (3), 2014.

Henning-Thurau T., Gwinner K.P., Walsh, G., Gremler D.D., *Electronic Word-of-Mouth Via Consumer-Opinion Platforms: What Motivates Consumers to Articulate Themselves on the Internet?*, Journal of Interactive Marketing, 18 (1), 2004.

Hennings N., Wiedmann K.P., Klarmann C., *Luxury Brands in the digital age: exclusivity versus ubiquity*, Marketing Review St. Gallen, 29 (1), 2012.

Herrington J.D., Capella L.M., *Practical Applications of Music in a Service Settings*, Journal of Services Marketing, 8 (3), 1994.

Hetzel P., *Le mise en scène de l'identité d'une marque de luxe sur lieu de vent: l'approche expérientielle des magasins Ralph Lauren*, Revue Française de Marketing, n. 187, 2002.

Higgins E.T., Scholer A.A., *Engaging the consumer: The science and art of the value creation process*, Journal of Consumer Psychology, 19 (2), 2009.

Hirschman E.L., Holbrook M.B., *The experiential aspects of consumption: consumer fantasies, feeling and fun*, Journal of Consumer Research, 9 (2), 1982.

Hoffmann D.L., Fodor M., *Can you measure the ROI of your social media marketing?*, MIT Sloan Management Review, 52, 2010.

Hoffmann D.L., Novak T.P., *Marketing in Hypermedia Computer-Mediated Environments: Conceptual Foundations*, Journal of Marketing, 60, 1996.

Hollebeek L.D., *Exploring Customer Brand Engagement: Definition and Themes*, Journal of Strategic Marketing, 19 (7), 2011.

Hollebeek L.D., Glynn M.S., Brodie R.J., *Consumer Brand Engagement in Social Media: Conceptualization, Scale Development and Validation*, Journal of Interactive Marketing, 28, 2014.

Huang Z., Benyoucef M., *From e-commerce to social commerce: A close look at design features*, Electronic Commerce Research and Applications, 12, 2013.

Huang Z., Benyoucef M., *User preferences of social features on social commerce websites: an empirical study*, Technological Forecasting & Social Change, 2014.

Hughes A.M., Sweetser A., *Successful E-Mail Marketing Strategies: from Hunting to Farming*, Racom Communications, Chicago, 2009.

Hur W.M., Kim H., Woo J., *How CSR Leads to Corporate Brand Equity: Mediating Mechanisms of Corporate Brand Credibility and Reputation*, Journal of Business Ethics, 125 (1), 2014.

Insch A., *Online communication of corporate environmental citizenship: a study of New Zealand's electricity and gas retailers*, Journal of Marketing Communications, 14 (2), 2008.

Ironico S., *Fashion Management*, Franco Angeli, Milano, 2014.

Jahdi K.S., Acikdilli G., *Marketing communications and corporate social responsibility (CSR): marriage of convenience or shotgun wedding?*, Journal of Business Ethics, 88 (1), 2009.

Jahn B., Kunz W., Meyer A., *The role of social media for luxury brands: motives for consumer engagement and opportunities for business*, Social Science Research Network, 2013.

Jansen B.J., Zhang M., Sobel K., Chowdury A., *Twitter power: tweets as electronic word of mouth*, Journal of the American Society for Information Science and Technology, 60 (11), 2009.

Janssen C., Vanhamme J., Lindgreen A., Lefebvre C., *The Catch-22 of Responsible Luxury: Effects of Luxury Product Characteristics on Consumers' Perception of fit with Corporate Social Responsibility*, Journal of Business Ethics, 119, 2014.

Jin S.A.A., *The potential of social media for luxury brand management*, Marketing Intelligence & Planning, 30 (7), 2012.

Jung Choo H. *et al.*, *Luxury customer value*, Journal of Fashion Marketing and Management: An International Journal, 16 (1), 81-101, 2012.

Kalakota R., Whinston A.B., *Electronic Commerce*, Addison Wesley, Reading (Mass.), 1997.

Kapferer J.N., *How the Internet impacts on brand management*, Journal of Brand Management, vol. 7, n. 6, 2000.

Kapferer J.N., *Managing luxury brands*, Journal of Brand Management, 4 (4), 251-259, 1997.

Kapferer J.N., Bastien V., *The Luxury Strategy: Break the Rules of Marketing to Build Luxury Brands*, Kogan Page Ltd, 2012 (2nd ed.).

Kapferer J.N., Bastien V., *Luxury Strategy*, Franco Angeli, Milano, 2009.

Kapferer J.N., Michaut-Denizeau A., *Is luxury compatible with sustainability? Luxury consumers' viewpoint*, Journal of Brand Management, 21 (1), 1-22, 2014.

Kaplan A.M., *If you love something, let it go mobile: mobile marketing and mobile social media*, Business Horizons, 55 (2), 2012.

Kaplan A.M., Haenlein M., *Users of the world, unite! The challenges and opportunities of Social Media*, Business Horizons, 53 (1), 2010.

Keller K.L., *Strategic Brand Management: Building, Measuring and Managing Brand Equity*, Prentice Hall, NY, 2008 (3rd ed.); Pearson Education, Harlow, 2013 (4th ed.).

Kietzmann K., Hermkens J.H., McCarthy I.P., Silvestre B.S., *Social media? Get serious! Understanding the functional building blocks of social media*, Business Horizons, 54, 2011.

Kim A.J., Ko E., *Impacts of Luxury fashion brand's social media marketing on customer relationship and purchase intention*, Journal of Global Fashion Marketing, 2010.

Kim A.J., Ko E., *Do social media marketing activities enhance customer equity? An empirical study of luxury fashion brand*, Journal of Business Research, 65, 2012.

Kim H., Lee M., Lee H., Kim N., *Corporate social responsibility and employee-company identification*, Journal of Business Ethics, 95, 2010.

Kim S., Park H., *Effects of various characteristics of social commerce (s-commerce) on consumers' trust and trust performance*, International Journal of Information Management, 33, 2013.

Kirtiş K., Filiz Karahan F., *To Be or Not to Be in Social Media Arena as the Most Cost-Efficient Marketing Strategy after the Global Recession*, Procedia Social and Behavioral Sciences, 24, 2011.

Klein L.R., Quelch J.A., *Business-to-business market making on the Internet*, International Marketing Review, 14 (5), 1997.

Kotler P., *Atmospherics as a Marketing Tool*, Journal of Retailing, vol. 49, n. 4, 1973.

Kotler P., Keller K., Ancarani F., Constable M., *Marketing per Manager*, Pearson, 2014.

Krasnova H., Spiekermann S., Koroleva K., Hildebrand T., *Online social networks: why we disclose*, Journal of Information Technology, 25, 2010.

Krugman D.M., Reid L.N., Dunn S.W., Barban A.M., *Advertising: its role in modern Marketing*, Dryden Press, New York, 1994.

La Cour A., Kromann J., *Euphemisms and hypocrisy in corporate philanthropy*, Business Ethics: A European Review, 20 (3), 267-279, 2011.
Lambin J.J., *Market-driven management. Marketing strategico e operativo*, McGraw-Hill Italia, Milano, 2012.
Larrson K., Watson R., *A Social Media Analytics Framework*, Thirty Second International Conference on Information Systems, Shanghai, 2011.
Lee E.M., Park S., Lee H.J., *Employee perception of CSR activities: Its antecedents and consequences*, Journal of Business Research, 66, 2013.
Lee J., Geistfeld L.V., *A hierarchy of store characteristics: a conceptual advancement*, 8ª International Conference on Research in the Distributive Trades, Cescom, Milano, September, 1995.
Lemoine J.F., *Vers une approche globale de l'atmosphère du point de vente*, Revue Française du Marketing, n. 194, set., 2003.
Lewis V.B. *et al.*, *Benchmark: Luxury sector ebusiness adoption*, Forrester Research, (2008).
Li F., Du T.C., *Who is talking? An ontology-based opinion leader identification framework for word-of-mouth marketing in online social blogs*, Decision Support Systems, 51, 2011.
Li J., Zhan L., *Online persuasion: How the written word drives WOM, evidence from consumer-generated product reviews*. Journal of Advertising Research, 51(1), 2011.
Liang T.P., Ho Y.T., Li Y.W., Turban E., *What Drives Social Commerce: The Role of Social Support and Relationship Quality*, International Journal of Electronic Commerce, 16 (2), 2012.
Linda S., *Social commerce: e-commerce in social media context*, Engineering and Technology, 72, 2010.
Lindquist J.K., *Meaning of Image*, Journal of Retailing, 50 (4), 1974.
Lohdia S., *The World Wide Web and its potential for corporate environmental communication: a study into present practices in the Australian mineral industry*, International Journal of Digital Accounting Research, 6 (11), 2006.
Loureiro S.M.C., Lopes R., *How to achieve affective commitment in luxury car brand communities*, Working paper presented at the 9th Annual Global Brand Conference, Hertfordshire Business School, Hatfield, Hertfordshire, UK. April 9-11, 2014.
Lovelock C., Wirtz J., Iacovone L., *Marketing dei servizi. Il caso Yoox*, Prentice Hall, Milano, 2007.
Luan G., *Cartier becomes first luxury brand to set up community on MySpace*, New Media Age, 2008.
Lusch R.F., Vargo S.L., *Service-Dominant Logic as a Foundation for Building a General Theory*, in *The Service-Dominant Logic of Marketing*, eds Armonk, M.E Sharpe, NY, 2006.
Luxury Institute WealthSurvey, *Social Networking Habits and Practices of the Wealthy*, 2009, in www.luxuryboard.com.

Macchi J., *Lusso 2.0*, Lupetti, Milano, 2011.

Malhotra N.K., *A Threshold Model of Store Choice*, Journal of Retailing, 59 (2), 1983.

Mandelli A., *Internet marketing*, McGraw-Hill, Milano, 1998.

Mangold W.G., Faulds D.J., *Social media: The new hybrid element of the promotion mix*, Business Horizons, 52, 2009.

Maple P., Casalegno C., Civera C., *An investigation of 'The Spectrum of Corporate Social Responsibility'. Or to be more precise: Over-communication – a comparative analysis of the UK and Italian banking sectors from the customers' perspective*, International Society for Information Studies, Vienna, 2015.

Matute-Vallejo J., Bravo R., Pina J.M., *The influence of Corporate Social Responsibility and Price Fairness on Customer Behaviour: Evidence from the Financial Sector*, Corporate Social Responsibility and Environmental Management, 18, 2011.

Maurya M., *Evolution of blogs as a credible marketing communication tool*, Journal of Case Research, 2 (1), 2010.

McAlexander J., Schouten J., Koenig H., *Building brand community*, Journal of Marketing, 66 (1), 2002.

McCusker G., *Can luxury brands ever shine online*, Revolution, Haymarket Business Pubblication, 2008.

McKnight D.H., Choudhury V., Kacmar C., *The impact of initial consumer trust on intentions to transact with a Web site: A trust building model*, Journal of Strategic Information Systems, 11 (4), 2002.

McWilliam G., *Building stronger brands through online communities*, Sloan Management Review, 41 (3), 2000.

McWilliams A., Siegel D.S., Wright P.M., *Corporate social responsibility: Strategic implications*, Journal of management studies, 43 (1), 1-18, 2006.

Mehrabian A., Russell J.A., *An Approach to Environmental Psychology*, MIT, 1974.

Miceli G., *La personalizzazione collaborativa dell'offerta: modelli e processi di marketing management*, McGraw-Hill, Milano, 2008.

Mohammed R. *et al.*, *Internet marketing: Building advantage in a networked economy*, New York, McGraw-Hill, Inc., 2003.

Mosca F., *Le strategie di distribuzione dei beni ad elevato valore simbolico*, Giappichelli, Torino, 2005.

Mosca F., *Casi ed Esperienze di marketing*, Giappichelli, Torino, 2000.

Mosca F., *Marketing dei beni di lusso*, Pearson Italia, Milano, 2010.

Mosca F. *et al.*, *Marketing e nuovi scenari competitivi*, Milan, McGraw-Hill, Inc., 2014.

Mosca F., Casalegno C., Civera C., *Luxury and corporate social responsibility communication strategies. How much does the web matter? A cross investigation on players and consumers' perception*, British Academy Management Conference, Newcastle (UK), 6-8 september, 2016.

Mosca F., Casalegno C., Feffin A., *Nuovi modelli di comunicazione nei settori dei beni di lusso: un'analisi comparata*, X Conference Società Italiana Marketing, Milano, 3-4 october, 2013.

Mosca F., Tamborrini P., Casalegno C., *Systemic Design: How to Compete by Leveraging the Value System*, Symphonya Emerging Issues in Management, 2, 2015.

Muñiz, A.L., O'Guinn T.C., *Brand community*, Journal of Consumer Research, 27 (3), 2001.

Nambisan S., Baron R.A., *Interactions in Virtual Customer Environments: Implications for Product Support and Customer Relationship Management*, Journal of Interactive Marketing, 21 (2), 2007.
Nasruddin E., Bustami R., *The Yin and Yang of CSR Ethical Branding*. Asian Academy of Management Journal, 12 (2), 2007.
Naylor R.W., Lamberton C.P., West P.M., *Beyond the "Like" Button; The Impact of Mere Virtual Presence on Brand Evaluations and Purchase Intentions in Social Media Settings*, Journal of Marketing, 76, 2012.
Nemzow M., *Building cyberstores: installation, trasaction processing and management*, McGraw-Hill, New York, 1997.
Nevin J.R., Houston M., *Images as a Component of Attractiveness to Intra-Urban Shopping Areas*, Journal of Retailing, 56 (1), 1980.
Nielsen J., *Designing Web Usability*, New Riders, 1998.
Nueno J.L., Quelch. J.A., *The mass marketing of luxury*, Business Horizons, 41 (6), 61-68, 1998.
Nyelk S., Roux E., *Does Product Category Matters in Marketing Luxury Brands via WWW: Contrasting Consumers and Manager Views*, Paris, 1997.
Nyeck S., Roux E., *WWW as a communication tool for luxury brands: compared perceptions of consumers and managers*, In van Raiij et al., *Proceedings of the Second International Research Seminar on Marketing Communication and Consumer Behaviour*, La Londe Les Maures, 1997.

Okonkwo U., *Can the luxury brand athmosphere be tranferred to the Internet?*, Brandchannel, 2005.
Okonkwo U., *Luxury Fashion Branding*, Palgrave Macmillan, 2007.
Okonkwo U., *Sustaining the luxury brand on the Internet*, Journal of Brand Management, 16 (5-6), 2009.
Okonkwo U., *Luxury Online: Style, Systems, Strategies*, Palgrave McMillan, 2010.
Okonkwo U., *Luxury Fashion Branding: trends, tatics, techiques*, Palgrave Macmillan, 2012.
Ortved J., *Is Digital killing the luxury brand? The democratizing power of the Web means figuring out how to go online without going downscale*, Adweek, 12 Sept. 2011.
Otto J., Chung Q., *A framework for cyber-enhanced retailing: integrating e-commerce*, Electronic Markets, 10 (4), 2000.

Park H., Kim Y.K., *The role of social network websites in the consumer– brand relationship*, Journal of Retailing and Consumer Services, 21 (4), 2014.
Park J., Song H., Ko E., *The Effect of the Lifestyles of Social Networking Service Users on Luxury Brand Loyalty*, Journal of Global Scholars of Marketing Science, 21 (4), 2011.
Patterson P., Yu T., De Ruyter K., *Understanding customer engagement in services*, Proceedings of ANZMAC Conference: Advancing Theory, Maintaining Relevance, Brisbane, 4-6 Dec. 2006.
Pauli G., *Blue economy. 10 anni. 100 innovazioni. 100 milioni di posti di lavoro*, Edizioni Ambiente, Milano, 2010.

Pellegrini L., *Luoghi di acquisto: strumenti chiave nelle strategie di marketing. Luoghi dell'acquisto e relazione con il consumatore*, Micro & Macro Marketing, 3, 2001.

Pellicelli G., *Il marketing*, Utet, Torino, 2012.

Pentina I., Prybutok V.R., Zhang X., *The Role of Virtual Communities as shopping reference Tools*, Journal of Electronic Commerce Research, 9 (2), 2008.

Phau I., Prendergast G., *Consuming luxury brands: The relevance of the 'Rarity Principle'*, Journal of Brand Management, 8, 2000.

Piron F., *A definition and empirical investigation of impulse purchasing*, Unpublished Dissertation, The University of South Carolina, 1989.

Pollack I., *Communication Corporate Ethics on the World Wide Web – A Discourse Analysis of Selected Company Web Sites*. Business and Society, 42 (2), 2003.

Pomering A., Dolnicar S., *Assessing the prerequisite of successful CSR implementation: are consumers aware of CSR initiatives?*, Journal of Business Ethics, 85 (2s), 2009.

Porter M.E., Kramer M.R., *Creating shared value*, Harvard Business Review, 89 (1), january 2011.

Porter M.E., Kramer M.R., *The competitive advantage of corporate philanthropy*, Harvard business review, 80 (12), 56-68, 2002.

Pöyry E., Parvinen P., Malmivaara T., *Can we get from liking to buying? Behavioral differences in hedonic and utilitarian Facebook usage*, Electronic Commerce Research and Applications, 12, 2013.

Rangaswamy A., Van Bruggen G.H., *Opportunities and Challenges in Multichannel Marketing: An Introduction to the Special Issue*, Journal of Interactive Marketing, 19 (2), 2005.

Rayport J.F., Sviokla J.J., *Managing in the marketspace*, Harvard Business Review, november-december, 72 (6), 2004.

Ricotta F., *Marketing Multicanale*, Pearson, Milano-Torino, 2009.

Rifkin J., *The Age of Access*, Tarcher/Putnam, New York, 2000.

Rohm A.J., Swaminathan V., *A typology of online shoppers based on shopping motivations*, Journal of Business Research, 57 (7), 2004.

Romano D.F., *Immagine, marketing e comunicazione*, Il Mulino, Bologna, 1988.

Rooke D.W., Gardner M.P., *In the mood: impulsive buying affective antecedents*, Research in Customer Behaviour, 6 (7), 1993.

Sansone M., Scafarto F., *Il ruolo comunicativo del punto vendita nel sistema moda. Un approccio semiotico al marketing*, Paper al Convegno Internazionale *Le Tendenze del Marketing*, Venezia, Università Ca' Foscari, 28-29 november 2003.

Schau H.J., Muñiz A.M., Arnould E.J., *How Brand Community Practices Create Value*, Journal of Marketing, 73 (5), 2009.

Schivinski B., Dabrowski D., *The effect of social media communication on consumer perceptions of brands*, Journal of Marketing Communications, 22 (2), 2014.

Schmitt B.H., *Experiential Marketing: how to get customer to sense, feel, think, act and relate to your company and brand*, The Free Press, New York, 1999.

Schultz D.E., Tannenbaum S., Lauterborn R.F., *Integrated Marketing Communications: putting it togheter & making it work*, NTC, 1993.

Schwartz S.H., *Universals in the content and structure of values: Theoretical advances and empirical tests in 20 countries*, Advances in experimental social psychology, vol. 25, 1-65, 1992.

Sciarelli S., Vona R., *L'impresa commerciale*, McGraw-Hill, Milano, 2000.

Sciarelli S., Vona R., *Management della distribuzione* (Milano, McGraw-Hill, Milano, 2009.

See-To E., Ho K., *Value co-creation and purchase intention in social network sites: The role of electronic Word-of-Mouth and trust – A theoretical analysis*, Computers in Human Behavior, 31, 2014.

Sen S., Bhattacharya C.B., *Does doing good always lead to doing better? Consumer reactions to corporate social responsibility*, Journal of Marketing Research, 38 (2), May 2001.

Seringhaus F.R., *Selling Luxury Brands Online*, Journal of Internet Commerce, 4 (1), 2005.

Shin D. H., *User experience in social commerce: in friends we trust*, Behaviour & Information technology, 32 (1), 2013.

Singh S., Sonnenburg S., *Brand Performance in Social Media*, Journal of Interactive Marketing, 26 (4), 2012.

Smith A., Fischer E., Yongjian C., *How Does Brand-related User-generated Content Differ across YouTube, Facebook, and Twitter?*, Journal of Interactive Marketing, 26, 2012.

Som A., Blanckaert C., *Road to Luxury*, Wiley, Singapore, 2015.

Spar D., Busgang J.J., *The Net*, Harward Business Review, May-June, 1996.

Sprangenberg E.R., Crowley A.E., Henderson P.W., *Improving the Store Environment: Do Olfactory Cues Affect Evaluations and Behaviors*, Journal of Marketing, 60 (2), 1996.

Stanley T., Sewall M., *Image Inputs to a Probabilistic Model: Predicting Retail Potential*, Journal of Marketing, 40 (3), 1976.

Steel E., *Luxury brands experiment with social media*, ft.com, 2013.

Steenkamp E., Wedel E.J., *Segmenting Retail markets on Store Image Using a Consumer-Based Methodology*, Journal of Retailing, 67, 1991.

Stephen A.T., Toubia O., *Deriving Value from Social Commerce Networks*, Journal of Marketing Research, 47 (2), 2010.

Swinyard W.R., *The effects of mood, involvement and quality of store experience on shopping intentions*, Journal of Consumer Research, 20 (2), 1993.

Tai S.H.C., Fung A.M.C., *Application of an environmental psychology model to in-store buying behaviour*, International Review of Retail Distribution and Consumer Research, 7 (4), 1997.

Tapscott D., Williams A.D., *Wikinomics 2.0, la collaborazione di massa che sta cambiando il mondo*, Rizzoli-Etas, Milano, 2008.

Thompson Jr. T., Hertzberg J., Sullivan M., *Social media and its associated risks*, Grant Thornton LLP, 2010.

Thomsen S.R., Straubhaar J.D., Bolyard D.M., *Ethnomethodology and the study of online communities: exploring the cyber streets*, Information Research, 4 (1), 1998.

Toffler A., *The third wave*, Bantam Books, 1980.
Toubia O., Stephen A.T., *Intrinsic vs. Image-Related Utility in Social Media: Why Do People Contribute Content to Twitter?*, Marketing Science, 32 (3), 2013.
Truong Y., McColl R., *Intrinsic motivations, self-esteem, and luxury goods consumption*, Journal of Retailing and Consumer Services, 18, 2011.
Trusov M., Bucklin R.E., Pauwel K., *Effects of Word-of-Mouth Versus Traditional Marketing: Findings from an Internet Social Networking Site*, Journal of Marketing, 73, September 2009.
Tuten T.L., Solomon M. R., *Social Media Marketing*, Pearson Italia, Milano, 2014.

Urban G.L., *Customer Advocacy: A New Era in Marketing?*, Journal of Public Policy and Marketing, Spring, 2005.
Uwins, S., *Creating Loyal Brands. A guide to earning loyalty in a connected world*, Publish Green, 2014.

Vallaster C., Lindgreen A., Maon F., *Strategically leveraging corporate social responsibility: A corporate branding perspective*, California management review, 54 (3), 2012.
Van de Ven B., *An Ethical Framework for the Marketing of Corporate Social Responsibility*, Journal of Business Ethics, 82 (2), 339-352, 2008.
Van Doorn J., Lemon K.L., Mittal V., Nass S., Peck D., Pirner P., Verhoef P.C., *Customer Engagement Behavior: Theoretical Foundations and Research Directions*, Journal of Service Research, 13 (3), 2010.
Veblen T., *The Theory of The Leisure Class*, Macmillan, Londra, 1899.
Venkatesan R., Kumar R., Ravishanker N., *Multichannel Shopping: Causes and Consequences*, Journal of Marketing, 71 (2), 2007.
Vernuccio M., *La rivoluzione digitale*, in Mattiacci A., Pastore A., *Marketing. Il management orientato al mercato*, Hoepli, Milano, 2014.
Vescovi T., Checchinato F., *Luoghi di esperienza e strategie competitive nel dettaglio*, Micro & Macro Marketing, 3, 2004.
Vianelli D., *L'atmosfera del punto vendita in un contesto multi-culturale: una ricerca empirica su consumatori di diversa nazionalità*, Industria & Distribuzione, 1, 2001.
Vickery G., Wunsch-Vincent S., *Participative web and user-created content. Web 2.0, wikis and social networking*, OECD, 2007.
Vigneron F., Johnson. L.W., *A review and a conceptual framework of prestige-seeking consumer behavior*, Academy of Marketing Science Review, 1, 1999.
Vigneron F., Johnson, L.W., *Measuring perceptions of brand luxury*, Journal of Brand Management, 11, 2004.
Villanueva J., Yoo S., Hanssens D.M., *The Impact of Marketing-Induced Versus Word-of-Mouth Customer Acquisition on Customer Equity Growth*, Journal of Marketing Research, 45, 2008.
Visser W., *The quest for sustainable business: an epic journey in search of corporate responsibility*, Greenleaf, Sheffield, 2012.
Visser W., *Corporate Sustainability & Responsibility: an introductory text on CSR theory & practice – past, present & future*, Kaleidoscope Futures, London, 2013.

Vivek S.D., Beatty S.E., Morgan R.M., *Customer Engagement: Exploring Customer Relationships Beyond Purchase*, Journal of Marketing Theory and Practice, 20 (2), 2012.

Wanderley L.S.O., Lucian R., Farache F., De Sousa Filho J.M., *CSR information disclosure on the web: a context-based approach analysing the influence of country of origin and industry sector*, Journal of Business Ethics, 82, 2008.

Wang C., Zhang P., *The evolution of social commerce: the people, management, technology and information dimensions*, Communications of the Associations for Information Systems, 31 (5), 2012.

Wang X., Yu C., Wei Y., *Social Media Peer Communication and Impacts on Purchase Intentions: A Consumer Socialization Framework*, Journal of Interactive Marketing, 26 (4), 2012.

Weber L., *Marketing to the social web: how digital customer communities build your business*, John Wiley & Sons, 2007.

Weinberg B.D., Pehlivan E., *Social spending: Managing the social media mix*, Business Horizons, 54, 2011.

Welcomer P.L., Cochran G.R., Rands G., Haggerty M., *Constructing a web: effects of power and social responsiveness on firm-stackeholder relationships*, Business and Society, 42 (1), 2003.

Westbrook R.A., Black W.C., *A motivation-based shopper typology*, Journal of Retailing, 61 (1), 1985.

Westbrook R.A., Oliver R.L., *Developing Better Measures of Consumer Satisfaction: Some Preliminary Results*, in NA – Advances in Consumer Research, Association for Consumer Research, 8, 1980.

Winer R.S., Dhar R., Mosca F., *Marketing Management*, Apogeo, Milano, 2013.

Yadav M.S., de Valck K., Hennig-Thurau T., Hoffman D.L., Spann M., *Social Commerce: A Contingency Framework for Assessing Marketing Potential*, Journal of Interactive Marketing, 27, 2013.

Yi X., Siqing P., *How do corporate associations influence customer relationship strength? The effects of different types of trust*, Journal Of Strategic Marketing, 19 (5), 443-454, 2011.

Yoon S.J., *A social network approach to the influences of shopping experiences on e-WOM*, Journal of Electronic Commerce Research, 13 (3), 2013.

Zaghi K., *Atmosfera e Visual Merchandising: ambienti relazioni ed esperienze. Il punto vendita come luogo e strumento di relazioni*, Franco Angeli, Milano, 2008.

Zaglia M.E., *Brand communities embedded in social networks*, Journal of Business Research, 51-60, 2013.

Zimmer M.R., Golden L.L., *Impressions of Retail Stores: A Content Analysis of Consumer Images*, Journal of Retailing, 64 (3), 1988.

Appendix 1
LITERATURE REVIEW

A1.1. Introduction

This first Appendix focuses on the main research topics about brand communities, on the idea of *User Generated Content* and on social media, examined by the literature so far, with particular attention to high symbolic value goods. Furthermore, it clarifies the methods used to better understand the above-mentioned phenomena, its outcome and the tools employed.

Research method. Research was carried out with the help of two main platforms:

- Search engine platform at the University of Turin;
- Databases and digital journals at the Luigi Bocconi Business University.

Intense research using keywords related to the work topic was implemented in both platforms from September 2014 to February 2016.

Research outcomes in the scientific literature. The main contributions of this work are: 93 scientific and managerial articles. A literature analysis was carried out paying attention to: main research topics (keywords), reference authors, content approach (orientation to academic research or managerial practice), source of the scientific contribution, journals ranking (according to AIDEA), used study method, publishing date, observations (a summary of the article) and the number of pages. Outcomes of the literature review are reported in the summary table.[1]

Main contributions and research topics can be placed in four macro areas:

- Web evolution, collecting articles about current phenomena.
- Social media strategies: referring to the approach currently adopted by companies to integrate social media with traditional marketing and promotion mix activities. In this regard, scientific debate on luxury brands focuses on how to turn the perception of exclusivity and rarity typical of luxury goods into a digital experience.
- Consumers' perception of digital activities: this aspect focuses on consumer-company relationships in the digital field, perceptions of brand's consumers and CRM.
- Measurement methods and digital marketing activities' metrics: the marketing function is constantly engaged in measuring each activity. This is particularly true for social marketing as it requires qualitative (more than quantitative) measurements, which are difficult to prove.

Table A1.1 Literature Review

Source: own processing

Article	Main topics (Keywords)	Author/s	Type of article and Source	Ranking Journal	Method	Date	Observations	Page
How Social Media Marketing Efforts Influence Brand Equity Creation and Its Consequences: The Case of Luxury Brands	Social Media Brand Equity Creation Luxury Brand WOM Customization	Aikaterini Manthiou, Joonas Rokka, Bruno Godey, Liang (Rebecca) Tang	Chapter Let's Get Engaged! Crossing the Threshold of Marketing's Engagement Era doi:10.1007/978-3-319-11815-4_169	–	Exploratory study with empirical outcomes	2016	This study investigates the impact of communication media on brand equity and its consequences, analyzing luxury brands. A model of structural equations sustaining the research hypothesis was developed on the basis of a survey involving 397 luxury customers. Social media marketing efforts can be globally identified and measured according to five aspects: entertainment, interaction, trendiness, personalization and word of mouth. Furthermore, the outcomes show the connection between social media marketing and brand equity and report its consequences, among which are preference and loyalty.	16
Pursuing the concept of luxury: Introduction to the *JBR* Special Issue on "Luxury Marketing from Tradition to Innovation"	Luxury; Segmentation; Definition; Internet	Jean-Louis Chandona, Gilles Laurenta, Pierre Valette-Florence	Academic article – Journal of Business Research doi:10.1016/j.jbusres.2015.08.001	A	Descriptive article	2016	Theoretical framework, emotion analysis system (qualitative), forecasting models, analysis systems on social media. The paper introduces a forecasting survey about the use of social media, providing a general summary on forecasting methods and factors.	5
Who's behind the screen? Segmenting social venture consumers through social media usage	Create; Connect; Control; Social venture; Social media site; Segmentation	Te-Lin (Doreen) Chunga, Nwamaka A. Anazab, Joohyung Parkc, Adrienne Hall-Phillips	Journal of Retailing and Consumer Services doi:10.1016/j.jretconser.2015.01.006	C	Exploratory study with empirical outcomes	2015	The outcome of a survey involving 305 social companies'consumers allowed the identification of four different segments of consumers – social observers, active participants, social connectors and moderate participants – on the basis of three dimensions social media use: content creation, connection with others and user-experience control.	7

Article	Main topics (Keywords)	Author/s	Type of article and Source	Ranking Journal	Method	Date	Observations	Page
Persuasive messages, popularity cohesion, and message diffusion in social media marketing	Persuasive messages; Social media marketing; Popularity cohesion; Message diffusion	Yu-Ting Chang, Hueiju Yu, Hsi-Peng Lu	Journal of business research doi:10.1016/j.jbusres.2015.11.027	A	Exploratory study with empirical outcomes	2015	This activity investigates how persuasive messages (i.e. quality, popularity and attractiveness of the topic) can make Internet users share social marketing activities.	8
Engaging consumers online through websites and social media: A gender study of Italian Generation Y clothing consumers	Facebook, Online shopping, trust	Waqar Nadeem, Daniela Andreini, Jari Salo, Tommi Laukkanen	International Journal of Information management doi:10.1016/j.ijinfomgt.2015.04.008	-	Descriptive Article	2015	The article highlights the importance of social media for luxury companies and introduces a general framework that, when discussing various managerial implications, describes the connection between social pages and customer loyalty.	8
Consumers' response to other consumers' participation in new product development	Brand uniqueness, brand attribution, brand schema, congruity, new product development, consumer behavior	Karina T. Liljedal, Micael Dahlen	Journal of Marketing communications doi:10.1509/jm.14.0199	C	Empirical study	2015	It is an empirical study on 386 consumers investigating consumer reactions to knowing that other consumers have taken part in the development of the product. Apparently the impact is more favorable when the product is not consistent with the brand.	15
Commodity and community in social networking: Marx and the monetization of User-Generated Content	Facebook, free labour, immaterial labour, internet, public space, social networking sites	Dal Yong Jin, Andrew Feenberg	The information Society doi:10.1080/0197243.2015.977635	-	Descriptive Article	2015	The article begins by describing the two perspectives on social media-generated free labor. According to one view, it is intangible work on intangible products. According to another, it is non-paid work consumers do for customers. The article goes beyond the mere economic perspective as this would not consider the democratic implications related to this phenomenon. Human aspect sits at the center of these online interactions in the public domain.	10

Article	Main topics (Keywords)	Author/s	Type of article and Source	Ranking Journal	Method	Date	Observations	Page
Fashion Retailing – past, present and future	Fashion, retail, technology, omni-channel, information and communication technology	Helen mcCormick, Jo Cartwright, Patsy Perry, Liz Barnes, Samantha Lynch, Gemma Ball	Textile Progress doi10.1080/00405167.2014.973247	-	Descriptive Article	2015	It is a real storiographic article describing the development of the retail channel for fashion, including the consequences ICT could have today on the one-channel approach typical of this sector. It investigates social networks (Facebook), analyzing Michael Kors' case and how he uses his own platforms.	96
Social media and human need satisfaction: Implications for social media marketing	Social media; Need satisfaction; Social media typology; Social media marketing	Yu-Qian Zhu, Houn-Gee Chen	Academic article –Business Horizons doi:10.1016/j.bushor.2015.01.006	B	Descriptive article	2015	The bottom line is that in order to be efficient, social media marketing should be in line with social media users' different needs. In that perspective, this article divides social media services in four categories: relationship, media, cooperation, creativity.	10
Listening In on Social Media: A Joint Model of Sentiment and Venue Format Choice	Social media, brand tracking, online word of mouth, social media analytics, social media research	David A. Schweidel, Wendy W. Moe	Academic article – Journal of Marketing Reasarch doi:10.1509/jmr.12.0424	A*	Empirical study	2014	According to this research, several marketers, on social media, use brand emotion metrics which do not reflect reality. Difficulties in assessing different social media often lead to the evaluation of a single one only, avoiding aggregates.	17
Mining Marketing Meaning from Online Chatter: Strategic Brand Analysis of Big Data Using Latent Dirichlet Allocation	Consumer satisfaction, quality, dimensions, brand mapping, big data, latent Dirichlet allocation, user-generated content	Seshadri Tirunillai, Gerard J. Tellis	Journal of Marketing Research doi:10.1509/jmr.12.0106	A*	Empirical study	2014	The study, involving 15 companies operating in five different markets over a time span of four years, highlighted the importance of UGC for the marketer. The information provided by this study is useful to understand consumers and their perception of brand quality.	18

Article	Main topics (Keywords)	Author/s	Type of article and Source	Ranking Journal	Method	Date	Observations	Page
Is Neutral Really Neutral? The Effects of Neutral User-Generated Content on Product Sales	User-generated content, mixed-neutral user-generated content, indifferent-neutral user-generated content, product sales, opportunity – motivation – ability framework	Tanya (Ya) Tang, Eric (Er) Fang, & Feng Wang	Articolo Accademico – Journal of Marketing doi:10.1509/jm.13.0301	A*	Empirical study	2014	The article illustrates the outcomes of empirical research aimed at analyzing the influence of consumer-generated contents – positive, negative and neutral – on sales. According to this research, neutral UGC effects on product sales are actually not really neutral and sales depend on both the type of UGC and the distribution of positive and negative UGC.	17
What We Know and Don't Know About Online Word-of Mouth: A Review and Synthesis of the Literature	Electronic word-of-mouth; Systematic review; Social media; c2c interactions; Social influences	Robert Allen King, Pradeep Racherla, Victoria D. Bush	Academic article – Journal of Interactive Marketing doi:10.1016/j.intmar.2014.02.001	A	Descriptive Article	2014	It illustrates the researchers' interest in the last ten years for online word of mouth. A multidimensional analysis of eWOM communication surfaces on the basis of a systematic revision of 190 studies. Current key and emerging issues are introduced to raise important questions about future research.	17
Content Sharing in a social broadcasting environment: Evidence from Twitter	Content sharing, social broadcasting, information diffusion, Twitter, weak tie	Zhan shi, Huaxia Rui, Andrew B. Whinston	Mis Quarterly doi:10.2139/ssrn.2341243	-	Market investigation	2014	Empirical study on tweet type and the relationship between consumers and brand/possible content creation.	27
Social network branding: branding in social networks era	Social network, Facebook, branding, social media	A. Gandolfo, L. Lupi	Academic article – Markets and competitiveness doi:10.3280/MC2014-002008	A	Descriptive article	2014	The article introduces a footwear company based in Tuscany that uses Facebook as a distribution channel along with traditional tools to promote its brand.	25
Building a Luxury Brand Image in a Digital World	Digital channels, brand promise, how to build a prestigious image, how to marry bricks and clicks	D. Dubois	Non-academic article – knowledge.insead.edu	-	Descriptive article	2014	The article explains how digital channels are nowadays an opportunity for luxury companies; Hermès and Burberry are taken as an example for their digital strategies.	2

Article	Main topics (Keywords)	Author/s	Type of article and Source	Ranking Journal	Method	Date	Observations	Page
Effects of intrinsic and extrinsic motivation on user-generated content	UGC, word-of mouth, intrinsic and extrinsic motivation	R. Poch, B. Martin	Academic article – Journal of Strategic Marketing doi:10.1080/0965254X.2014.926966	B	Descriptive article	2014	The study investigates consumers' intrinsic and extrinsic motives for creating video content.	-
Luxury Brands are winning on Instagram	Luxury brand engagement, hashtag, product images, benefits of a platform-specific approach	E. Adler	Non-academic article – businessinsider.com	-	Descriptive article	2014	It focuses on the importance of Instagram for luxury companies and lists some strategies to win over social networks.	2
Web 2.0: Consumer empowerment through the Internet evolution brings implications for marketers	The Internet as a billboard, the consumer empowerment era, how marketers can best adapt to reach consumers in web 2.0	R. Korthenius	Non-academic article – brandba.se	-	Descriptive article	2014	This article follows the Internet's evolution to understand the implications between the power of "consumer 2.0" and marketing experts.	6
How Can Luxury Brands use Social Media?	Digital generation, social media, brand's reputation, social influencers	I. Vermeren	Non-academic article – brandwatch.com	-	Descriptive article	2014	The article analyzes the recent networking era and highlights 6 points in which luxury companies should focus to best develop their Web strategy.	3
Social Media Marketing for Luxury products	Social media channels, Facebook advertising, word-of-mouth, social media campaigns	J. Tan	Non-academic article – business2community.com	-	Descriptive article	2014	The article reports 3 steps to follow on social media for "not-yet-established luxury brands".	3

Article	Main topics (Keywords)	Author/s	Type of article and Source	Ranking Journal	Method	Date	Observations	Page
The Informational Value of Social Tagging Networks	User-generated content, social tags, social media, brand equity, firm valuation	Hyoryung Nam & P.K. Kannan	Journal of Marketing doi:10.1509/jm.12.0151	A*	Empirical study	2014	This article investigates how the information on social tags can be considered as a measurement of a brand's performance and somehow forecasts the financial assessment of a company. Using data gathered by a social tagging and bookmarking the website (Delicious), the authors have analyzed social tagging data for 44 companies in 14 markets. The analysis shows that as tag-based brand management social metrics capture a brand's familiarity, association advantage, and – as brand association competitiveness – can explain sudden equity returns.	15
Targeted Online Advertising: Using Reciprocity Appeals to Increase Acceptance Among Users of Free Web Services	free web services, targeting, advertising, privacy concerns, reciprocity	Jan H. Schuinanii, Florian von Wangenheim, & Nicole Groene	Journal of Marketing doi:10.1509/jm.11.0316	A*	Descriptive Article	2014	The article highlights the importance of taking care of the relationship between consumers and the website as a free tool for interaction and content generation.	18
The effect of social media comunication on consumer perceptions of brands	Brand equity, brand attitude, purchase intention, Facebook	B. Schivinski; D. Dabrowski	Academic article – Journal of marketing communications doi:10.1080/13527266.2013.871323	C	Empirical study	2013	Survey involving 504 Facebook users and 60 brands operating in different fields (soft drinks, clothing and mobile network providers). The article investigates the effects of social media on consumers' brand perceptions. Study has shown how both brand equity and brand attitude affect positively consumers' purchasing intentions.	20

Article	Main topics (Keywords)	Author/s	Type of article and Source	Ranking Journal	Method	Date	Observations	Page
Brand community embedded in social networks	Brand community, brand-related community, social network, social identity, netnography	M.E. Zaglia	Academic article – Journal of Business Research doi:10.1016/j.jbusres.2012.07.015	A	Descriptive article	2013	Ideal qualitative approaches to scrutinize the existence of community brands within social networks. This survey values the netnography's approach in investigating virtual communities. The document investigates the advantages of social networks in terms of time and financial savings.	9
Can fashion blogs function as a marketing tool to influence consumer behaviour? Evidence from Norway	Blog as new a channel of marketing, communicationa and publication of information through user-generated contents.	K. Halvorsen, J. Hoffmann, I. Coste-Manière, R. Stankeviciute	Academic article – Journal of Global Fashion Marketing doi:10.1080/20932685.2013.790707	D	Empirical study	2013	The article introduces a research project from three different angles: readers, fashion blogs and companies investing in fashion blog marketing. The study demonstrates fashion blogging's significant role in brand and products' communication and its effect on customer purchasing behavior. Fashion blogs are a powerful communication tool for marketing products.	13
Utilization of Relationship-Oriented Social	B2B, B2C, professional sales, professional selling process, social media	J.N. Moore, C.D. Hopkins, M.A. Raymond	Academic article– Journal of Internet Commerce doi:10.1080/15332861.2013.763694	D	Empirical study	2013	Social Media divided in 15 categories; with a sample of 395 B2B and B2C sellers, social media effects in companies are presented. The article introduces a study aimed at understanding social media use among professionals.	27
Consumption and communication of luxury brands online – Illustrating a qualitative online case study	Online environment, Online research, Study	A. Radón	International Journal of Cyber Society and Education	-	Descriptive article	2013	Case study – qualitative online research (discussion groups, website visitor, tracking systems, e-mail consumer panels, online surveys and online focus groups). This paper illustrates an online qualitative marketing study on consumption and brand communication.	6

Article	Main topics (Keywords)	Author/s	Type of article and Source	Ranking Journal	Method	Date	Observations	Page
Materialism, Attitudes, and Social Media Usage and Their Impact on Purchase Intention of Luxury fashion Goods Among American and arab Young Generations	Social Media Advertising, Purchase intention, Arab consumers	S. Kamal, S.C. Chu, M. Pedram	Academic article – Journal of Interactive Advertising doi:10.1080/15252019.2013.768052	-	Empirical study	2013	Online questionnaire, investigations, 400 students e-mailed and invited to take part in the survey. 347 completed interviews, 306 used. This study investigates whether materialism, an important component of consumer behavior, is a consequence of social media use affecting user attitude towards Web advertising.	13
The Effects of Online Brand Community on Brand Equity in the Luxury Fashion Industry	Online brand community, Web 2.0, Online marketing, Research model	S.Brogi, A.Calabrese, D. Campisi, F.Di Pillo, G.Capece, R.Costa	International Journal of Engineering Business Management	-	Empirical study	2013	Research model; variables: brand community participation, perceived brand quality, brand community's generated content, brand loyalty, brand associations, brand awareness. The article aims at creating a research model to analyze the effects of OBCs (Online Brand Community) dynamics on brand value.	9
The role of Social Media for luxury brands – motives for consumer engagement and opportunities for business	How social media brand pages affect the customer-brand relationship, value of social media for luxury brands	B. Jahn, W. Kunz, A. Meyer	Academic article – Social Science Research Network doi:10.1007/978-3-8349-4060-5_14	-	Theoretical discussion, general framework	2013	The article highlights the importance of social media for luxury companies and introduces a general framework that, when discussing various managerial implications, describes the connection between social pages and customer loyalty.	15
Why Social Media is Luxury's best friend?	Business strategies, dream, core value, social media platform	D. Dubois	Non-academic article – knowledge.insead.edu	-	Descriptive article	2013	This articles focuses on the importance of social media and suggests three ways of being effective on the Web.	2
How Luxury Brands are using social media to earn new customers	Social media marketing strategy, memory-making experience, social presence, customer engagement	J. Fishaw	Non-academic article – digitalsherpa.com	-	Descriptive article	2013	This article explains the importance of social media for luxury brands and provides some examples about Burberry, Ritz-Carlton and Tiffany&Co.	1

Article	Main topics (Keywords)	Author/s	Type of article and Source	Ranking Journal	Method	Date	Observations	Page
Luxury brands experiment with social media	Social media marketing, social media as a priority, Facebook page, digital outlets, engaging with customers	E. Steel	Non-academic article – ft.com	-	Descriptive article	2013	The article explains today's importance of social media for the marketing of Swiss luxury watches.	3
Understanding consumers' responses toward social media advertising and purchase intention toward luxury products	Advertising, beliefs, social media, luxury brand, structural equation model, purchase intention	S.C. Chu, S. Kamal, Y. Kim	Academic article – Journal of Global Fashion Marketing doi:10.1080/20932685.2013.790709	D	Empirical study	2013	The study explores young users (18-35 years old)'s benefits and behaviors deriving from social media use. The paper investigates consumer's reactions through social network advertising and their purchasing intentions towards luxury products.	16
Managing Brands in the Social Media Environment	Multi-Vocal, Co-created nature of brand stories, A conceptual framework of Social Media's impact on brand management, Current knowledge and future research questions	S. Gensler, F. Völckner, Y. Liu-Thompkins, C. Wiertz	Academic article – Journal of Interactive Marketing doi:10.1016/j.intmar.2013.09.004	A	Descriptive article	2013	The article introduces a framework about social media impact on brand management.	14
The challenges of luxury brands' positioning on social media	Definition of UGC, Difference between Brands and Luxury Brands, Inherent exclusivity, Example, Discussion, Communication platform	C. Zhang	Non-academic article – brandba.se	-	Descriptive article, theoretical framework, empirical exemple (Burberry)	2013	The paper intends to explore how luxury brands build their own image using social networks.	5

Article	Main topics (Keywords)	Author/s	Type of article and Source	Ranking Journal	Method	Date	Observations	Page
Rising to Stardom: An Empirical Investigation of the Diffusion of User-generated Content	Network analysis, Spread of user-generated videos online, YouTube, Viral marketing	Y. Liu-Thompkins, M. Rogerson	Academic article – Journal of Interactive Marketing doi:10.1016/j.intmar.2011.1 1.003	A	Proportional rates model	2012	The article examines the diffusion of videos on YouTube.	11
Brand Performances in Social Media	Brands in social media, Managing brands, Co-creation, Storytelling	S. Singh, S. Sonnenburg	Academic article –Journal of Interactive Marketing doi:10.1016/j.intmar.2012.0 4.001	A	Descriptive article	2012	The paper explains the importance of company-customer cooperation for value creation.	8
Social Media in an Alternative Marketing Communication Model	W.o.m, CRM, brand community, Email marketing, SEO, Viral marketing, guerrilla marketing, mobile marketing, UGC, blogs	C. Castronovo, L. Huang	Journal of Marketing Development and Competitiveness	-	Theoretical framework	2012	This document provides an overview on social media and integrated communication. Moreover, it develops an alternative conceptual marketing model that companies can adopt to reach their marketing goals.	18
Do Social media marketing activities enhance customer equity? An empirical study of luxury fashion brand	Social Media Marketing activities, Customer equity and its drivers, Purchase intention, Study	A.J. Kim, E. Ko	Academic article – Journal of Business Research doi:10.1016/j.jbusres.2011.1 0.014	A	Empirical study	2012	Preliminary test to select survey sample, data analysis, CFA (Confirmatory factor analysis) model, conceptual mode, structural equation mode. The outcomes of this study allow luxury brands to accurately predict consumers' future purchasing behaviors and can be used as a guideline to best manage marketing activities.	7
The luxury consumer in the new digital world: then & now	The future of digital technology innovation in luxury travel	S. Helstab	Non-academic article – Four Seasons Luxury Trend Report	-	Descriptive article	2012	This document collects data about luxury hotels and resorts industry trends, investigating the relationship between the website FourSeasons and the main social media like Facebook, Tumblr and YouTube.	9

Article	Main topics (Keywords)	Author/s	Type of article and Source	Ranking Journal	Method	Date	Observations	Page
Luxury Brands in the Digital Age – Exclusivity versus Ubiquity	Value of Luxury online, leaders in online luxury, Luxury e-tailing: blessing or curse?	N. Hennigs, K.P. Wiedmann, C. Klarmann	Academic article – Marketing Review doi:10.1007/s11621-012-0108-7	C	Descriptive article	2012	The document explores the value of online luxury objects and monitors web strategies adopted by the main players.	6
The potential of social media for luxury brand management	Social media marketing potential, UGC and social networking sites (SNSs) for luxury brands management. Correlation between online research and offline purchase	S-A.A. Jin	Academic article – Marketing Intelligence & Planning doi:10.1108/02634501211273805	C	Empirical study	2012	Survey carried out to encourage participants to explore Louis Vuitton's Facebook page and fill out a questionnaire on their satisfaction in relation to the company's page and other endogenous variables. The paper focuses on the potential of social media in luxury brands management.	12
If you love something, let it go mobile: mobile marketing and mobile social media	Social Media, Mobile marketing, Mobile social media, geo-localization, smartphone, Foursquare	A.M. Kaplan	Academic article – Business Horizons doi:10.1016/j.bushor.2011.10.009	B	Descriptive article	2012	The article aims at highlighting the importance of mobile phones and introducing mobile marketing and mobile social media in general.	10
Brand in the hand: a cross-market investigation of consumer acceptance of mobile marketing	Mobile marketing, Branding, Marketing communications, wireless communications, consumer acceptance of new technology, global marketing	A.J. Rohm, T.T. Gao, F. Sultan, M. Pagani	Academic article – Business Horizons doi:10.1016/j.bushor.2012.05.004	B	Descriptive article	2012	Considering the significant evolution of communication technology, this article investigates those factors influencing mobile marketing use in three important markets: United States, China and Europe. These three markets are influenced by perceived usefulness, consumer's innovation and personal attachment.	8

Article	Main topics (Keywords)	Author/s	Type of article and Source	Ranking Journal	Method	Date	Observations	Page
Diffusion and success factors of mobile marketing	Mobile data services, SMS, mobile commerce, online marketing, Web content analysis	A. Scharl, A. Dickinger, J. Murphy	Academic article – Electronic commerce research and application doi:10.1016/j.elerap.2004.10.006	D	Quantitative analysis	2012	This article investigates SMS, the most effective form of mobile communications. Multinational organizations use SMS for their mobile marketing campaigns.	14
Unintended Brand Endorsers' Impact on Luxury Brand Image	Luxury brands, brand endorsement, brand image	A. Radón	International Journal of Marketing Studies	-	Two case studies, online and offline interviews with consumers	2012	This article offers in-depth interviews (online) with luxury consumers reporting their perceptions on brand's image.	8
Managing luxury brands	Luxury goods, up-market brand, ordinary brand, luxury brand's nature	J.N. Kapferer	Academic article – Journal of Brand Management doi:10.1057/bm.1997.4	C	Descriptive article	2012	The article draws attention to luxury brandOs' characteristics and highlights their essential management difference in relation to non-luxury brands.	8
A survey of prediction using Social Media	Social networking service, UGC, prediction methods, social media, marketing	S. Yu, S. Kak	Non-academic article – arxiv.org	-	Descriptive article	2012	Theoretical framework, emotions analysis system (qualitative), forecasting models, analysis system on social media. The paper introduces a forecasting survey about the use of social media, providing a general summary on forecasting methods and factors.	20
Social Media and Luxury Brand Management: The Case of Burberry	Growing importance of social networks, Web 2.0, Creation of UGC, Blogs, Forums, Potential of social media, Burberry's social media strategy	M. Phan, R. Thomas, K. Heine	Academic article – Journal of Global Fashion Marketing doi:10.1080/20932685.2011.10593099	D	Descriptive article about British brand Burberry	2011	It describes Burberry's luxury image revamp over the last ten years.	9

Article	Main topics (Keywords)	Author/s	Type of article and Source	Ranking Journal	Method	Date	Observations	Page
The Effect of the Lifestyles of Social Networking Service Users on Luxury Brand Loyalty	Marketing application potential of social networking services by analyzing their influence on brand loyalty, Statistics, Exploratory factor analysis, Cluster analysis	J. Park, H. Song, E. Ko	Academic article – Journal of Global Scholars of Marketing Science doi:10.1080/21639159.2011.9726521	-	Empirical study	2011	The article focuses on social networking services (SNSs)'s marketing potential, studying its influence on brand's loyalty.	10
Top 10 Need-to-Knows about Social Networking and where it's headed	Social networking behaviour, Facebook, microblogging, digital natives, mobile devices	T. Toy	Non-academic article – comscore.com	-	Descriptive article	2011	The report is a summary of social networking activities drafted by observing digital consumers' behavior.	27
Social marketing and New Media Predictions	Predictions for the biggest social marketing developments, role of big data, key technologies to impact social marketing, role of mobile in social, top challenges for social marketers	34 Authors (among them: B. Solis, J. Falls, D. Peck, M. Lewis, A. Patterson, D. Haslam)	Non-academic article – brandchannel.com	-	Interview with 34 marketing experts, analysts, consultants and agencies	2011	Interview with 34 marketing experts, analysts, consultants and agencies. The paper gathers marketing experts' opinions on social media.	30

Article	Main topics (Keywords)	Author/s	Type of article and Source	Ranking Journal	Method	Date	Observations	Page
Report on Social Media: Swiss Luxury watches	Integration of social media channels, opportunity to interact, online community, co-creation of value, twitalyzer, social engagement, quality of relationship in social media of the Swiss watch brands, presence online	J. Araoz, J. Bandick, P. Berg Per, D. Gumiel, P. Melo, M. Pozzoli, D. Stavitskiy, M. Verna	Non-academic article – swiss-smm.blogspot.it	-	Descriptive article	2011	An analysis of brand and social media forms followed by assessment forms based on 7 variables: social presence, customer management with commitment/ dialogue, support, innovation, value connection, communication leadership, emotion management/awareness. The article investigates how Rolex, Patek Philippe and Omega have integrated social media on their websites. The three companies' YouTube channel, Facebook, LinkedIn and Twitter profiles, Forum and Blog are analyzed.	10
The Facebook App Economy	Active users, connections, Facebook platform, "like", Canvas App	II-H. Hann, S. Viswanathan, B. Koh	Non-academic article – billboard.com	-	Theoretical framework	2011	An assessment of Facebook's impact on the USA job market is given using 4 mathematical models. The paper highlights the importance of Facebook in people's relationships.	7
Luxury Brands in Social Media. How to maintein the allure of luxury online	Internet users, behaviour luxury brands online, bloggers, Storytelling 2.0, Social platforms	C. Lesage	Non-academic article – synthesio.com	-	Case study	2011	The document aims at understanding how luxury companies can maintain Web prestige.	9
Co-creating value for luxury brands	Types of value for luxury brands, case study	C. Tynan, S. McKechnie, C. Chhuon	Academic article – Journal of Business Research	A	Theoretical frameworks, reasearch case study	2010	The authors develop a theoretical framework in relation to luxury brand's value types and use a case study to identify value creation processes.	7
Predicting the Future with Social Media	Social media content, Twitter, sentiment analysis, movies	S. Asur, B.A. Huberman	Non-academic article – International Conference on Web Intelligence and Intelligent Agent Technology	-	Experimental study	2010	The paper shows how to use social media content to foresee real world outcomes; in particular, the authors focus on Twitter's chat to predict film's revenues and demonstrate how emotions can be used to improve social media's prediction power.	8

Article	Main topics (Keywords)	Author/s	Type of article and Source	Ranking Journal	Method	Date	Observations	Page
Luxury online: Style, Systems, Strategies	Web 2.0, E-experience, Art of selling the dream online, E-people, Best and worst practices of luxury online	U. Okonkwo	Palgrave Macmillan	-	Descriptive paper with case analysis	2010	The reason why luxury should be online is no longer relevant today. Instead, the author considers how luxury should be presented online, in particular how it should take into account consumers' virtual experiences. The document reveals how digital challenges can be overcome without loosing sight of luxury brands' intrinsic characteristics.	385
The Impact of New Media on Customer Relationship	New media, customer relationship, electronic word-of-mouth, online community, recommendation systems, mobile technologies	T. Hennig-Thurau, E.C. Malthouse, C. Friege	Academic article – Journal of Service Research doi:10.1177/109467051037 5460	A	Descriptive article with theoretical framework	2010	The paper introduces a framework on social media impact on customer relationships.	20
Who's Author, Editor and Publisher in User-generated Content? Apllying Traditional Media Concepts to UGC Providers	UGC, liability, platform provider	P. Valcke, M. Lenaerts	Academic article – International Review of Law, Computers & Technology doi:10.1080/1360086100364 4533	-	Descriptive article	2010	This study analyzes UGC legal accountability focusing both on the role of traditional players in the information chain value and on new intermediaries.	12
Evolution of blogs as a credible marketing communication tool	two-way marketing conversation, dialogue, blog, virtual world, digital medium	M. Maurya	Journal of Case Research	-	Descriptive article with case study	2010	The article discusses blogs' growing influence, their evolution and adoption by marketing for communication purposes.	20

Article	Main topics (Keywords)	Author/s	Type of article and Source	Ranking Journal	Method	Date	Observations	Page
Impacts of Luxury fashion Brand's Social Media Marketing on Customer Relationship and Purchase Intention	Use of social media, effect of social media marketing (SMM), Properties of social media, Regression analysis	A. Jiyoung Kim, E. Ko	Academic article – Journal of Global Fashion Marketing doi:10.1080/20932685.2010.10593068	D	Experimental study	2010	Preliminary test: 150 questionnaires distributed, 133 used for statistical analysis; multiple regression analysis to test the effects of social media marketing. The study in the article investigates the effect of social media marketing on customer's relationships and purchasing intentions.	7
The effect of consumer-to consumer interactions on idea generation in virtual brand community relationships	C2C interaction, human capital, brand knowledge, idea generation	C. Wus, W. Fang	Academic article – Technovation doi:10.1016/j.technovation.2010.07.005	B	Experimental study	2010	This document investigates C2C and the relationship between brand knowledge and generation of ideas in the brand's virtual communities. The outcome shows how consumers' interactions are positively associated with the creation of new ideas. Therefore human capital should be given significant importance.	11
Luxury wine brand visibility in social media: an exploratory study	Ascendance of social media, Study of Bordeaux first growth	M. Reyneke, L. Pitt, P.R. Berthon	Academic article – International Journal of Wine Business Research doi:10.1108/17511061111121380	-	Experimental study	2010	The paper gathers data from howsociable.com; 13 social media websites (MySpace, LinkedIn...) and with the creation of contingency tables, the latter used to start the analysis using Xistat. The paper describes wine luxury brands in a multi-dimensional space.	15
Crafting integrted multichannel retailing strategies	Retail strategy, cross-channel synergy, Internet retailing, consumer behaviour, channel format, retail mix decision	J. Zhang, P. Farris, J. Irvin, T. Kushwaha, T. Steenburgh	Academic article – Journal of Interactive Marketing doi:10.1016/j.intmar.2010.02.002	A	Descriptive article	2010	The authors give an overview of the opportunities offered by multichannel sales to create synergies between channels and the challenges for new strategies.	12

Article	Main topics (Keywords)	Author/s	Type of article and Source	Ranking Journal	Method	Date	Observations	Page
User-Generated Content	Definition of UGC, Forms, Drivers, Product recommendation	N. Balasubramaniam	Seminar of Advanced Topics	-	Descriptive article	2009	The paper explains the the development of social platforms like Facebook and Wikipedia.	6
Anti-branding on the Internet	Anti-consumption, online consumption, two empirical studies	S. Krishnamurthy, S. Umit Kucuk	Academic article –Journal of Business Research doi:10.1016/j.jbusres.2008.09.003	A	Experimental study	2009	The article investigates causalities in the two empirical studies on anti-branding.	7
The anatomy of the luxury fashion brand	Luxury fashion branding, brand management	A.M. Fionda, C.M. Moore	Academic article – Journal of Brand Management doi:10.1057/bm.2008.45	C	Descriptive article	2009	This document explores criticalities brands should consider to be successful in luxury markets, exploring connections and experiences in association with companies' managers.	16
Sustaining the luxury brand on the Internet	Luxury ant the Internet, webmosphere, e-business, sensory goods	U. Okonkwo	Academic article – Journal of Brand Management doi:10.1057/bm.2009.2	C	Descriptive article	2009	The paper instigates the core and goals of luxury business, with particular attention to branding in digital environments.	9
Does Internet really matter for the luxury goods industry?	Rise of the Internet and its impact on business, Distribution and branding strategies	R. Chadel	Non-academic article – www.chadel.ch	-	Descriptive article	2009	The article considers the importance of the Web for luxury companies.	4
Twitter Power: Tweets as Electronic Word of Mouth	Research results investigating microblogging as a form of electronic word-of-mouth for sharing consumer opinions concerning brands	B.J. Jansen, M. Zhang, K. Sobel, A. Chowdury	Academic article – Journal of the American Society for Information Science and Technology doi:10.1002/asi.21149	-	Experimental study	2009	The article collects the main outcomes of the survey on micro-blogging as word of mouth to share consumers' opinions about the brand. More than 150 micro-blogs reporting comments and opinions have been examined. Graphics and tables are available.	19

Article	Main topics (Keywords)	Author/s	Type of article and Source	Ranking Journal	Method	Date	Observations	Page
Social media: the new hybrid element of the promotion mix	Integrated marketing communications, Social media, Consumer-generated media	W. Glynn Mangold, D.J. Faulds	Academic article – Business Horizons doi:10.1016/j.bushor.2009.03.002	B	Descriptive article	2009	The article explains the importance of social media for companies in relation to the larger audience they can reach through the Internet.	8
Being Immersed in Social Networking Environment: Facebook Groups, Uses and Gratifications, and Social Outcomes	Facebook Groups users' gratifications, socializing, entertainment, self-status seeking, user demographics, civic and political involvement	N. Park, K.F. Kee, S. Valenzuela	Academic article – Cyber Psichology & Behavior doi:10.1089/cpb.2009.0003.	-	Reasearch carried out on 1,715 college students between 18 and 29 years of age	2009	The article investigates users' level of gratification in Facebook groups and its relationship with users' offline participation.	5
Co-creation and User-generated Content-Elderly People´s User Requirements	Elderly people, UGC, online community, user requirements	A. Karahasanovic, P.B. Brandtzaeg, J. Heim, G. Jans	Non-academic article – Computers in human behavior	-	Exploratory studies conducted in several countries (Norway, Belgium)	2009	This article introduces three studies on users' needs in relation to UGC co-creation, use and consumption. The first study focuses on Internet use and the need of taking part in online communities. The second one defines the social needs leading to production of UGCs. The third study investigates both users and environment's needs at an individual level.	23
User-Generated Content: The case for Mobile Services	User-generated mobile services, mobile Internet, invisible computing	C.S. Jensen, C.R. Vicente, R. Wind	Academic article – IEEE Computer	-	Descriptive article with case study	2009	Web applications, as well as mobile devices, encourage users to produce content. The document investigates the effects on the supply of mobile devices to users and the possibility of producing and sharing content.	-
Small versus big stories in framing consumption experiences	Experience, consumer research, consumer behaviour	A. Carù, B. Cova	Academic article – Qualitative Market Research doi:10.1108/13522750810864422	C	Descriptive article	2008	The document analyzes changes in consumers' purchasing habits as they become more self-aware. They are story makers, talk about their inner feelings and experience and share them through the Internet.	10

Article	Main topics (Keywords)	Author/s	Type of article and Source	Ranking Journal	Method	Date	Observations	Page
Exploring consumer motivations for creating user-generated content	Impact of UGCs on consumers, media providers and marketing preofessionals; and short and long term effects of using this multimedia content	T. Daugherty, M.S. Eastin, L. Bright	Acaddemic article – Journal of Interactive Advertising doi:10.1080/15252019.2008. 10722139	-	Experimental study	2008	Exploratory study/Survey: 325 participants over a period of 7 days with 1,000 emails sent out from the first day, 1,500 in 3 days and 500 on the fifth day. The survey concluded after only receiving 325 filled-out questionnaires. The paper aims at uncovering the attitudinal factors at the origin of creation and consumption of UGCs.	9
Multichannel shopper segments and their covariates	Multichannel, Internet, shopping behaviour, segmentation, retailing, innovativeness	U. Konus, P.C. Verhoef, S.A. Neslin	Academic article – Journal of Retailing doi:10.1016/j.jretai.2008.09. 002	A	Experimental study	2008	Channels' proliferation is a new challenge for research, which can now segment consumers on the basis of their need for information and their purchasing habits in a multichannel environment.	15
Partecipative web and user-generated content	UGC, worldwide communication, implications for policy	G. Vickery, S. Wunsch-Vincent	OECD	-	Descriptive article	2008	This study describes the rapid growth of UGCs and their ever-increasing communication role around the world. The large variety of smart web services and applications enables an increasing number of people to create, distribute and use UGCs as part of a more active web.	74
Multichannel Shopping: Causes and Consequences	Customer profitability, channel adoption duration, multichannel marketing resources, multichannel shopping	R. Venkatesann, V. Kumar	Academic article – Journal of Marketing doi:10.1509/jmkg.71.2.114	A	Descriptive article	2007	Hypothesis on the impact of customer-company different interaction characteristics can be formulated considering the social exchange theory and the customer database of a clothing manufacturer selling its products on three channels. Authors explore multichannel shopping drives and the impact of commercial multichannel activities on customers' profitability.	18

Article	Main topics (Keywords)	Author/s	Type of article and Source	Ranking Journal	Method	Date	Observations	Page
Measuring the value of electronic word of mouth and its impact in consumer community	Message boards, Chat rooms, Virtual brand community, word of mouth, social network	P. Dwyer	Academic article – Journal of Interactive Marketing doi:10.1002/dir.20078	A	Descriptive article	2007	The study introduces a new measurement unit (APR, adapted PageRank) which measures the value communities place on Word-of-Mouth and on their own creators. The article focuses on electronic word-of-mouth and its impact on online communities.	16
Motivations to produce User Generated Content:Differences between Webbloggers and Videobloggers	UGC, motivations, video content, Web 2.0	R. Stoeckl, P. Rohrmeier, T. Hess	Non-academic article – Proceedings of 20th Bled eConferences eMergence	-	Exploratory investigation	2007	This exploratory study investigates what motivates Webloggers and Videobloggers to create UGCs. There are several motivations. Video production is associated with fun, weblogging is considered a way of sharing information and expressing personality.	16
I Tube, You Tube, Everybody Tubes: Analyzing the World's Largest User Generated Content Video System	UGC sites, social interactions, popularity life-cycle of videos	M. Cha, H. Kwak, P. Rodriguez, Y.Y. Ahn, S. Moon	Non-academic article – dl.acm.org	-	Descriptive article	2007	The article focuses on social YouTube, investigating videos' popularity lifecycle, request's intrinsic statistic properties and their connection with the age of the video.	14
Personalized content recommendation and user satisfaction: Theoretical synthesis and empirical findings	Personalized services, Internet world, user satisfaction	T.P. Liang, H.J. Lai, Y.C. Ku	Academic article – Journal of Management Information Systems doi:10.2753/MIS0742-1222230303	B	Descriptive article	2006	This study identifies theories linked to the use of personalized services and their effect on customers' satisfaction. Customers' satisfaction is higher when customers are explicitly involved in the content generation process.	25

Article	Main topics (Keywords)	Author/s	Type of article and Source	Ranking Journal	Method	Date	Observations	Page
Impact of personal orientation on luxury-brand purchase value: an international investigation	Antecedents and consequence of personal orientation towards luxury brand consumption	S.P. Tsai	Market Research Society	-	Theoretical frameworks, empirical results	2005	The article identifies a model about personal orientation to luxury goods' consumption. The study gathers data from Asia, Europe and America.	25
Free-riding and customer retention across retailers' channel	Free-riding rate, retailing, cross-channel consumer behaviour, channel management, elationship between retailers and manufacturers	S. Van Baals, C. Dach	Academic article – Journal of Interactive Marketing doi:10.1002/dir.20036	A	Explorational investigation	2005	When consumers use more than one channel within a single transaction, they benefit from several retailers. The authors claim that more than 20% of consumers use several channels at the same time according to the selected product (research, speed of technological change, frequency of purchase).	10
Selling Luxury Brands Online	Online selling of luxury brands, Internet presence, Survey of 190 luxury brands	F.H. Rolf Seringhaus	Academic article – Journal of Internet Commerce doi:10.1300/J179v04n01_01	D	Explorational investigation	2005	The paper examines luxury brands' online sales issues.	25
Can the luxury fashion brand store atmosphere be transferred to the Internet?	Customisation and personalisation, Luxury consumers, Interactive flash animation	U. Okonkwo	Non-academic article – brandchannel.com	-	Descriptive article	2005	The document analyzes the most important elements needed to transfer luxury brand's prestige into the Web.	5
Luxury branding on the Internet: lost opportunity or impossibility?	Internet and the luxury sector, Managers' attitudes, Consumers' perceptions, Web content analysis	F. Dall'Olmo Riley, C. Lacroix	Academic article – Marketing Intelligence & Planning doi:10.1108/02634500031046 5407	C	Descriptive article	2003	The study is divided in three parts: the first one investigates luxury companies' aptitudes to promoting their brands on the Internet; the second one assesses consumers' behaviors and opinions. Finally, the third part investigates companies' inclination to use the Internet to promote luxury brands.	9

Article	Main topics (Keywords)	Author/s	Type of article and Source	Ranking Journal	Method	Date	Observations	Page
The market valuation of Internet channel addition	Distribution channel, Internet channel, performance potential	I. Geyskens, K. Gielens, M.G. Dekimpe	Academic article – Journal of Marketing doi:10.1509/jmkg.66.2.102.18478	A	Exploratory study with empirical outcomes	2002	Internet proliferation led several well-established companies to explore this new distribution channel. According to the authors, Internet investments show, in average, a positive value because of a higher advertising presence.	17
Branding matters more on the Internet	Brand equity, e-branding, e-tailing, brand-building, personality, Internet	H. Rubinstein, C. Griffiths	Academic article –Journal of Brand Management doi:10.1057/palgrave.bm.2540039	B	Descriptive article	2001	This document examines how the Internet has changed companies' brand management. On the Internet, the brand is the core of the strategy. The emphasis is shifted to so-called "brand experience". The authors investigate the process of building a brand's image, both online and offline, trying to integrate internal and external values.	10

A summary of the main scientific academic journals and related number of articles, taken from the previous table, is reported here:

-   *Ranking A* (23 articles): Mercati e Competitività, Journal of Business Research, Journal of Interactive Marketing, Journal of Service Research, Journal of Retailing, Journal of Marketing;
-   *Ranking B* (8 articles): Journal of Strategic Marketing, Business Horizons, Technovation, Journal of Management Information Systems;
-   *Ranking C* (10 articles): Journal of marketing communications, Marketing Review, Marketing Intelligence & Planning, Journal of Brand Management, Qualitative Market Research;
-   *Ranking D* (7 articles): Journal of Global fashion Marketing, Journal of Internet Commerce, Electronic Commerce Research and Application, Journal of Internet Commerce.

The 93 articles listed in the previous table can then be divided in four categories:

-   *Brand community*: collects mostly academic articles investigating different grouping options for consumers' web communities distinguishing between physical communities, first online communities and more recent communities of online consumers.
-   *Digital media, the Internet and luxury brands*: it gathers articles on digital marketing phenomena applied to luxury brands.
-   *Social media*: collects articles aimed at understanding new digital channels, especially social networks. In particular the following topics are discussed: the power of Twitter as an electronic word-of-mouth, the use of social media and their impact on young American and Arab people's purchasing intentions, the brand's online management and performances, the importance of electronic word-of-mouth, the impact on communities and the economy revolving around the main social network (Facebook).
-   *Luxury and social media*: it includes articles about the relationship between brand and digital channels. Articles in this category investigate the relationship between luxury fashion brand communities, luxury wines visibility on social media and its implications, online luxury communication and consumption, Internet as an opportunity (or a threat) to luxury companies, exclusivity and ubiquity in the digital era, luxury atmospheric presence on websites, challenges of luxury positioning on social networks and e-commerce. Brands focusing their strategies on digital channels (for example Burberry) are mentioned as an example.

Research work will now be displayed in a chronological-conceptual order. In fact, we will focus on the notion of brand community and its development by describing user-created content, the relationship between users and companies – in particular high symbolic value brands – and their use to promote company's brands.

A1.2. Brand community

Definition. The term *"brand community"* was created in 2001 by Muniz and O'Guinn who defined it as *"a specialized community with no specific geographical location created as a result of the social interactions among users"*.

Mc Alexander *et al*. in 2002 clarified how in today's ultracompetitive markets, the traditional product differentiation model is no longer the best solution. One of the best solutions to differentiate is, in fact, to develop and foster brand communities.

In 2008, Keller gave a useful and complete definition of brand community: *"A name, word, sign, symbol or sketch, or their combination, identifying a seller or a group of sellers' products or services aimed at distinguishing them from the competition's"*. According to this definition, brands can be assessed and measured. This is the objective of brand equality which can be defined as the *"aggregate of resources"* (or costs) associated with the brand's name and symbol and is added to (or subtracted from) the value offered to customers or companies by a good or service (Aaker, 1991).

Companies develop branding strategies aimed at increasing their products' perceived value in a specific market. This mainly involves the development of symbols and the so-called brand storytelling, which allows for a special emotional link between consumers and the *"narrating"* company (Fournier, 1998).

Brand communities foster emotional relationships between consumers and companies and develop effectively high and sustainable levels of brand equity. Muñiz and O'Guinn have shown how the most important brand communities thrive in highly competitive markets and around brands with a significant heritage. Therefore, brand practices and brand communities are undeniably intertwined.

The development of online brand communities. The first studies on brand communities date back to the end of the XX century, when most of the literature was focused on physical communities. Back then, people would actually meet up to share their experiences as consumers. Academics pointed out that these online communities shared some common features, which are still valid today in spite of the changes precipitated by digital technologies:

- Members' sense of belonging and their differentiation from non-members;
- Members are considered a means to transmit the brand's values;
- Members tend to show respect and loyalty to other members and the community itself.

The Internet and information and communication new technologies (ICT) prompted literature to acknowledge the brand communities milestone switch from physical to virtual. Researchers are trying to understand what motivates people to engage in these communities, analyzing the attributes of virtual communities as opposed to physical ones' (Granitz and Ward, 1996).

Communication among individuals far away from each other is now possible on the Internet. This enriches interactions and new connections between customers and customers and brand (Thomsen *et al.*, 1998).

De Valk *et al.* (2009) provide a good definition of online brand communities. These are: *"geographically free, based on social communication and relationships between consumers and brand"*. Brand communities have shown a strong ability to spread around and influence the non-virtual world more than physical brand communities.

The development of online brand communities expands the concept of brand community itself. Mc Alexander *et al.* (2002)'s perspective – defined customer-centric – builds on Muñiz and O'Guinn (2001)'s vision. In fact, according to the formers, brand communities are not a mere group of consumers sharing the same interest in a brand but offer significant consumer experiences through companies. These experiences strengthen consumers' interactions and are cheaper and easier to grow digitally than physically. In fact, through the Internet, companies could decrease their branding practices' costs and reach a potentially larger audience.

Consumer Brand Engagement. A fundamental concept must be considered when analyzing the interactions between consumers and reference brands (in brand communities and not): consumer brand engagement (CBE). Gambetti *et al.* (2012) talk about CBE as a multidimensional concept aimed at establishing a long-lasting relationship with its target through emotions, a strong and easy-to-feed component in the current global market.

Brand engagement is based on the idea of reciprocity and is expressed through three main elements: knowledge, courtship and living together.

- Knowledge represents the transparency with which consumers can access information in relation to the brand and its values. The brand's degree of accessibility and availability in everyday life is very important.
- Courtship, which has to do with the brand's charm. This concept has two specific aspects: egocentrism and non-conventional communication. The first one has to do with the effect of brand's charm on consumers. Through the brand, consumers are willing to feel unique, stating their identity and vanity. Non-conventional communication involves the charm of a new brand, still perceived as original.
- Living together, where brand engagement happens: brand and consumer interact, represent and influence each other. Consumers express themselves through the brand and, vice versa, the brand makes itself visible in everyday life through consumers.

CBEs allow companies to enter their customers' houses and share their history and values, getting in touch with what Gambetti *et al.* call society's "soul".

Brand community and value creation. According Schau *et al.* (2009), brand communities contribute to value creation. Brand-consumer closeness created by brand communities can generate a process of value co-creation, which, sometimes, represents the whole company's marketing plan (Lusch and Vargo, 2006). This can simply be a process of content creation with the customers but can go beyond that, becoming a real co-creation, more or less intense, of products or services. In some cases, customers' influence on goods' general appearance is limited. In other cases, however, customers directly take part in the creation process. Using this kind of shared process, companies can develop messages and images which will be promoted by consumers themselves, who also influence marketing strategies.

This is arguably a very powerful tool, which helps companies to avoid branding strategies mistakes when launching new products (Bacon, 2013).

Brand communities are quite closed and difficult to access (and sometimes not for free) while online brand communities are more widely spread, open and visible (Brodie *et al.*, 2011): more widely spread as they can avoid geographical limitations; more open as they are free of charge; more visible because of the Internet.

At the same time, consumer's reasons for being part of a community have become stronger. This is due to the transparency of the brand identity, which is available online but cannot be found in offline communities (Naylor *et al.*, 2012).

Online communities' visibility and popularity leave less room for inaccuracy in relation to brand identity. Brands and companies are more exposed to comments and criticism. This, in return, encourages customers to commit as they know they will get real feedback about the brand and its authenticity.

The impact of brand communities on marketing strategies. Online brand communities are completely transforming marketing methods and processes. Branding activities in the digital era tend to be complex due to consumers' increasing level of influence: brand-consumer relationships have become more promiscuous on the web and interactions have multiplied on blogs and social media. Therefore, marketers need to integrate their marketing strategies with social media, blog and forum activities when managing customers.

Mc William (2000) has proved that fostering relationships within brand communities strengthens brands. He pointed out an important difference between spontaneous and commercial communities: spontaneous communities can generate a strong enthusiasm about the brand but are more difficult to control than commercial communities. The success of spontaneous communities springs from the trust its members put on each other. All members feel equal without that information gap typical of brand-managed communities. In this regard, Mc William highlights the importance of content for the so-called marketed brand communities (managed by the brand itself). They are more appealing when their content is more spontaneous and less commercial or controlled. According to Mc William, companies should borrow their content from non-marketed communities in order to be successful in their online branding practices.

Therefore, each customer-brand interaction through social media, blogs and website is precious: Naylor *et al.* (2012) support this theory and stress the importance of mini-connections within the online community. Their positive effects on the brand are often more significant than the relationship/interaction established between customer and brand at the moment of purchasing.

Marketed vs. non-marketed brand community. The difference between consumer-created and marketed-created online communities is a recurrent topic. In order to distinguish them, several research studies focus on customer involvement strategies. Doohwang *et al.* (2011) state that consumers achieve different goals on the basis of brand community types: personal gain or altruism.

As proved, consumers value altruism, thus preferring consumer-created communities, which are used by companies to address some specific communities and plan their strategies in accordance with the expectations of the community itself. These communities allow marketing managers to plan their strategies on the basis of customers' lifestyles and not only age, gender or income (Bacon, 2013).

A1.3. User Generated Content

Definitions. The phrasing *User Generated Content* (UGC) started being popular in 2005 to describe the active, and sometimes fundamental, role of users in the creation of website content.

Christodoulides *et al.* (2012) define UGC as content that: *"Is available to the public through means of communication, for example the Internet, entails a sort of creative effort and is created for free and non-professionally"*.

This definition, based on users' creative effort, is similar to the definition of *Consumer-Generated Media* (CGM) given by Maurya (2010): *"A series of new online information sources created (...) and used by consumers willing to educate other consumers on products, brands, services"*. Both definitions highlight the importance of communication and dialogue for user-generated content. Consumers dialogue with brands through their comments online about product characteristics, advertisement strategies and even their perception of the brand.

OECD (Organisation for Economic Cooperation and Development) in 2007 endorsed these definitions and outlined some characteristics:

- Publication requirements: it has to be user-generated content available on a web platform (an Internet website or a social network group). Thus, they do not include content sent via chats, emails, etc.
- Creative effort: a certain amount of effort is put in creating new material or

adapting old material to generate something new. Users are required to add their own value to the work. UGC's creative effort is often cooperative. An example of this is the cooperation between users and websites aimed at changing content. It is, however, difficult to establish the minimum creative effort required.

- Creation outside professional practices and routines: content created in the framework of economic and professional activities is excluded.

UGC classification. OECD research classifies *User Generated Content* on the basis of distribution platforms. Types of UGC are:

- Text: original texts, novels, poems;
- Photos and images: digital pictures posted online by users; photos or images created or edited by users;
- Music and audio: digital audio recordings;
- Videos and films: video recordings including remix or existing content;
- Active journalism: reports on current events communicated by ordinary people;
- Educational content: content created in schools and universities with an educational purpose;
- Mobile-created content: content created on cell phones or other wireless devices, like text messages, photos and videos. They are usually sent via MMS, emailed or uploaded to the Internet;
- Content created within the context of an online virtual environment or integrated into it.

Table A1.2 shows the listed UGC types and gives some examples of them.

Table A1.2 UGC Types

Type of Content	Description	Examples
Text, novel and poetry	Original writings or expanding on other texts, novels, poems	Fanfiction.net, Quizilla.com, Writely
Photo/Images	Digital photographs taken by users and posted online; Photos or images created or modified by users	Photos posted on sites such as Ofoto and Flickr; Photo blogging; Remixed images
Music and Audio	Recording and/or editing one's own audio content and publishing, syndicating, and/or distributing it in digital format	Audio mash-ups, remixes, home-recorded music on bands websites or MySpace pages, Podcasting
Video and Film	Recording and/or editing video content and posting it. Includes remixes of existing content, homemade content, and a combination of the two	Movie trailer remixes; Lip synching videos; Video blogs and videocasting; Posting home videos; Hosting sites include YouTube and Google Video; Current TV
Citizen journalism	Journalistic reporting on current events done by ordinary citizens. Such citizens write news stories, blog posts, and take photos or videos of current events and post them online.	Sites such as OhmyNews, GlobalVoices and NowPublic; Photos and videos of newsworthy events; Blog posts reporting from the site of an event; Cooperative efforts such as CNN Exchange

Educational content	Content created in schools, universities, or with the purpose of educational use	Syllabus-sharing sites such as H20; Wikibooks, MIT's OpenCourseWare
Mobile content	Content that is created on mobile phones or other wireless devices such as text messaging, photos and videos. Generally sent to other users via MMS (Media Messaging Service), emailed, or uploaded to the Internet	Videos and photos of public events, environments such as natural catastrophes that the traditional media may not be able to access; Text messages used for political organising
Virtual content	Content created within the context of an online virtual environment or integrated into it. Some virtual worlds allow content to be sold. User-created games are also on the rise	Variety of virtual goods that can be developed and sold on Second Life including clothes, houses, artwork

Source: Vickery G., Wunsch-Vincent S., *Participative web and user-created content. Web 2.0, wikis and social networking*, OECD, 2007, p. 15.

UGC distribution platforms are:

- Blogs: websites with content organized in a chronological order. Blogs are usually managed by bloggers who publish multimedia content as text or posts. This idea reminds us of a newspaper article.
- Wikis: a collection of web pages created with cooperation between users (for example Wikipedia).
- Websites where users can give each other feedback on written works.
- Aggregators: websites whose content is organized through virtual bookmarks (for example Digg, a social bookmarking website born in 2004, where news and connections are fed by users and make it to the top page on the basis of a non-hierarchical system based on other users' evaluation).
- Podcasting websites: websites where audio and video files can be downloaded from (for example iTunes, an Apple application used to reproduce and organize multimedia files which allows users to buy songs, videos and films online on their iTune Store).
- Social networks: social interaction websites (for example Facebook, Twitter, Instagram).
- Virtual environments: virtual simulation of environments. [2]
- Websites for content exchange/sharing among users and artists.

Table A1.3 shows the listed UGC distribution platforms and gives some examples of them.

Table A1.3 UGC distribution platforms

Type of Platform	Description	Examples
Blogs	Web pages containing user-created entries updated at regular intervals and/or user-submitted content that was investigated outside of traditional media	Popular blogs such as BoingBoing and Engadget; Blogs on sites such as LiveJournal; MSN Spaces; CyWorld; Skyblog
Wikis and Other Text-Based Collaboration Formats	A wiki is a website that allows users to add, remove, or otherwise edit and change content collectively. Other sites allow users to log in and cooperate on the editing of particular documents	Wikipedia; Sites providing wikis such as PBWiki, JotSpot, SocialText; Writing collaboration sites such as Writely
Sites allowing feedback on written works	Sites which allow writers and readers with a place to post and read stories, review stories and to communicate with other authors and readers through forums and chat rooms	FanFiction.Net
Group-based aggregation	Collecting links of online content and rating, tagging, and otherwise aggregating them collaboratively	Sites where users contribute links and rate them such as Digg; Sites where users post tagged bookmarks such as del.icio.us
Podcasting	A podcast is a multimedia file distributed over the Internet using syndication feeds, for playback on mobile devices and personal computers	iTunes, FeedBruner, iPodderX, WinAmp, @Podder
Social Network Sites	Sites allowing the creation of personal profiles	MySpace, Facebook, Friendster, Bebo, Orkut, Cyworld
Virtual Worlds	Online virtual environment	Second Life, Active Worlds, Entropia Universe, and Dotsoul Cyberpark
Content or Filesharing sites	Legitimate sites that help share content between users and artists	Digital Media Project

Source: Vickery G., Wunsch-Vincent S., *Participative web and user-created content. Web 2.0, wikis and social networking, OECD*, 2007, p. 15.

New tendencies and development of UGC concept. The volume of content created by consumers has grown exponentially over the past years and research has increased accordingly. Research shows an improvement in the quality of created content. The reasons identified for it are mainly two. On the one hand today's consumers are more self-aware and up for expressing and sharing their purchasing experience (Carù and Cova, 2008), on the other hand – contrary to OECD definition – more and more content is professionally created.

Companies realized the large impact of non-commercial content on consumers and have implemented new strategies borrowing tools and content from non-commercial platforms. Brand's fan pages on social networks are one of the most interesting features of this strategy as they gather the whole community around a wide company-controlled space which, at the same time, is a free area for consumers to express their own opinions.

From content creation to diffusion: Word of Mouth (WOM). The definition of UGC does not cover all content created by consumers on the web and thus it is not the only kind of user-generated information which can influence brands. Word-of-

Mouth (WOM) can have a big influence on the consumer's perceptions of a brand (Allsop *et al.*, 2007).

WOM is very powerful: even the best commercial is less influential than a friend's recommendation. Commercials are suspicious as they are clearly aimed at selling products or services. On the contrary, other people's recommendations are trustworthy as they usually come from people whose taste and habits we know. Customers can then contextualize the recommendation and refer it to their needs. This point relates to what was previously mentioned about the influence of marketed communities in comparison with non-marketed communities.

Emotional reviews are most appreciated (Li and Zhan, 2011). Marketing managers know that and have used some of these reviews' features to increase the success of their communication campaigns. Adjusting their traditional format to whatever is popular on the Internet, brands place their products nearer customer's expectations.

Brands should therefore develop a new model of communication and engagement aimed at increasing conversations between customers on the Internet. Conversations bring along a greater brand awareness and feed online and offline word of mouth. Brands' main challenge is then keeping the tone of conversations as positive as possible (Keller, 2008). This leads to the so-called "integrated marketing communication" (IMC). Born at the end of the eighties, it is the answer to these new communication needs.

A1.4. Social media

From brand community to social media based brand community. Studies have so far focused on the concept of brand community and its influence – especially with the advent of the virtual world – on content and company's strategic approaches.

Social media are nowadays the brand communities' main distribution platforms through dedicated fan pages and they have become a new meeting place for customers and brands.

In 2014, more than 70% of social media users followed their favorite brands on these platforms. Keeping this in mind, companies have invested more in this direction for an estimated cost in 2016 of 4.3 billion dollars (Williamson, 2011).

Kaplan and Haenlein (2010) defined social media as "*a group of Internet-based applications based both ideologically and technologically on web 2.0, allowing bottom-up content sharing*". They are related to two fundamental concepts: web 2.0 and UGC.[3]

Several social media platforms are available today and include social networks, photo sharing websites, wikis, and forums. However, the most popular social media are Facebook, Twitter, YouTube and Wikipedia (Kim and Ko, 2012). They facilitate content and information sharing, strengthen a brand's history and culture and influence brand loyalty by fostering mutual assistance among users and brand advocacy.

According to this definition, with the advent of new technologies, the thin line separating brand communities – as defined by literature – and social media is becoming even thinner. Facebook brand fan pages, Youtube brand channels or Twitter profiles have become virtual communities for consumers following their favorite brands on interactive platforms and can be defined as social media based brand communities.

Companies' use of social media. Literature provides significant information about the use of social media within companies.

The different uses have in common an increasing importance of customer's interactions with the company.

Customers are on social media because they feel the urge of being informed and communicating (Kietzmann *et al.*, 2011), and they consider social platforms as an essential part of their purchasing experience (Larrson and Watson, 2011).

Communication on social media should be bidirectional. Companies should offer their content and at the same time answer customers' requests (Weinberg and Pehlivan, 2011) in a kind of Ping-Pong typical of equal relationships.

The use of social media as marketing tools helps companies to achieve their goals more quickly and effectively: brand awareness, brand engagement and word of mouth have become measurable and traceable indicators in social media (Hoffmann and Fodor, 2010) and reach out to an audience which is much larger than in the past. Again, customer's active participation is fundamental to spreading brand awareness and company's products. Companies do not need to engage in direct actions as some users take up a role of advocacy and evangelization among other users (Altimeter Group, 2010).

Lastly, social media have partially replaced traditional call centers as customer service tools (TNS, 2011): companies need to constantly check social media and interact with customers in real time in order to avoid negative feedback and support their customer base quickly and effectively (Zaglia, 2013).

Mangold and Faulds (2009) summarize this idea describing social media as essential tools for companies' marketing and communication strategies. They do not work as stand-alone products but are part of a whole system, which includes traditional tools and social platforms and aimed at achieving common goals.

Social media and companies: benefits and criticalities. Social media are a powerful tool to reach out to customers and directly communicate with them. The massive use of social media in terms of time spent on these platforms (in particular social networking) has to do with the gratification users receive from activities like informing, communicating and socializing with family and friends in a fun way on the web (Krasnova *et al.*, 2010).

This spontaneous and non-compelled use of social networks is what allows companies to better reach users/customers in terms of marketing and communication.

In general, companies can benefit from social media use for the following reasons:

-   Efficiency: if used for marketing purposes, they allow for more efficient strategies and much higher viral effects than traditional media; similarly, social media can gather data for marketing research at a lower cost than traditional data-collection methods (Kirtiş and Karahan, 2011).
-   Community building: social media gather people living in different social and geographical environments in the name of a common interest – the companies and their products in this case – creating a community where people can express themselves and compare their ideas with others members' (Weber, 2007).
-   Brand awareness: this is facilitated by the extremely high number of social media users who make a large audience at lower costs for companies. Users become, in fact, indirect promoters for companies and their products (Harvard Business Review, 2010).
-   Word of Mouth: social media users take up a central role in company's success creating a word-of-mouth effect which is amplified by web 2.0 potential (Li and Du, 2011).
-   Customer interaction and involvement: customers become part of the company's product realization cycle. They are co-creators in the design phase, developers and testers in the intermediate phase and continuous feedback providers in the after-sales phase (Foux, 2006; Mangold and Faulds, 2012).
-   Loyalty: promotion of loyalty and long-term relationships leads to economic benefits for companies (Harvard Business Review, 2010).

According to the Grant Thornton LLP report Social media and its associated risks (2010), the main criticalities for companies are:

-   Diffusion of proprietary information: one of the main problems associated with social media is the risk of spreading information protected by copyright.
-   Negative comments about the company: they can come from unsatisfied customers or employees and can propagate on social media at a much faster pace than they would on traditional media.
-   Exposure of personal information.
-   Fraud.
-   Obsolete information.

A1.5. Focus: UGC, social media and luxury brand

Luxury brands in digital environments. The concept of luxury can have several definitions. Despite some small differences, most definitions encompass the feeling of fulfillment generated by luxury goods. Even if part of the literature associates their value to high quality standards (Keller, 2008), several authors place the intrinsic value of a luxury brand beyond the product's tangible aspects. According to them, this has primarily to do with symbolic values, like exclusivity and status, and entails luxury as a way of thinking and a lifestyle.

This perspective is both a threat and an opportunity for high symbolic value goods. On the one hand, once a strong brand image has been created, value is generated by association to it. On the other hand, brands should carefully safeguard their image. In fact a loss of exclusivity or status would affect the brand itself, even if the quality of the products has remained unchanged.

This is a challenge for luxury brands – creating and developing digital strategies. As mentioned by Steel (2013), until recently luxury fashion brands were suspicious of digital media. The main concern was the impossibility of accurately representing the brand's image and its emotional connotation in a digital format. Moreover, the Internet conflicted with luxury brands' sacred connotations: the idea of a product that is untouchable, unattainable and out of reach.

Keller describes several intangible aspects related to luxury brands whose online rendering proves difficult (for example the idea of belonging to a restricted and privileged club). He stresses the importance of consistency in luxury brands management strategies. Finally, he highlights that many people still consider the Internet as a bargaining space, on the basis of what the e-commerce used to be. These are the main elements preventing fashion luxury brands from entering the digital arena.

Challenges for luxury companies' management. Challenges springing from shifting products and services from a physical to a digital environment are not new. Some companies simply use the Internet as an information tool, aimed at closing the sale at the store (for example the automobile sector). Despite these difficulties, technological progress and consumer's acceptance of online markets have boosted the digital market.

However, what is at stake for luxury brands is quite significant. In fact, all brands invest in creating an online image to support their identities and values. However, for luxury brands, their image is their actual essence.

Okonkwo (2009) refers to luxury not as a product, service or lifestyle but as an identity, philosophy and culture. According to him, the Internet could over-expose brands whose desirability largely depends on the perception of limited availability. The author still identifies the sensory nature of luxury products based on sight, touch and smell as an essential part of the sales process. This supports the notion of incompatibility between luxury and the Internet.

In spite of the validity of these issues, the need for an online presence of luxury brands is nowadays certain. It is important to keep an open approach to virtual experiences and consider the importance of the ever-growing digital world for the future of luxury.

Keller (2008) defines ten significant luxury brand's characteristics and talks about their management as a precise and controlled process. The Internet, as a place where messages can become "viral", is apparently the inverse of control.

Besides exclusivity, high-end fashion brands sport originality and creativity. The nature of the Internet is threatening for a sector that is traditionally very protective of its design. Artists and stylists represent the essence of many luxury brands whose risk of being copied has been amplified by the advent of the digital era.

Luxury players' change of attitude. As proven by social media, in the last few years several luxury brands have changed their approach to the Internet and web 2.0 technologies. In fact, some important brands have created official Facebook pages and Twitter accounts.

According to some authors, the 2008 economic recession was an impetus in this direction (Clark, 2010; Ortved, 2011). In fact, luxury brands had to find new growth opportunities and the use of the relatively unexplored digital channel was a necessary step for several companies.

The anonymity guaranteed by the Internet was in favorable to high-income people who could keep buying luxury goods in time of recession without being exposed. For example, website Net-A-Porter reported an extraordinary 53% sales increase during 2008 (Grose, 2011).

According to Okonkwo (2009), several brands started to explore the online world only after 2007 and they did so to satisfy their customers' expectations. This is a clear indicator of a change in the top-down relationship between luxury brands and consumers. In fact, while company's websites have been part of their marketing strategies for a long time, luxury brands' acceptance of the Internet is indicated by their more recent investment in social media. Despite the obvious need for image control, campaigns like *Art of the Trench* by *Burberry* and *Poppy* by *Coach* (Kim and Ko, 2010) are examples of creative projects designed by luxury brands to involve consumers.

The literature points out advantages and disadvantages of this approach. However, it is a fact that luxury brands have now discovered new opportunities through web 2.0 and have acknowledged the need for an online presence to create their own content and gain control of online messages, at least partially (Kaplan, 2012).

The Internet and the ever-evolving new digital technologies have increased the debate on the online presence of luxury companies. Some luxury brands have made a big leap over the last 3 to 5 years: from a passive position to active engagement with

Internet and web 2.0 technologies. Even if motives for such a change can differ among the different companies involved, this leap might point at a change in how luxury brands perceive and position themselves in the Internet's open world where anything is no longer private and exclusive.

At this stage, it is not clear whether technologies have evolved to the point of making all the worries associated to a possible image loss on the web groundless or companies have understood the real power of digital media and have consciously decided to use their potential for their communication strategies.

Much literature can be found on the implications of the web for companies but little has been written on what this means for consumers. In fact, one of the main aspects of web 2.0 is its interactive nature and ability to deeply involve users. This has brought along a significant change in consumer behaviors and society in general.

Is this the beginning of a new series of rules for luxury or is it its actual end? According to Okonkwo (2009), the search for excellence is a common feature of all societies and is independent from economic status; if this is true, luxury brands are likely to go through a significant re-definition but will maintain their online presence. Possibly, the next generation of luxury consumer, having grown up with the Internet, will better understand how to access these products and what makes them more or less desirable.

Notes

1   AIDEA (Italian Academy of Business Economics) in 2007 started a project aimed at ranking the best international scientific journals (Journal Rating AIDEA). Ranking criteria include specific and objective characteristics, international rating and bibliometric indicators. Journals are ranked combining these factors and are labeled according to their quality, with A indicating the highest degree of quality.

2   For example Second Life, a new media platform integrating synchronous and asynchronous communication tools and often used in several creative fields: entertainment, art, education, music, cinema, role-play games, architecture, planning, business, etc. or Active Worlds, a 3D virtual reality platform. Users enter the universe of Active Worlds with an alias and explore the virtual world created by other users. Users can chat and use available tools to build houses and areas. Once connected, users can avail of a browser, a voice chat and an instant messaging service.

3   Web 2.0 started in 2004 and is a platform whose software and contents are not only created by companies and official bodies but are generated by different users, in a constant work-in-progress formula. UGC, as mentioned, has to do with how consumers can create content and make it available to other users through social media. They are thus the ideal platforms for the development of creative and co-creative interactions between users and between consumers and brands.

APPENDIX 2
SAMPLE AND METHODOLOGY

This monograph research document aims at establishing some key points in relation to web and social media development. It is a conceptual synthesis of scientific works, discussed at international conferences and in journals, about the use of web as a digital channel and social media by luxury brands: in particular, the research focuses on online presence, reference models, adopted strategies, best and worst places, identification of digital channels and e-commerce alternate approaches, assessment of social-activity-generated traffic.

The Research Questions underpinning the exploratory investigation of a sample of companies, increased over time, are: has the online presence of the considered sample changed over the time span considered? What was the approach to the development of web e-commerce activities on digital channels and what are the reference models? Which social media have the highest number of fan/followers and web and social media activities? Is there any connection between business field and user base? Is there a direct relationship between the extent of the community and the level of interaction? What are the social media strategies adopted by luxury brands? What best practices have been adopted in relation to each social media?

The research data base has included, over time, more new brands, market segments and groups and has consequently selected luxury centers and premium brands as follows: 39 brands in the fashion industry, 15 in the watch and jewelry sector, 15 in perfumery and cosmetics, 16 in the automotive sector and 15 in the wine and spirits sector.

The period of observation and analysis spanned from April 2013 to September 2016 and involved an ever-growing number of brands. The subject of the analysis: the presence of luxury brands on four websites and official websites. The social networks involved were Facebook, Twitter, YouTube, Instagram and, for some analysis, Pinterest. With regard to Facebook, four parameters were taken into consideration: Fans – the number of people who "liked" the brand's official page, showing interest and establishing a connection. As a consequence of that, the Fan Page was visible on the profile of the user whose name was then added to the list of "likers" and in social plug-ins. Furthermore, the page's last posts were showing in the user's news section. This parameter thus shows the number of potential readers of the brand's published content. According to Cosenza (2013) and Gentili (2015), however, only a few posts make it to the fans' news feed (about 10%). In fact, Facebook indexation algorithm selects content on the basis of a series of parameters, which consider user's interests and their friends' behaviors. Therefore, a wider distribution is a direct consequence of a greater generated stimulus. In fact, we cannot limit our analysis to the fan base but should consider more deeply the content quantity and quality and the generated engagement.

People talking about it: users who have created a story in relation to the page (by "liking" a content, writing on the wall, sharing a Post, answering a question, interacting with an event, tagging or mentioning the page). The number reported is updated daily but always refers to the previous seven days. This parameter was introduced to minimize Facebook's fan trade phenomenon thus providing a more reliable figure about the page's quality and the activity of its administrators. Number of posts: it is the total amount of links, photos and videos published by a company in a given day. It is an indicator of the activity and how frequently the page is updated. Types of posts: it is the number of photos, videos and links published in a given day. It provides information on the company's editorial strategy. Post content: this indicator divides posts on the basis of their content: promotional or entertaining. Promotional posts are photos, links or videos aimed at selling a product or a service. In this category: links to e-commerce, photos of the stars wearing a certain product, albums showing the last collection, advertisement videos and everything that is traditional business. Entertainment posts aim at creating an experience for the consumer establishing a long-lasting connection after purchase, increasing awareness and encouraging conversation. This category includes backstage videos, exclusive interviews, significant photos of the brand's history and heritage, sponsorships and sport, art and current affairs news related to the brand. Number of user's likes (average): it is the average number of users who liked the posts published by the company in a given day. This indicator shows which content is most appreciated by the target audience. Number of user's sharings (average): it is the sum of all sharings divided by number of published posts. A high volume of sharings points at strong interest in the page, an established relationship and content appreciation. In fact, along with the number of "likes" and comments, sharings are one of the factors making up the post engagement rate.

In relation to Twitter, the following indicators were considered. Number of followers: it is the number of people following the company's account. Similarly to what happened on Facebook, this relationship allows the company's tweets to get a higher visibility. Moreover, the company will show in the user's following list and, conversely, the user will be added to the company's follower's list. However, the number of followers is not the most important aspect for a social network like Twitter, which is based on real time activities: in fact, there is a high possibility that users do not see all tweets as they are not constantly on line. Number of tweets: it's the number of tweets published by a company in a given day. A tweet does not exceed 140 characters and is a means for companies to share links, images and videos with their followers. The total tally includes re-tweets, i.e. external users' tweets shared by the company on its account. Types of tweets: it is the number of photos, videos and links published by the company in a given day. Tweet content: this indicator divides tweets on the basis of their content: promotional or entertaining. The meaning of these two categories is similar to Facebook's: however, the few luxury accounts using tweets for their customer care practices should be added to the entertaining content. These tweets are meant to answer users' questions and solve some of their problems. Their purpose is to improve the customer's experience and foster their loyalty to the brand. For this reason, they have been included in the entertainment category. Number of re-tweets (average): it is the average number of people who has shared the company's tweets. This indicator identifies the generated interest and the relevance of published content for the company's target.

With regard to You Tube, the monitored parameters were: Number of subscribers: it is the number of users following the company's channel. It is important to analyze and monitor this figure in order to understand the extent and the interest of the community. In fact, brands should keep expanding their catchment area as long as subscribers fall within the business objectives' targets. Number of videos: it s the amount of videos published by a company in a given day. It refers to the frequency of publication and provides information on the channel activity. Video views (average): it reports the average viewings of the videos published in a given day. The number of views per video provides useful information about a company's users' taste. In this perspective, using YouTube Analytics, companies can identify which videos have prompted users' subscriptions. Total views: it is the total number of views since the channel has started operating and it is made up of the number of views per video published by the company.

The parameters considered for Instagram were the following. Followers: it is the number of people following the company's account. As it happens on Facebook and Twitter, company's posts are visible on the user's home page. The company gains popularity by appearing in the user's followed list and the user's account will be added to the company's followers' list. Followed: it is the number of business or personal profiles followed by the company. Number of overall posts: it is the total number of posts published by the company ever since joining Instagram. It is an indicator of the channel activity. Number of daily posts: it is the number of posts published by a company in a given day. It shows the frequency with which a brand produces specific content for this channel. Type of posts: it refers to the aim of the content: entertaining or promotional. Definitions of these categories used above may also apply here. Number of user's likes (average): it is the average number of users who liked the posts published by the company in a given day. It is the sum of all "likes" from different posts divided by the number of published posts. It points to what kind of content the audience likes most. Number of comments (average): it is the average number of user's comments related to the posts published daily by a company. It shows the followers' level of involvement and, through hashtags, the whole Instagram community's.

The following pages are a summary of the analysis carried out in the context of the different research that was conducted and published.

Table A2.1 Sample analysis

Company	Brand	Logo	Date of birth	Social network
Aston Martin Lagonda Limited	Aston Martin		1913	8: Facebook, Twitter, YouTube, Pinterest, Google+, Un dln, Instagram, Vimeo
Volkswagen	Bentley		1919	5: Facebook, Twitter, YouTube, LinkedIn, Instagram
Bmw	Bmw		1917	5: Facebook, Google+, Twitter, Instagram, YouTube
Volkswagen	Bugatti		1909	6: Facebook, Linkedin, Twitter, Instagram, Google+, You Tube
General Motors	Cadillac		1902	7: Facebook, Twitter, Instagram, YouTube, Pinterest, Tumblr, Google+
Fiat Chrysler Automobiles	Ferrari		1947	7: Facebook, YouTube, Instagram, Linkedin, Twitter, Google+, Flickr
Harley - Davidson Motor Company	Harley Davidson		1903	4: Facebook, Twitter, Instagram, YouTube
Nissan Motor Company	Infiniti		1989	5: Facebook, Twitter, Instagram, YouTube, Google+
Tata Motors	Jaguar		1945	5: Facebook, Twitter, YouTube, Instagram, Linkedin
Audi	Lamborghini		1963	9: Facebook, Google+, Twitter, YouTube, Pinterest, Instagram, Linkedin, Weibo, Youku
Toyota	Lexus		1989	7:Facebook, Twitter, YouTube, Instagram, Google+, Tumblr, Vimeo
Fiat Chrysler Automobiles	Maserati		1914	7: Facebook, Twitter, YouTube, Pinterest, Google+, Instagram, LinkedIn
McLaren Group	McLaren		1963	5: Facebook, Twitter, YouTube, Instagram, Google+
Gruppo Daimler	Mercedes-Benz		1926	4: Facebook, Twitter, YouTube, Instagram
Volkswagen	Porsche		1931	7: Facebook, Twitter, Pinterest, Linkedin, Instagram, Google+, YouTube
Bmw	Rolls-Royce		1906	7: Facebook, Twitter, Pinterest, Tumblr, Instagram, Google+, YouTube
LVMH SA	Acqua di Parma		1916	5: Facebook, YouTube, Instagram, Twitter, Pinterest
Parfums Caron	Caron Paris		1904	5: Facebook, Twitter, YouTube, Instagram, Google+
Estée Lauder Companies Inc.	Clinique Laboratories, Inc.		1968	6: Facebook, Twitter, YouTube, Instagram, Google+, Pinterest

(Rows from Aston Martin through Rolls-Royce are grouped under the vertical label **Automotive**.)

	Company	Brand	Logo	Founded	Social Media
Perfumes & Cosmetics	Estée Lauder Companies Inc.	Estée Lauder		1946	6: Facebook, Twitter, YouTube, Instagram, Google+, Pinterest
	LVMH SA	Guerlain		1828	6: Facebook, Twitter, Pinterest, Google+, Instagram, YouTube
	L'Oréal	Helena Rubinstein		1902	5: Facebook, Twitter, YouTube, Instagram, Google+
	Procter & Gamble	Jean Patou		1910	4: Facebook, Twitter, YouTube, Instagram
	L'Oréal	Lancôme		1935	5: Facebook, Twitter, YouTube, Instagram, Google+
	Shiseido Company, Limited	Shiseido		1872	5: Facebook, Twitter, YouTube, Instagram, Pinterest
	LVMH SA	Christian Dior S.A.		1946	6: Facebook, Instagram, YouTube, Twitter, Google+, Tumir
	L'Oréal	Biotherm		1952	5: Facebook, Google+, YouTube, Instagram, Twitter
	Amouage	Amouage		1983	3: Facebook, Instagram, Twitter
	Beiersdorf	La Prairie		1954	5: Facebook, Google+, YouTube, Instagram, Twitter
	Creed	Creed		1760	3: Facebook, Instagram, Twitter
	L'Oréal	Shu Uemura		1965	5: Facebook, twitter, Instagram, YouTube, Pinterest
	Gruppo Richemont	Cartier		1847	6: Facebook, Twitter, Instagram, YouTube, Tumblr, Pinterest
	Tiffany and Co.	Tiffany and Co.		1837	7: Facebook, Twitter, Instagram, YouTube, Tumblr, Pinterest, Google+
	Gruppo Richemont	Mont Blanc		1906	6: Facebook, Twitter, Instagram, YouTube, Pinterest, Google+
	Rolex SA	Rolex		1905	5: Facebook, YouTube, Youku, Pinterest, Douban
	LVMH SA	Bulgari		1884	4: Facebook, Twitter, Instagram, YouTube
	Chopard	Chopard		1860	8: Facebook, Twitter, Pinterest, Google+, Instagram, Tumblr, YouTube, Weibo
	Franck Muller Watchland SA	Frank Muller		1992	5: Facebook, Twitter, YouTube, Instagram, Google+
	Vhernier	Vhernier		1984	4: Facebook, Twitter, Instagram, Pinterest
	LVMH SA	Zenith		1865	5: Facebook, YouTube, Linkedin, Pinterest, Instagram

Jewelry & Watches	Kering	Pomellato	*Pomellato*	1967	4: Facebook, Instagram, YouTube, Twitter
	David Yurman Inc.	David Yurman	DAVID YURMAN	1980	6: Facebook, Twitter, Instagram, Google+, YouTube, Pinterest
	Gruppo Richemont	Van Cleef & Arpels	Van Cleef & Arpels	1896	7: Facebook, Twitter, Instagram, YouTube, Google+, Tumblr, Pinterest.
	LVMH SA	Hublot	HUBLOT GENEVE	1980	7: Facebook, Twitter, Pinterest, Instagram, YouTube, Weibo, Google+
	Swatch	Longines	LONGINES	1832	7: Facebook, Twitter, Linkedin, Instagram, YouTube, Weibo, Google+
	Patek Philippe & Co.	Patek Philippe	PATEK PHILIPPE GENEVE	1851	4: Facebook, Instagram, YouTube, Twitter
	LVMH SA	Moët & Chandon	MOËT & CHANDON CHAMPAGNE	1743	4: Facebook, YouTube, Instagram, Twitter
	Bollinger	Bollinger		1828	6: Facebook, Twitter, Instagram, Google+, YouTube, Pinterest
	Cà del Bosco	Cà del Bosco	Ca'del Bosco	1964	6: Facebook, Twitter, Instagram, Google+, YouTube, Pinterest
	LVMH SA	Dom Pérignon	Dom Pérignon	1921	3: Facebook, YouTube, Instagram
	LVMH SA	Chateau Cheval Blanc	CHATEAU CHEVAL BLANC	1832	1: Facebook
	Ferrari f.lli Lunelli S.p.A.	Ferrari	FERRARI	1902	5: Facebook, Twitter, Instagram, YouTube, Google+
	Gaja Distribuzione	Gaja	GAJA	1977	–
	Louis Roederer	Louis Roederer	LOUIS ROEDERER	1776	5: Facebook, Twitter, YouTube, Instagram, Google+
	Pernod Ricard	Martell	MARTELL	1715	4: Facebook, YouTube, Instagram, Twitter
	Chateau Margaux	Chateau Margaux		1705	2: Facebook, Twitter
	Rémy Martin & Co.	Rémy Martin	RÉMY MARTIN	1724	3: Facebook, Twitter, YouTube
	LVMH SA	Glenmorangie	GLENMORANGIE SINGLE MALT SCOTCH WHISKY	1843	5: Facebook, Twitter, YouTube, Instagram, Google+
	LVMH SA	Krug	KRUG	1843	5: Facebook, Twitter, YouTube, Instagram, Google+

Wine & Spirits	LVMH SA	Numanthia	NUMANTHIA	-	1: Twitter
	LVMH SA	Belvedere Vodka	BELVEDERE VODKA	1910	5: Facebook, Twitter, YouTube, Instagram, Google+
	Burberry Limited	Burberry	BURBERRY	1856	5: Facebook, Twitter, YouTube, Instagram, Google+
	Chanel SA	Chanel	CHANEL	1909	5: Facebook, Twitter, YouTube, Instagram, Google+
	Kering	Bottega veneta	BOTTEGA VENETA	1967	8: Facebook, Twitter, Tumblr, Pinterest, YouTube, Google+, Linkedin, Instagram
	Hermès	Hermès	HERMÈS PARIS	1837	7: Facebook, Twitter, Instagram, YouTube, Pinterest, Tumblr, Google+
	Prada S.p.A.	Prada	PRADA	1913	4: Facebook, Twitter, Instagram, YouTube
	Moschino	Moschino	MOSCHINO	1983	5: Facebook, YouTube, Pinterest, Twitter, Instagram
	LVMH SA	Fendi	FENDI	1925	6: Facebook, YouTube, Google+, Pinterest, Twitter, Instagram
	Dsquared²	Dsquared²	DSQUARED²	1996	6: Facebook, Instagram, Twitter, YouTube, Pinterest, Vimeo
	OTB	Diesel	DIESEL	1978	6: Facebook, Instagram, Twitter, YouTube, Pinterest, Google +
	Kering	Balenciaga	BALENCIAGA	1919	7: Facebook, Instagram, Twitter, YouTube, Tumblr, Pinterest, Fancy
	Manolo Blahnik	Manolo Blahnik	JIMMY CHOO	1973	4: Facebook, YouTube, Instagram, Twitter
	J. Choo Limited	Jimmy Choo	MANOLO BLAHNIK	1996	6: Facebook, Twitter, Instagram, Google+, YouTube, Pinterest
	Kering	Alexander Mc Queen	MC Q	1992	6: Facebook, Google+, Twitter, Instagram, YouTube, Linkedin
	Christian Louboutin Switzerland SA	Christian Louboutin	Louboutin	1992	5: Facebook, Google+, Twitter, Instagram, YouTube
	LVMH SA	Emilio Pucci	EMILIO PUCCI	1984	5: Facebook, Twitter, Instagram, Tumblr, YouTube
	LVMH SA	DKNY	DKNY	1947	7: Facebook, Twitter, Google+, YouTube, Instagram, Pinterest, Tumblr
	Moncler S.r.l.	Moncler	MONCLER	1952	7: Facebook, Twitter, Google+, YouTube, Instagram, Pinterest, Weibo
	Tod's S.p.A.	Tod's	TOD'S	1920	5: Facebook, YouTube, Pinterest, Instagram, Google+
	LVMH SA	Ermenegildo Zegna	Ermenegildo Zegna	1910	8: Facebook, Twitter, YouTube, Google+, Pinterest, Instagram, Weibo, Wechat

Giorgio Armani S.p.A.	Giorgio Armani	GIORGIO ARMANI	1975	7: Facebook, Twitter, YouTube, Pinterest, Google+, Instagram, Tumblr
Dolce & Gabbana	Dolce&Gabbana	DOLCE & GABBANA	1985	12: Facebook, Twitter, YouTube, Pinterest, Instagram, Google+, Tumblr, Weibo, Linkedin, Youku, Vk, Livejournal
LVMH SA	Louis Vuitton	LV	1854	8: Facebook, YouTube, Google+, Twitter, Instagram, Pinterest, Foursquare, Snapchat
Brunello Cucinelli S.p.A.	Brunello Cucinelli		1978	3: Facebook, Twitter, Instagram
Etro S.p.A.	Etro	ETRO	1968	5: Facebook, Twitter, Pinterest, YouTube, Instagram
Kering	Gucci	GUCCI	1921	6: Facebook, Twitter, YouTube, Pinterest, Google+, Instagram
LVMH SA	Givenchy	GIVENCHY	1952	5: Facebook, Instagram, Twitter, Google+, YouTube
Valentino Fashion Group	Hugo Boss AG	BOSS	1923	6: Facebook, Twitter, Instagram, YouTube, Pinterest, Google+,
LVMH SA	Marc Jacobs	MARC JACOBS	1984	7: Facebook, Twitter, Instagram, YouTube, Google+, Pinterest, Tumblr
Michael Kors Inc	Michael Kors	MK MICHAEL KORS	1981	5: Facebook, Twitter, Instagram, YouTube, Pinterest
Missoni S.p.A.	Missoni	MISSONI	1953	7: Facebook, Twitter, Instagram, YouTube, Google+, Pinterest, Tumblr
Ralph Lauren Corporation	Ralph Lauren	RALPH LAUREN	1967	7: Facebook, Twitter, Instagram, YouTube, Google+, Pinterest, Tumblr
Tory Burch	Tory Burch	TORY BURCH	2004	7: Facebook, Twitter, Instagram, YouTube, Google+, Pinterest, Tumblr
Kering	Stella McCartney	STELLA McCARTNEY	2001	9: Facebook, Twitter, Instagram, YouTube, Google+, Pinterest, Tumblr, Vimeo, Fancy
Kering	Sergio Rossi	sergio rossi	1960	4: Facebook, YouTube, Instagram, Twitter
Salvatore Ferragamo S.p.A.	Salvatore Ferragamo	Salvatore Ferragamo	1927	7: Facebook, Twitter, Instagram, YouTube, Google+, Pinterest, Tumblr
Ted Baker Plc	Ted Baker London	TED BAKER	1988	6: Facebook, Twitter, Instagram, YouTube, Google+, Pinterest
Giovanni Versace S.p.A.	Versace	VERSACE	1978	8: Facebook, Twitter, Instagram, Weibo, Pinterest, Linkedin, Google+, YouTube
Valentino S.p.A.	Valentino	VALENTINO	1957	7: Facebook, Twitter, Instagram, Pinterest, YouTube, Weibo, Youku
Kering	YSL	YvesSaintLaurent	1961	4: Facebook, Instagram, YouTube, Twitter

Fashion & Accessories

Social network and online presence. Presence in social media and websites is reported in the following table.

Accessories	BRAND	Web site	ONLINE DISTRIBUTION			BUSINESS MODEL		Integration with physical channel	Integration with Social Media						Web Atmosphere
			Direct E-commerce	Indirect Outlet	Indirect Full Price	Single Channel	Multi Channel		Facebook	Twitter	Instagram	Youtube	Linkedin	Pinterest	
1	ALEXANDER McQUEEN	✓	✓	✓	✓		✓	♦	✓	✓	✓	✓	✓	✓	♦♦
2	BALENCIAGA	✓	✓	✓	✓		✓		✓	✓	✓	✓	✓	✓	♦♦
3	BOTTEGA VENETA	✓	✓	✓	✓		✓		✓	✓	✓	✓	✓		♦♦
4	BRUNELLO CUCINELLI	✓	✓	✓	✓		✓	♦♦♦	✓	✓	✓	✓	✓	✓	♦♦♦
5	BURBERRY	✓	✓	✓	✓		✓	♦♦♦	✓	✓	✓	✓	✓	✓	♦♦
6	CHANEL	✓	✓	✓	✓		✓	♦♦♦	✓	✓	✓	✓	✓		♦♦♦
7	CHRISTIAN LOUBOUTIN	✓	✓	✓	✓		✓		✓	✓	✓	✓	✓	✓	♦♦
8	DOLCE & GABBANA	✓	✓	✓	✓		✓	♦♦	✓	✓	✓	✓	✓	✓	♦♦
9	EMILIO PUCCI	✓	✓	✓	✓		✓	♦	✓	✓	✓	✓	✓	✓	♦
10	ERMENEGILDO ZEGNA	✓	✓	✓	✓		✓	♦♦	✓	✓	✓	✓	✓		♦♦♦
11	FENDI	✓	✓	✓	✓		✓	♦♦	✓	✓	✓	✓	✓	✓	♦♦
12	GIORGIO ARMANI	✓	✓	✓	✓		✓	♦♦	✓	✓	✓	✓	✓	✓	♦♦
13	GUCCI	✓	✓	✓	✓		✓	♦♦♦	✓	✓	✓	✓	✓	✓	♦♦♦
14	HELMUT LANG	✓	✓	✓	✓		✓	♦	✓	✓	✓	✓	✓		♦♦♦
15	HERMES	✓	✓	✓	✓		✓	♦	✓	✓	✓	✓	✓		♦
16	HUGO BOSS	✓	✓	✓	✓		✓	♦♦	✓	✓	✓	✓	✓	✓	♦♦
17	JIMMY CHOO	✓	✓	✓	✓		✓		✓	✓	✓	✓	✓	✓	♦♦
18	LOUIS VUITTON	✓	✓	✓	✓		✓	♦♦♦	✓	✓	✓	✓	✓	✓	♦♦♦
19	LUCAS HUGH	✓	✓	✓	✓		✓		✓	✓	✓	✓	✓		♦♦
20	MANOLO BLAHNIK	✓	✓	✓	✓		✓	♦♦	✓	✓	✓	✓			♦♦
21	MARC JACOBS	✓	✓	✓	✓		✓	♦♦	✓	✓	✓	✓	✓	✓	♦♦
22	MICHAEL KORS	✓	✓	✓	✓		✓	♦♦	✓	✓	✓	✓	✓	✓	♦♦
23	MISSONI	✓	✓	✓	✓		✓	♦	✓	✓	✓	✓	✓		♦♦
24	MONCLER	✓	✓	✓	✓		✓	♦♦♦	✓	✓	✓	✓	✓	✓	♦♦
25	MOSCHINO	✓	✓	✓	✓		✓	♦♦	✓	✓	✓	✓	✓		♦♦
26	PRADA	✓	✓	✓	✓		✓	♦♦♦	✓	✓	✓	✓	✓		♦♦
27	RALPH LAUREN	✓	✓	✓	✓		✓	♦♦	✓	✓	✓	✓	✓	✓	♦♦♦
28	SALVATORE FERRAGAMO	✓	✓	✓	✓		✓	♦♦	✓	✓	✓	✓	✓	✓	♦♦
29	SERGIO ROSSI	✓	✓	✓			✓	♦	✓	✓	✓	✓	✓	✓	♦
30	TED BAKER	✓	✓	✓	✓		✓	♦	✓	✓	✓	✓	✓	✓	♦♦♦
31	TOD'S	✓	✓	✓	✓		✓	♦♦	✓	✓	✓	✓	✓		♦♦
32	TORY BURCH	✓	✓	✓	✓		✓	♦♦	✓	✓	✓	✓	✓	✓	♦♦
33	VALENTINO	✓	✓	✓	✓		✓	♦♦♦	✓	✓	✓	✓	✓	✓	♦♦
34	VERSACE	✓	✓	✓	✓		✓	♦♦	✓	✓	✓	✓	✓	✓	♦♦♦
35	YSL	✓	✓	✓	✓		✓	♦	✓	✓	✓	✓	✓	✓	♦
% of use in 2016		100%	100%	100%	94%	0%	100%		100%	100%	100%	94%	89%	80%	

Parfumes & Cosmetics	BRAND	Web site	ONLINE DISTRIBUTION			BUSINESS MODEL		Integration with Social Media						Web Atmosphere
			Direct E-commerce	Indirect Outlet	Indirect Full Price	Single Channel	Multi Channel	Facebook	Twitter	Instagram	Youtube	Linkedin	Pinterest	
1	ACQUA DI PARMA	✓		✓	✓		✓	✓	✓	✓	✓	✓	✓	♦♦♦
2	CARON PARIS	✓	✓	✓	✓		✓	✓	✓	✓	✓			♦♦
3	ESTEE' LAUDER	✓	✓		✓		✓	✓	✓	✓	✓	✓	✓	♦
4	GIVENCHY	✓		✓	✓		✓	✓	✓	✓	✓	✓		♦♦
5	GUERLAIN	✓			✓	✓		✓	✓	✓	✓	✓	✓	♦♦
6	HELENA RUBISTEIN	✓	✓		✓		✓	✓	✓	✓	✓			♦♦
7	JEAN PATOU	✓		✓	✓		✓	✓	✓	✓	✓	✓	✓	♦♦
8	LANCOME	✓	✓		✓		✓	✓	✓	✓	✓			♦♦
9	SHISEIDO	✓		✓	✓		✓	✓	✓	✓	✓	✓	✓	♦
% of use in 2016		100%	44,45%	66,67%	100%	11,11%	88,89%	100%	100%	100%	89%	67%	56%	

Watches & Jewelry	BRAND	Web site	ONLINE DISTRIBUTION			BUSINESS MODEL		Integration with Social Media						Web Atmosphere
			Direct E-commerce	Indirect Outlet	Indirect Full Price	Single Channel	Multi Channel	Facebook	Twitter	Instagram	Youtube	Linkedin	Pinterest	
1	AUDEMARS PIGUET	✓			✓	✓		✓	✓	✓	✓	✓		◆◆
2	BULGARI	✓		✓		✓		✓	✓	✓	✓	✓		◆◆
3	CARTIER	✓	✓	✓	✓	✓	✓	✓	✓	✓	✓	✓	✓	◆
4	CHOPARD	✓			✓	✓		✓	✓	✓	✓	✓	✓	◆◆
5	FRANCK MULLER	✓			✓	✓		✓	✓	✓	✓	✓	✓	◆◆◆
6	MONTBLANC	✓	✓			✓		✓	✓	✓	✓	✓	✓	◆◆
7	OMEGA	✓		✓		✓		✓	✓	✓	✓	✓		◆◆◆
8	PATEK PHILIPPE	✓			✓	✓						✓		◆
9	PIAGET	✓	✓			✓		✓	✓	✓	✓	✓	✓	◆◆
10	ROLEX	✓			✓	✓		✓	✓	✓	✓	✓	✓	◆◆
11	TIFFANY	✓	✓	✓			✓	✓	✓	✓	✓	✓	✓	◆◆◆
12	VACHERON CONSTANTIN	✓						✓	✓	✓	✓	✓		◆◆
13	VAN CLEEF AND ARPLES	✓						✓	✓	✓	✓	✓	✓	◆◆
14	VHERNIER	✓						✓	✓	✓		✓	✓	◆◆
15	ZENITH	✓						✓	✓	✓	✓	✓	✓	◆◆
% of use in 2016			26,67%	26,67%	40%	60%	13,34%	93%	93%	93%	87%	100%	67%	

Automotive	BRAND	Web site	ONLINE DISTRIBUTION			BUSINESS MODEL		Integration with Social Media						Web Atmosphere
			Direct E-commerce	Indirect Outlet	Indirect Full Price	Single Channel	Multi Channel	Facebook	Twitter	Instagram	Youtube	Linkedin	Pinterest	
1	ASTON MARTIN	✓	◆		◆		◆	✓	✓	✓	✓	✓	✓	◆◆
2	BENTLEY	✓	◆		◆		◆	✓	✓	✓	✓	✓	✓	◆◆
3	FERRARI	✓	◆	◆	◆		◆	✓	✓	✓	✓	✓	✓	◆◆◆
4	JAGUAR	✓						✓	✓	✓	✓	✓		◆◆
5	LAMBORGHINI	✓	◆	◆	◆		◆	✓	✓	✓	✓	✓	✓	◆◆◆
6	LEXUS	✓						✓	✓	✓	✓	✓	✓	◆◆◆
7	MASERATI	✓	◆	◆	◆		◆	✓	✓	✓	✓	✓	✓	◆◆
8	MCLAREN	✓	◆	◆	◆		◆	✓	✓	✓	✓	✓	✓	◆◆◆
9	PORSCHE	✓	◆	◆			◆	✓	✓	✓	✓	✓	✓	◆◆
10	TESLA	✓	◆			◆		✓	✓	✓	✓	✓	✓	◆◆
% of use in 2016		100%	80%	50%	60%	10%	70%	100%	100%	100%	100%	100%	90%	

◆ Is referred to the accessories linked to the brand.

Pleasure Boats	BRAND	Web site	ONLINE DISTRIBUTION			BUSINESS MODEL		Integration with Social Media						Web Atmosphere
			Direct E-commerce	Indirect Outlet	Indirect Full Price	Single Channel	Multi Channel	Facebook	Twitter	Instagram	Youtube	Linkedin	Pinterest	
1	AMELS	✓						✓	✓	✓	✓	✓		♦
2	AZIMUT YACHTS	✓						✓	✓	✓	✓	✓	✓	♦♦♦
3	BAGLIETTO YACHTS	✓						✓	✓	✓	✓	✓		♦♦♦
4	CABO YACHTS	✓						✓						♦
5	FEADSHIP	✓						✓	✓	✓	✓	✓		♦♦
6	FERRETTI YACHTS	✓						✓	✓	✓	✓	✓	✓	♦
7	HEESEN YACHTS	✓						✓	✓	✓	✓	✓	✓	♦♦♦
8	LÜRSSEN	✓						✓		✓	✓			♦♦♦
9	OCEANCO	✓						✓		✓	✓	✓		♦♦
10	WALLY YACHTS	✓						✓	✓					♦♦♦
% of use in 2016		100%	0%	0%	0%	0%	0%	100%	70%	80%	70%	70%	30%	

Wine & Spirits	BRAND	Web site	ONLINE DISTRIBUTION			BUSINESS MODEL		Integration with Social Media						Web Atmosphere
			Direct E-commerce	Indirect Outlet	Indirect Full Price	Single Channel	Multi Channel	Facebook	Twitter	Instagram	Youtube	Linkedin	Pinterest	
1	ARMAND DE BRIGNAC	✓			✓	✓		✓	✓	✓		✓		♦♦♦
2	BOLLINGER	✓			✓	✓		✓	✓	✓	✓		✓	♦♦♦
3	CA' DEL BOSCO	✓			✓	✓		✓	✓	✓	✓		✓	♦♦
4	CHATEAU CHEVAL BLANC	✓			✓	✓		✓	✓					♦♦
5	DOM PERIGNON	✓			✓	✓		✓	✓	✓				♦♦♦
6	LOUIS ROEDERER	✓			✓	✓		✓	✓	✓	✓	✓		♦♦
7	MARTELL	✓			✓	✓		✓	✓	✓	✓	✓	✓	♦♦
8	MOET & CHANDON	✓			✓	✓		✓	✓	✓	✓	✓		♦♦♦
9	RUINART	✓			✓	✓		✓	✓	✓	✓	✓		♦♦♦
10	VEUVE CLICQUOT	✓			✓	✓		✓	✓		✓	✓		♦♦♦
% of use in 2016		100%			100%	100%		100%	100%	80%	70%	60%	30%	

Furniture	BRAND	Web site	ONLINE DISTRIBUTION			BUSINESS MODEL		Integration with Social Media						Web Atmosphere
			Direct E-commerce	Indirect Outlet	Indirect Full Price	Single Channel	Multi Channel	Facebook	Twitter	Instagram	Youtube	Linkedin	Pinterest	
1	ARTEMIDE	✓		✓	✓		✓	✓	✓	✓	✓	✓	✓	♦♦
2	BOCA DO LOBO	✓		✓		✓		✓	✓	✓	✓	✓	✓	♦♦
3	BOFFI	✓								✓		✓	✓	♦♦
4	EDRA	✓		✓	✓		✓	✓	✓	✓	✓			♦♦♦
5	FLOS	✓		✓	✓		✓	✓	✓	✓	✓	✓	✓	♦♦
6	HENREDON	✓	✓			✓		✓	✓	✓			✓	♦
7	KARTELL	✓	✓	✓	✓		✓	✓	✓	✓	✓	✓	✓	♦♦
8	KNOLL	✓	✓	✓	✓		✓	✓	✓	✓	✓	✓	✓	♦
9	POLIFORM	✓		✓	✓		✓	✓	✓	✓	✓	✓	✓	♦♦♦
10	POLTRONA FRAU	✓		✓	✓		✓	✓	✓	✓	✓	✓	✓	♦♦
11	RESTORATION HARDWARE	✓	✓			✓					✓			♦♦♦
% of use in 2016			36,36%	72,73%	63,64%	27,27%	63,64%	91%	82%	91%	73%	82%	82%	

Top brand Analysis Automotive Facebook/Twitter/YouTube/Instagram

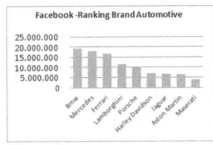

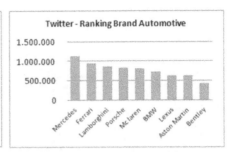

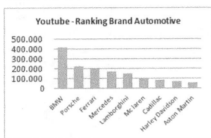

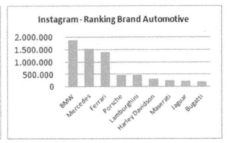

Top brand Jewelry & Watches Facebook/Twitter/YouTube/Instagram

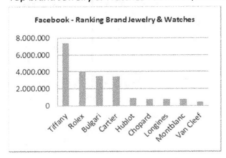

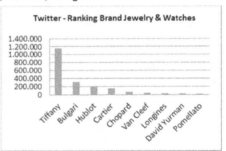

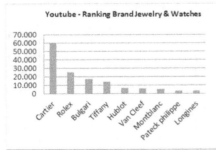

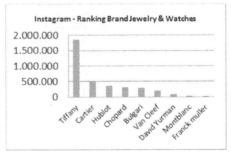

Top brand Wine & Spirits Facebook/Twitter/YouTube/Instagram

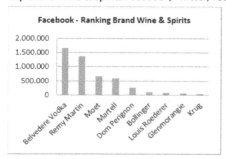

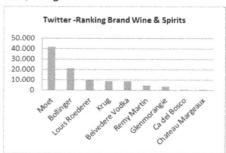

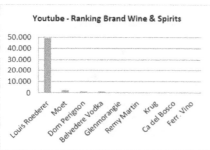

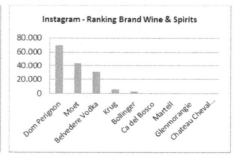

Top brand Perfume&Cosmetics Facebook/Twitter/YouTube/Instagram

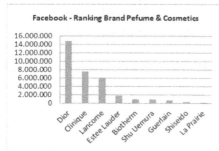

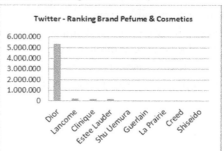

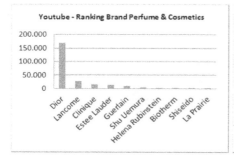

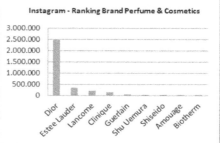

Top brand Fashion Facebook/Twitter/YouTube/Instagram

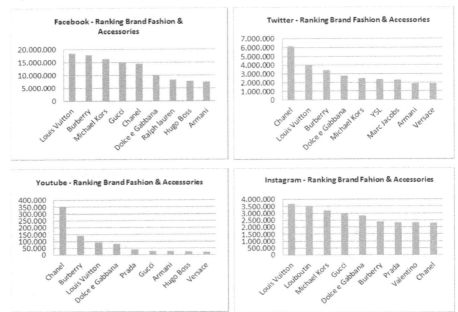

Social media adoption map. The Digital media adoption map identifies four strategic possible approaches to social media for luxury brands. The framework highlights these strategic approaches: social brand ambassador, social showcases, social seller, social infotainers.

The four categories were identified on the basis of two dimensions: percentage of promotional content and social commerce score.

Categories (right-side icons): Fashion & Accessories · Automotive · Perfume & Cosmetics · Jewelry & Watches · Wine & Spirits

FANBASE

FACEBOOK		TWITTER		YOUTUBE		INSTAGRAM		PINTEREST	
Bmw	18.565.928	Chanel	6.959.058	Bmw	439.996	Louis Vuitton	4.358.172	Aston Martin	335.401
Mercedes	18.010.665	Dior	5.680.500	Chanel	393.688	Christian Louboutin	3.994.296	D&G	177.468
Louis Vuitton	17.664.875	Louis Vuitton	4.264.184	Porsche	237.531	Michael Kors	3.782.686	Valentino	173.376
Burberry	16.730.046	Burberry	3.751.334	Ferrari	213.708	D&G	3.586.052	Michael Kors	167.647
Ferrari	16.588.227	D&G	3.041.913	Dior	189.373	Chanel	3.529.945	Tory Burch	157.272
Michael Kors	16.216.146	Michael Kors	2.718.963	Mercedes	187.429	Gucci	3.425.949	Bottega Veneta	141.973
Gucci	14.351.966	Marc Jacobs	2.675.679	Lamborghini	164.333	Dior	3.240.177	Burberry	130.345
Dior	14.256.898	YSL	2.598.316	Burberry	160.326	Burberry	3.094.639	Marc Jacobs	99.403
Chanel	14.069.268	Armani	2.079.720	Louis Vuitton	99.535	Prada	2.916.089	Tiffany & Co	95.037
Lamborghini	11.620.720	Versace	2.068.485	D&G	92.777	Valentino	2.881.494	Louis Vuitton	67.953

ENGAGEMENT RATE

FACEBOOK		TWITTER		YOUTUBE		INSTAGRAM		PINTEREST	
Rolex	4,56%	Ferrari	1,68%	n.a.		Aston Martin	6,63%	n.a.	
Christian Louboutin	3,72%	Bmw	1,34%	n.a.		Bentley	6,33%	n.a.	
Chanel	3,56%	Porsche	1,31%	n.a.		Porsche	5,88%	n.a.	
Maserati	2,99%	Tiffany & Co	1,27%	n.a.		Rolls-Royce	5,67%	n.a.	
Tiffany & Co	2,55%	Lamborghini	1,21%	n.a.		Bugatti	5,61%	n.a.	
Harley Davidson	2,55%	Maserati	1,13%	n.a.		Moët & Chandon	5,59%	n.a.	
Jimmy Choo	2,54%	Cadillac	1,12%	n.a.		Dom Perignon	5,41%	n.a.	
Jaguar	2,41%	Balenciaga	1,10%	n.a.		Jaguar	5,30%	n.a.	
Rolls-Royce	2,17%	Krug	1,09%	n.a.		Mercedes	5,00%	n.a.	
David Yurman	1,94%	Belvedere Vodka	1,09%	n.a.		Maserati	4,91%	n.a.	

SOCIAL COMMERCE

FACEBOOK		TWITTER		YOUTUBE		INSTAGRAM		PINTEREST	
Tiffany & Co	3,69	David Yurman	3,06			Clinique	2,69	Ferrari	3,95
Clinique	3,64	Tiffany & Co	2,91			Michael Kors	2,40	Tiffany & Co	3,90
David Yurman	3,49	Clinique	2,82			Tiffany & Co	1,57	Van Cleef	3,70
Shiseido	3,08	Shiseido	2,44			Van Cleef	1,50	Vhernier	3,40
Michael Kors	2,90	Michael Kors	2,25			Emilio Pucci	1,23	David Yurman	3,20
Christian Louboutin	2,81	Christian	2,22			Ferragamo	1,19	Creed	3,10
Stella McCartney	2,80	Louboutin	2,21			D&G	1,12	Dsquared	3,00
La Prairie	2,69	Marc Jacobs				Versace	1,12	Burberry	2,97
Estee Lauder	2,42	Bottega Veneta	2,18	n.a.		Donna Karan	1,03	Clinique	2,90
Ted Baker London	2,42	Ted Baker	2,12	n.a.		Tod's	1,03	Moschino	2,80
		La Prairie	2,10						

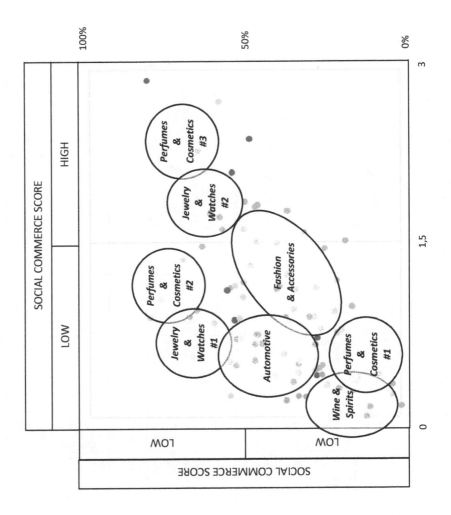